THE EVOLUTION OF A CONSTITUTION

The Evolution of a Constitution: Eight Key Moments in British Constitutional History casts light upon the British constitution of today by means of an in-depth consideration of eight key moments in British constitutional history. The historical perspective adopted in this book facilitates an informed and contextual understanding of the intricacies of the contemporary British constitution. Indeed, the book is based upon the premise that it is impossible to fully comprehend the nature, content and implications of today's constitution without a firm grasp on how it evolved into its present form.

Each of the eight main chapters focuses upon a different event in constitutional history which has contributed certain principles or practices to the modern-day constitution, and explains how these principles or practices evolved and highlights their contemporary significance. Historical events covered include the 1688 Glorious Revolution, the 1707 Union between England and Scotland, the 1911 Parliament Act, and the 1972 European Communities Act.

The Evolution of a Constitution

Eight Key Moments in British Constitutional History

ELIZABETH WICKS

·HART·
PUBLISHING

OXFORD AND PORTLAND, OREGON
2006

Published in North America (US and Canada) by
Hart Publishing
c/o International Specialized Book Services
920 NE 58th Avenue, Suite 300
Portland, OR 97213-3786
USA
Tel: +1 503 287 3093 or toll-free: (1) 800 944 6190
Fax: +1 503 280 8832
Email: mail@hartpub.co.uk
Website: www.isbs.com

Hart Publishing, Salter's Boatyard, Folly Bridge, Abingdon Rd, Oxford, OX1 4LB
Telephone: +44 (0)1865 245533 Fax: +44 (0) 1865 794882
Email: mail@hartpub.co.uk
Website: http//:www.hartpub.co.uk

British Library Cataloguing in Publication Data
Data Available

ISBN-13: 978-1-84113-418-5 (paperback)
ISBN-10: 1-84113-418-X (paperback)

Typeset by Forewords, Oxford
Printed and bound in Great Britain by
Biddles Ltd, Kings Lynn, Norfolk

Acknowledgements

I have benefited from many interesting discussions with my public law colleagues at the University of Birmingham, notably Sophie Boyron and Adrian Hunt, and I am also grateful to the current Head of the School of Law, Professor John Baldwin, for many years of support and encouragement. Danny Nicols of London Metropolitan University kindly read and commented upon an early draft of chapter one. I owe a continuing debt of gratitude to Professor David Feldman, now of the University of Cambridge and formerly my PhD supervisor at Birmingham, who started me on the road towards this book with his inspirational advice and unparalleled expertise on all things constitutional. Richard Hart has been the ideal publisher, offering encouragement and advice when needed but also giving me the space and time to write this book as I envisaged it.

I am also grateful to my partner Frank for many fruitful discussions about the issues covered in this book. He hid his instinctive boredom about constitutional history remarkably well and has contributed far more to this book than even he realises. Finally, I am grateful to my parents for their continued love, support and encouragement. Their belief in me is unwavering and enables me to follow my dreams wherever they take me. I am sure that my Dad will be the first, and keenest, reader of this book, and I sincerely hope he enjoys it.

In a book about the evolutionary nature of the constitution, it will immediately be apparent that any statement of the current law of the constitution is vulnerable to future change. Nevertheless, I have sought to state the law as it stood in September 2005, although some later developments, including the House of Lords' decision in *Jackson v Attorney-General*, have been included.

Liz Wicks
Birmingham, March 2006

Contents

Introduction

The constitution of the United Kingdom has evolved into its modern form over many centuries. Unlike the more common codified constitution,[1] it retains sufficient flexibility to allow adaptation to suit the changing circumstances of society with minimum procedural restraints. This ability to change carries with it a danger that nothing is sacred; no principle secure from the priorities of the current government. Flexibility need not be so unrestrained, however. An ability to evolve can be constrained by existing core principles of the constitution so that the evolution is a development – perhaps a restructuring – but never a fundamental break with the existing constitutional order. If such a break occurs it amounts to a constitutional revolution. The UK has encountered these in the past, as for example during the civil war in the seventeenth century, but the period covered in detail in this book is characterised by evolution rather than revolution of the constitutional order.

This book seeks to investigate the evolution of the UK constitution since 1688 to the present day (2005) by means of consideration of the key moments during that period which have developed the constitution in a significant way. These 'moments' include the enactment of statutes; the ratification of international treaties; the settlement of a revolution; and the ministry of a leading minister. They all led to fundamental changes in the existing constitution and thus acted as landmark moments in the continuous evolution of the constitution. This book is not intended as merely a history of the UK constitution since 1688 – valuable though that would be – instead, it is hoped to use the historical investigation to cast new light upon the constitution of today. In an uncodified constitution we cannot refer to a preamble setting out the core principles of the constitution. We may sometimes fear that the constitution has no fundamental principles but is rather a mere description of the governing of the state.[2] But by understanding the way in which the constitution has evolved into its modern state we can begin to appreciate the values which underlie it and the priorities which govern its development.

It will be instructive to see the potential relevance of historical evidence to the

---

[1] Codified/uncodified are better descriptors than written/unwritten to distinguish the UK's constitution from that of other countries because, as will be seen throughout the following chapters, much of the UK constitution is written, but it has never been codified into one document.

[2] This is the view of Griffiths: 'The constitution of the United Kingdom lives on, changing from day to day, for the constitution is no more and no less than what happens. Everything that happens is constitutional. And if nothing happened, that would be constitutional also' (JAG Griffiths, 'The Political Constitution' (1979) 42 *MLR* 1 at 19).

evolution of some currently topical constitutional issues. First, the protection of individual rights may be identified as an issue of great contemporary significance. The enactment of the Human Rights Act in 1998 brought the implications of human rights protection to the fore and raised seemingly insurmountable problems of balancing the rights of individuals with the needs of society. The evolution of the constitution since 1688 reveals, however, that these are not new issues. The 1689 settlement included some limited protection for individual rights and liberties and, in the twentieth century, the European Convention for the Protection of Human Rights and Fundamental Freedoms (the European Convention on Human Rights, or ECHR) provided groundbreaking international protection and enforcement of human rights. Analysis of earlier events may provide some answers to today's dilemma. Second, the role of Parliament and, especially, its relationship with the executive is a very topical issue in a political system dominated by party politics. An understanding of the history of the Westminster Parliament, its constitutional role and the development of the parliamentary executive cast light upon the modern institutions and their respective roles under the constitution. Third, House of Lords reform remains on the political agenda at the beginning of the twenty-first century but only by looking back a century to the Parliament Act 1911 can we understand how it became the body that it is today, in terms of its role, powers and composition.[3] Fourth, the role of a hereditary monarchy at the apex of the UK constitutional framework is continually the subject of debate. To what extent is hereditary influence a legitimate part of the constitution of a modern, democratic state? To answer this, the constitutional role of the monarch in the past must be considered, especially its development from the exercise of absolute power to acting as a referee of constitutional disputes. Fifth, the survival of the union state in the midst of the turmoil generated by devolution, decentralisation and growing nationalism begs the question of its origins. To understand why the union between England and Scotland survives, for example, we must surely enquire into its origins 300 years ago. Finally, the sovereignty of the state of the United Kingdom is perceived as under threat from an increasingly globalised world in which traditional constitutional doctrines, such as parliamentary sovereignty, are not always appropriate. One of the main threats to sovereignty of both the state and Parliament is posed by UK membership of the European Union (EU), and thus an appreciation of the EU's development and the views of the UK's government, legislature and populace upon voluntary entry into the EU's predecessor organisation helps to formulate an understanding of the UK's place in Europe today and the constitutional implications of this.

---

[3] Indeed, the Parliament Act 1911 provides perhaps the most striking indication of modern-day significance for seemingly historical events as, at the time of writing, the House of Lords is currently hearing a case based on this very statute and its judgment may have profound implications for the constitutional significance of this statute. See *R (Jackson) v Attorney-General* [2005] 3 WLR 733.

As indicated by the above, the subsequent chapters seek to retain a focus upon the UK's modern constitution while considering the historical moments which have forced the constitution to evolve into this modern form. Hindsight has not been entirely eliminated, therefore, and historians may regret this. This book is written by a lawyer, albeit one with an avid interest in constitutional history, and is aimed primarily (although not exclusively) at other lawyers but an attempt has been made to be sensitive to the demands of historical research and thus I have depended upon the views of historians (rather more than lawyers) and sought to provide a taste of differences in opinion within the historiography where appropriate. The resulting analysis of eight key moments in British constitutional history seeks to illuminate the core principles and strengths of the modern constitution but also its weaknesses, contradictions and impotence in the face of modern government. It is a story with a mixed outcome, but an awareness of this legacy of limitations can only serve to strengthen reliance upon positive aspects of the modern constitution and perhaps direct future evolution in that beneficial direction.

The remainder of the introduction seeks to present a picture of the constitution before the first key moment considered in chapter 1. As British history pre-1688 is far too immense a topic to do justice to it here, the following pages will focus upon two central themes: the relationship between individuals and the government (at this point in history, predominantly the Crown), and between the Crown and Parliament.[4] These two themes will be addressed by means of analysis of two fundamental events in early constitutional history: the sealing of the Magna Carta in 1215 and the seventeenth-century civil war.

Magna Carta – Individual Liberties and the Rule of Law

The Rule of Law has long been recognised as a central feature of the English constitution, albeit one with an ambiguous meaning. Even today, academics dispute the requirements of the principle of the Rule of Law,[5] but there is no doubt that at its core lies the principle that government must operate according to the law. Despite its inherent limitations within the modern government system, in which the parliamentary executive can also determine the law by which it must abide, it offers a basic minimum protection for individuals against the government. It is difficult to imagine the modern UK constitution without this principle at its heart, and the first steps towards it can be traced back to 1215

---

[4] To some extent this mirrors the relationship between the executive and legislative branches of government, with the Crown as executive, although the extensive power of the Crown pre-1688 extends to legislative influence beyond that of the Parliament.

[5] See P Craig, 'Formal and Substantive Conceptions of the Rule of Law: An Analytical Framework' [1997] *PL* 467.

and the Magna Carta which 'sought to establish the rights of subjects against authority and maintained the principle that authority was subject to law.'[6]

The Magna Carta is part of an agreement reached between King John and rebellious barons in 1215. John has been described as having 'the mental abilities of a great king, but the inclinations of a petty tyrant.'[7] The rebellion began with a baronial plot to kill the King during a military expedition to Wales in the summer of 1212. The plot's failure did not stem the tide of dissatisfaction, and the failure of a military expedition to France in 1214 only increased John's unpopularity and emboldened the barons.[8] Opposition to John was concentrated in East Anglia, the North and the West. While the number of barons who rebelled in the spring of 1215 was small,[9] they were joined by a larger number of knights, and not only those who were obliged to do so by the ties of fealty. Both the barons and the knights had personal grievances and, while the barons' grievances could perhaps have been redressed through private arrangements with the King, those of the knights required more generalised remedies.[10] It is this fact that led to wide-ranging terms in the Magna Carta and enabled its application in future diverse situations. In 1215 the King summoned a great council of barons to meet in Northampton after Easter. The barons arrived with a list of non-negotiable demands and were accompanied by armed men; the King failed to arrive at all. On 5 May the rebels formally renounced their fealty to John and named Robert Fitz Walter (a member of the earlier plot to kill John) as their leader. John was in a conciliatory mood as, by taking vows as a crusader in March, he had placed both his person and property under the protection of the Church and wished to retain the support of the Pope. The King thus continued to make proposals for settlement, but by mid-May the rebels had the city of London on their side. In July, the Pope offered his support by excommunicating all 'disturbers of the King' and their supporters.[11] Finally, the conflict reached Runnymede Meadow – a place chosen as an intermediary point between Windsor Castle and the rebels' camp at Staines – and under Archbishop Langton negotiations for a settlement commenced. The so-called 'Articles of the Barons' served as a discussion paper, and on 15 June 1215[12] a Charter, in the form of the King's grant of concessions to 'all the free men of our kingdom, for ourselves and our heirs for ever', was agreed. Copies were made of the Charter and sent throughout the kingdom, but Holt

---

[6] JC Holt, *Magna Carta*, 2nd edn (Cambridge, Cambridge University Press, 1992), p 19.

[7] WL Warren, *King John*, 2nd edn (London, Eyre Methuen, 1978), p 259. The origins of the 1215 rebellion predated John's reign, however, and 'lay much deeper than the shallows of his character' (Holt, n 6 above, p 36).

[8] RV Turner, *Magna Carta: Through the Ages* (London, Pearson, 2003), p 58.

[9] Only 39–45 (*ibid*, p 55).

[10] *Ibid*, pp 55–56.

[11] *Ibid*, p 61.

[12] This is now widely regarded as merely a nominal date, and Warren argues that 'it took several days after the 15th for the precise wording in proper legal terms to be worked out' (Warren, n 7 above, p 236).

argues that the Charter is not a dispositive document but an evidentiary one: the record of a transaction agreed verbally at Runnymede.[13] The agreement faced immediate difficulties, however, because, as Holt notes, 'not all the men involved were men of good will, the King least of all.'[14] Fighting broke out again in September, and soon afterwards the rebels offered the English crown to Louis of France. In May 1216 he landed in England with a large army, but John held the west of the country until his death in October 1216. He was succeeded by his young son, Henry III, whose supporters finally defeated the rebels. The Charter agreed to at Runnymede was reissued in a new form: the forestry clauses were withdrawn, expanded and issued in a separate charter called the 'little charter', while the remainder took the name of the 'big charter' or 'Magna Carta'. Further reissues followed in later years and reinterpretations of its terms left a legacy which still remains. So, what does the Magna Carta say which has given it such longevity?

As Warren has acknowledged, it is 'an unrewarding document for the general reader. It bristles with the technicalities of feudal law, and when these are cleared away most of its provisions seem very mundane.'[15] There is no high-sounding statement of principle or clearly defined political theory within its terms.[16] The Charter can be divided into six categories of provisions:[17] those relating to freedom of the English Church; those concerning John's lordship over his barons (defining the services and payments due to him); those on administrative matters, including the effective functioning of the common law courts; those granting concessions to England's towns; those creating machinery for enforcing the Charter, including innovatively the establishment of a committee of 25 barons to ensure John's observance of the Charter; and finally those establishing principles of lasting political importance. It is this last category of provisions which has had enduring influence. Two basic principles are established: 'that royal government must function both through judicial processes and with the counsel of the great men of the kingdom.'[18] The obligation to take counsel is ensured by the requirement that no scutage or aid is to be levied 'except by the common counsel of our realm.'[19] The principle that the Crown will act through judicial processes can be seen in chapters 39 and 40, the most famous of the Magna Carta's provisions. Chapter 39 states that 'No free man shall be arrested or imprisoned or disseised or outlawed or exiled or in any way victimised … except

---

[13] Holt, n 6 above, p 258.

[14] *Ibid*, p 228. Holt continues by arguing that 'even when he sealed Magna Carta, John had not the slightest intention of giving in or permanently abandoning the powers which the Angevin Kings had come to enjoy.' Turner agrees that the Magna Carta 'was an unworkable compromise between a King who accepted it only grudgingly and a group of angry, aggressive and wary barons' (Turner, n 8 above, p 77).

[15] Warren, n 7 above, p 236.

[16] *Ibid*.

[17] See Turner, n 8 above, pp 68–71.

[18] *Ibid*, p 67.

[19] Chapters 12 and 14 of the Magna Carta.

by the lawful judgement of his peers or[20] by the law of the land.' This requirement of due process is important but we should not forget that the overwhelming majority of the population at this time were not 'free men' and so did not enjoy the benefit of this provision. Chapter 40 complements chapter 39 by declaring that 'To no one will we sell, to no one will we refuse or delay right or justice.' It is largely through these two provisions that the Magna Carta has come to symbolise the Rule of Law, as it marked 'one of the earliest attempts to impose the limitations of law on a ruler's sovereign authority.'[21] Furthermore, as Turner argues, chapters 39 and 40 established the basic principle that the Rule of Law ensures personal liberty:

> First, the executive power must proceed by recognised legal process, never unlawfully, when taking action against an individual. Second, no one is above the law, however high his or her status, a concept capable of evolving into the principle of equality under the law.[22]

This capacity for the terms and significance of the Magna Carta to evolve was seen at its most striking during the seventeenth century when lawyers interpreted, or arguably misinterpreted,[23] the Magna Carta to require trial by jury and the consent of representatives for taxation. Such ideas certainly went beyond the original purposes of the Charter, but then it has always 'meant more than it said.'[24] As Warren explains, the Magna Carta, by its mere existence, 'was a standing condemnation of the rule of arbitrary will,' and thus an appeal to Magna Carta throughout the ages has been 'a shorthand way of proclaiming the Rule of Law.'[25] Even though it originated as merely an attempt to protect baronial interests, by establishing the principles inherent in the Rule of Law, the Magna Carta left a legacy for individuals of future ages to ensure that their governments acted according to the law and legal processes.

Parliament versus Crown

The evolution of the Westminster Parliament, now the sovereign body within the UK constitution, has been a gradual and incremental story. During the eleventh and twelfth centuries, the King's 'crown wearings' (thrice-yearly sessions during which the King wore his crown) served as a reason for gatherings of the King's

---

[20] There is some debate over whether the correct word here is 'or' or 'and' because the original 'vel' could be translated as either word. Obviously the meaning of the chapter is entirely changed depending upon which word is used.

[21] Turner, n 8 above, p 1.

[22] *Ibid*, pp 1–2.

[23] This is Warren's view. See Warren, n 7 above, p 240.

[24] *Ibid*.

[25] *Ibid*.

counsellors and can perhaps be regarded as early precursors of the establishment of a parliament. During the thirteenth century, in the reign of King John's son, Henry III, a more recognisable parliament began to emerge from the earlier King's Council. Representation originally comprised merely bishops and magnates, but the so-called Model Parliament of 1265, summoned by Simon de Montfort following the capture of Henry during the Barons' War, introduced the idea of representation from the shires and boroughs. By the fourteenth century, the presence of knights representing the shires and burgesses (or merchants) representing the boroughs became established as a permanent feature. In 1376, the so-called Good Parliament chose a representative to take its complaints to the King. Sir Peter de la Mare, the representative chosen, is widely regarded as the first speaker of the House of Commons, and the modern post retains this original role of representing the House of Commons in its dealings with the monarch. By the fifteenth century, Parliament was beginning to look recognisable, with a House of Lords comprising lords temporal and lords spiritual, and a House of Commons comprised of knights and burgesses elected, in some fashion, by the shires and boroughs of the country. However, the summoning of a parliament remained an infrequent occurrence, usually dependent upon the King needing supply of funds, and the issues of the powers of Parliament and its relationship with the Crown remained unresolved until the seventeenth century. The final resolution of these issues occurred as part of the constitutional settlement following the 1688 Revolution and will be discussed in detail in the first chapter. However, earlier in the seventeenth century the issues exploded into a bloody civil war. A brief overview of these events will help to place the 1688 events in their seventeenth-century context.

On one side of the mid-seventeenth-century conflict, royalists believed that the monarch ruled by virtue of the divine right of kings – that is, that God had conferred powers (or sovereignty) directly on the King alone – and, on the other side, parliamentarians preferred the view that powers were conferred on the community as a whole, which was then represented by the King, Lords and Commons working together.[26] During a tempestuous century in which religious conflict polarised Europe,[27] these two differing theories of government authority provided the theoretical framework for unprecedented military conflict and constitutional revolution. Military conflict began in 1638 when, in Scotland, representatives of nobility and the Kirk signed a National Covenant which required its signatories to resist innovations in religion, and an army of Covenanters ignited the 'First Bishops' war' necessitating the summoning of a parliament by King Charles in 1640 in order to obtain funds to counter the rebellion in Scotland. The parliament summoned refused, however, and was quickly

[26] See J Goldsworthy, *The Sovereignty of Parliament: History and Philosophy* (Oxford, Clarendon Press, 1999), ch 5.
[27] See J Scott, *England's Troubles – Seventeenth Century English Political Instability in European Context* (Cambridge, Cambridge University Press, 2000) for an account of seventeenth-century conflict within a European context.

dissolved, earning it the name 'Short Parliament'. The army of Covenanters moved south across the border and occupied Newcastle. Charles was forced to summon another parliament and this one, appropriately called the 'Long Parliament', would continue to sit until after the King's execution nine years later. The Long Parliament was united in seeking reform and the King was persuaded to sign the Triennial Act in 1641, which required parliaments to be held every three years for a minimum period of 50 days. The Long Parliament also drafted a 'Grand Remonstrance' specifying details of its grievances against King Charles (even those already remedied). The debates on this document in November 1641 saw the first division of Parliament into royalists and parliamentarians. The Grand Remonstrance was passed by eleven votes, but Charles rejected its demands and disastrously sought to impeach leading parliamentary leaders. He then abandoned his seat of government in London and moved north. Both sides gathered forces of over 20,000 each, and in 1642 civil war finally commenced. The country was divided, with the North and West largely royalist and the South and East largely parliamentarian, but the boundaries of loyalty were not so clear cut, and counties, towns and even families were split. Kishlansky explains what each side was fighting for:

> Royalists fought for the traditions of religion and monarchy that their ancestors had preserved and passed onto them as a sacred inheritance … Their fundamental principle was loyalty … Parliamentarians fought for true religion and liberty. They too defended an ancient inheritance – a church purified of recent innovations and a government that respected the inviolability of property … Their fundamental principle was consent – an ingrained belief in the cooperation between subject and sovereign that maintained the delicate balance between prerogatives and liberties.[28]

Kishlansky further explains that both sides believed in both sets of values, but the civil war forced everyone to choose one set over the other: 'The civil war turned a stable marriage of beliefs into irreconcilable differences.'[29]

In 1645, the parliamentarian armies were united into a New Model Army under a central authority and, under a self-denying ordinance, all Members of Parliament were stripped of their commands. The New Model Army achieved a famous victory at the Battle of Naseby on 14 June 1645, inflicting great losses upon the royalists. A parliamentarian victory in the war became likely and, a year later, the King surrendered to the Covenanter Army. Discontent in the army grew, especially as its pay was months in arrears, and it soon became a hotbed for extremism, as grievances over lack of pay combined with radical political demands. When Parliament ordered the army's disbandment with only eight weeks' arrears of wages, the army's rank and file refused to comply and the army moved beyond the control of Parliament. In 1647, Charles escaped confinement

---

[28] M Kishlansky, *A Monarchy Transformed – Britain 1603–1714* (London, Penguin Books, 1996), p 151.

[29] *Ibid*, p 152.

and a combination of local risings and an invasion from Scotland ignited a second civil war. The royalists lost for a second time. The Army Remonstrance presented to Parliament after hostilities had ceased again in November 1648 demanded a trial for Charles, a purge of the Long Parliament, and the establishment of a successor parliament chosen on the basis of a reformed franchise and with its powers limited. The Long Parliament was indeed purged of all members sympathetic to the King, leaving a rump of 150 members, to be known as the Rump Parliament. Charles was placed on trial, convicted and executed on 30 January 1649. A revolution had occurred.

The Rump Parliament wasted no time in abolishing both the House of Lords and the monarchy. Meanwhile, the army, led by Oliver Cromwell, viciously conquered Ireland and also won victories against the Scottish. The relations between army and Parliament remained precarious and, when the Rump Parliament failed to achieve any social or religious reform, Cromwell forcibly expelled the Rump on 20 April 1653. Its replacement was the Nominated, or 'Barebones', Parliament whose membership was divided between moderates and radical religious enthusiasts. Attendance fell until the radicals were able to pass several Bills on church reform. This frightened the moderates into joining together to resign their power and deliver civil authority directly into the hands of the army and Cromwell. Cromwell, however, was reluctant to lead a military government and instead established a written constitution – the UK's first and only encounter with one (to date). The 'Instrument of Government' of 1653 divided power between the Protector (Oliver Cromwell), who would exercise executive power; the Council (of between 13 and 21 members), which advised the Protector on civil and military matters; and the Parliament (a single chamber of 460 members, meeting at least triennially for at least five months' duration) with the power to make laws. Bills passed by Parliament could even become law without the Protector's signature after a 20-day delay, although the Instrument of Government itself could not be amended without the Protector's consent.[30] The first Parliament met on 3 September 1654 but was largely critical of the Instrument, claiming that it lacked authority. Cromwell was forced to call a second Parliament in 1656 for war revenue and, even though opponents of the regime were now excluded, the Parliament still urged reforms. It requested Cromwell to take the crown, thus returning to a known and understood form of government, and it prepared the 'Humble Petition and Advice', which amended the Instrument, including by creating a bicameral legislature, establishing hereditary succession and enhancing Parliament's power at the expense of the army-dominated Council. Cromwell again refused to take the crown but accepted the Petition in May 1657. When Parliament reconvened in the following year, those who had previously been excluded attacked the new settlement and once more, in exasperation, Cromwell dissolved the Parliament. He died on 3 September 1658, naming his son, Richard, as his successor (and thus retaining the hereditary principle despite refusing to

---

[30] See *ibid*, p 207 for more detail on these institutions.

rule as a monarch). Richard Cromwell acceded peacefully but it has been said that he 'possessed neither the ambition nor the ruthlessness necessary to hold the government together',[31] and by July 1659 he had been ousted from power. The Rump Parliament was recalled, followed by the Long Parliament, and finally a Convention Parliament opened in April 1660. It restored both the House of Lords and the monarchy. Charles' eldest son, now Charles II, returned to England as the new King. Despite diverse efforts over 20 years to find a new constitution to replace the pre-1640 one, all attempts had failed.

The restoration of Charles II meant that in many ways government returned to its pre-civil war nature. England's brief encounter with a written constitution and a republican government was short-lived and would not be repeated, but the conflict between Crown and Parliament remained unresolved with the differences, papered over in the restoration settlements, to re-emerge later in the century. Indeed, the Stuart monarchy, and its belief in the divine rights of kings, survived less than three decades after the restoration. But while many of the issues which had ignited the conflict remained unresolved, a stronger legislative institution also boded ominously for the future of absolute monarchy. As Kishlansky notes, 'If it had ever been an event, Parliament was now an institution.'[32] Furthermore, the political turmoil of the civil war had led to the emergence of political parties as the traditional consensus decision-making was gradually replaced by the increased use of divisions.[33] Today, of course, the influence of party politics is ubiquitous. The emergence of adversary politics was not reversed with the restoration and therefore this remains one of the key legacies of the civil war period for the modern constitution. The transformation of a council into a genuine legislature was achieved by the 13 years of continuous sittings in the absence of any executive authority.[34] Parliament obtained and secured a constitutional role as a permanent and distinct political institution. And this institution had unsettled business with the institution of the Crown. It is to this unresolved conflict and its eventual resolution which we will now turn in the following chapter.

---

[31] *Ibid*, p 217.
[32] *Ibid*, p 226.
[33] See M Kishlansky, 'The Emergence of Adversary Politics in the Long Parliament' in R Cust and A Hughes (eds), *The English Civil War* (London, Arnold, 1997).
[34] *Ibid*, p 80.

1

1688 – Glorious Revolution; Enduring Settlement: Sovereignty, Liberty and the Constitution

The significance of the English Revolution of 1688 is not widely appreciated today and yet many of the constitutional facts taken for granted in modern Britain are a direct legacy of this Revolution and the settlement which followed it. The year 1688 lives on in our constitution through the principles of liberty, parliamentary supremacy, and constitutional monarchy. The constitution, and the way in which individuals are governed under it, has undergone some radical transformations since the seventeenth century – the growth in the executive, the role of Prime Minister, union with Scotland, democratic suffrage and the increasing influence of international and European obligations – and yet the contemporary relations between Crown and Parliament, and between individual and government, still rest upon the foundations of this seventeenth-century revolution settlement.[1]

I. Setting the Scene – A Strange 'Revolution'

The 'Glorious Revolution' of 1688 was, in a narrow sense, a change in succession to the Crown. King James II fled abroad and was replaced by his daughter, Mary, and her husband, William of Orange. In a wider sense, the revolution transformed the English constitution in numerous ways, not least by establishing a constitutional monarchy. It also had significant implications throughout Europe as England, now ruled by William of Orange, joined the Dutch in the war against

---

[1] See GM Trevelyan, *The English Revolution 1688–89* (London, Thornton Butterworth Ltd, 1938), pp 16–17: 'The relation of the Crown to Parliament and to the Law; the independence of Judges; the annual meeting of Parliament; the financial supremacy of the Commons; the position of the Church of England; the Toleration of religious Dissent; freedom of political speech and writing …: in short, a Constitutional Monarchy for a free people, these are the bases of our polity and they were well and truly laid [by the 1688 Settlement].'

Catholic France.[2] The subtext was religion. A religious war was waging across Europe, and in Protestant England, a Catholic sat on the throne.

King James II was a deeply religious man, and it is this characteristic more than any other which led to his removal/desertion from the throne. His 'moral and intellectual shortcomings' have been well documented.[3] He exercised his prerogative powers without caution or restraint and set himself against the popular will of his people. But his underlying fault was no more and no less than his religion – James II was a Catholic and it has been claimed that '[h]is religion came first: the welfare of his country a bad second.'[4] The King's own Catholicism, his Catholic Queen and Catholic conversions amongst his senior ministers, when added to the perceived 'royal assault, by means of the dispensing power, upon the monopoly of legal worship'[5] created a fear of popery that was not hard to foresee. As Scott has stated, 'short of erecting billboards on the roadside proclaiming "Protestantism in Danger", it is difficult to see what else could have been done to reignite public fears.'[6] James' desire to convert his people to Catholicism was always destined to failure but, as Schama notes, by 1687 James was no longer listening to reason,[7] and opposition to his rule was growing. Schama perceptively reminds us, however, that history is written by the victors:

> Much of the stereotype of the brutal autocrat is a projection backwards from the story written by the winners … The *cause* for which James was apt to get stirred up was, after all, toleration, that 'liberty of conscience' that Cromwell had so often warbled about, only extended, unlike the Cromwellian state, to Catholics.[8]

The irony here is almost palpable. A revolution fought on the basis of liberty and freedom removed a King whose greatest crime was religious tolerance.[9] The Revolution Settlement's centrepiece Bill of Rights, which identified and protected many of the modern human rights, even incorporated the concept of religious

----

[2] See J Scott, *England's Troubles – Seventeenth Century English Political Instability in European Context* (Cambridge, Cambridge University Press, 2000) for convincing analysis of the wider European context of the events of 1688.

[3] WS Holdsworth, *A History of English Law, Volume VI* (London, Methuen & Co, 1924), p 192. See also S Schama, *A History of Britain, Volume 2, The British Wars 1603–1776* (London, BBC Consumer Publishing, 2001), p 308, and CR Lovell, *English Constitutional and Legal History* (New York, Oxford University Press, 1962), pp 389–90.

[4] Holdsworth, n 3 above, p 192.

[5] Scott, n 2 above, p 209.

[6] *Ibid.*

[7] 'By 1687 James was no longer listening – at least with any degree of attentiveness – to the voices of reason … James was listening to the voices in his head. And they were singing Hosannas' (Schama, n 3 above, pp 308–9).

[8] Schama, n 3 above, pp 309–10.

[9] As Nenner states, 'what made James' prerogative powers especially menacing was that they were being used in furtherance of an obnoxious religious design. Had the dispensing power not been used to advance Catholics to office, it is more than likely that any protests against its use would have been muted, if heard at all' (H Nenner, 'Liberty, Law, and Property: The Constitution in Retrospect from 1689' in JR Jones (ed), *Liberty Secured? Britain Before and After 1688* (Stanford, Stanford University Press, 1992), p 104).

discrimination into its terms, for in the seventeenth century the idea of liberty, so fundamental to the revolution, was not yet linked to equality.[10] It should be noted, however, that James' toleration was tactical. His priority was to convert England to Rome, infamously intolerant of other religions.[11]

A particularly controversial example of James' misuse of the suspending power was the Declaration of Indulgence, which purported to suspend the restraints upon liberty of worship. An Order in Council required bishops to distribute the Declaration to their clergy to be read from the pulpit. Seven bishops refused to do so and presented a petition to the King. They were arrested and put on trial for seditious libel. At trial, the legality of the King's suspending power was a secondary issue, but the jury's acquittal of the bishops represented a rare judicial loss by the monarch.[12] On that very day, a committee of seven English peers, representing both Whigs and Tories, sent a fateful invitation to William of Orange. The so-called 'invitation' expressly stated the dissatisfaction which 'the people' felt at 'the present conduct of the government, in relation to their religion, liberties and properties.'[13] The invitation also emphasised the widespread desire for a change in ruler: 'your Highness may be assured there are nineteen parts of twenty of the people throughout the kingdom who are desirous of change.'[14] While this statistic suggests that the impetus for change was internal to the kingdom, the European context of the invitation, and William's rapid response, must not be overlooked.

Although James' domestic policies 'succeeded in alienating nearly every segment of the political nation,' this was not, in itself, sufficient to cause a revolution. As Kishlansky notes, James' downfall came only because 'he allowed himself to become a pawn in the power politics of Europe.'[15] James' policy of siding with Catholic France rather than Protestant Holland proved to be a risky venture. The battle for supremacy between Catholicism and Protestantism preoccupied the whole of Europe.[16] The invitation to William can thus only be fully understood in the light of developments in Europe and as the product of lengthy negotiations with William, who sought English support in his war against France.[17] William's

---

[10] On this issue, see Part III below.

[11] Schama, n 3 above, pp 309–10.

[12] See Sir DL Keir, *The Constitutional History of Modern Britain since 1485* (London, Adam & Charles Black, 1969), pp 266–67 for discussion of the Trial of the Seven Bishops.

[13] 'The Invitation to William', 30 June 1688. This document (along with many others) is reproduced in EN Williams, *The Eighteenth Century Constitution, 1688–1815 – Documents and Commentary* (Cambridge, Cambridge University Press, 1960), pp 8–10.

[14] *Ibid.*

[15] M Kishlansky, *A Monarchy Transformed – Britain 1603–1714* (London, Penguin Books, 1996), p 266.

[16] Indeed, Scott argues that even the English fear of popery is only explainable within a European context, for it would be illogical within a solely national context in which Protestantism was already secure. It is only within the European context, where Protestantism was under threat from a counter-reformation led by Spain and France, that the strength of feeling inherent in the English fear of popery makes sense (Scott, n 2 above, pp 29–30).

[17] DL Smith, *A History of the Modern British Isles 1603–1707 – The Double Crown* (Oxford, Blackwell Publishers, 1998), p 283. Indeed, Schama argues that the critical event of 1688 – the

reply, therefore, comes as no surprise. Declaring 'so great an interest in this matter, and such a right, as all the world knows, to the succession of the Crown,' William committed himself to travelling to England to rectify the situation.[18] He acknowledged the moves towards arbitrary government in England and claimed his 'expedition' to England was 'intended for no other design, but to have a free and lawful Parliament assembled as soon as is possible.'[19] The threat to the laws and liberties of the state were repeatedly emphasised, as was the overwhelming complaint that 'a religion, which is contrary to law, is endeavoured to be introduced.'[20] It is, therefore, not hard to understand why William's reply has been described as 'one of the greatest and most decisive propaganda coups of early modern times.'[21]

William and his forces landed at Torbay on 5 November and, in the ensuing month, he gathered support across the country as they slowly proceeded towards London. It has been said that 'the overwhelming response of the nation was to keep their heads down.'[22] The memories of the civil war early in the century were still fresh and meant that the public were keen to avoid further bloodshed.[23] It was at this stage that James 'lost his nerve'[24] and sought to flee the country (succeeding on his second attempt). This was the turning point in a revolution which had never really got started, and it was the 'worst thing that James could have done'[25] for it 'created a power vacuum into which William could step.'[26] On the very day that James left the kingdom (11 December), a group of peers issued a declaration from Guildhall giving their support to William. This was a policy which was formalised two weeks later, when an assembly, summoned by William, asked him to 'take upon the Administration of public Affairs, both Civil and Military, and the Disposal of the public Revenue.'[27] In effect, James had been deposed and replaced by William and 'what remained was to give this accomplishment constitutional form.'[28]

A month later, on 22 January 1689, a Convention of Lords and Commons met to determine the future of the Crown. The key issue facing the Convention was

---

replacement of James II with William and Mary – is better described as an invasion, on the basis that it was contemplated by William long before he received his official invitation (Schama, n 3 above, p 313).

[18] 'William's Reply', 30 September 1688, reproduced in Williams, n 13 above, pp 10–16.
[19] *Ibid.*
[20] *Ibid.*
[21] JI Israel (ed), *The Anglo-Dutch Moment – Essays on the Glorious Revolution and its World Impact* (Cambridge, Cambridge University Press, 1991), p 14.
[22] Smith, n 17 above, p 284.
[23] In England bloodshed was, indeed, largely avoided. The Irish were not so fortunate. As Trevelyan chillingly expresses it, Ireland 'had to be reconquered before she would submit to the change of sovereigns' (Trevelyan, n 1 above, p 205).
[24] Smith, n 17 above, p 286.
[25] *Ibid.*
[26] *Ibid*, p 287.
[27] 'Address of the Assembly', 16 December 1688, reproduced in Williams, n 13 above, p 18.
[28] Scott, n 2 above, p 221.

whether the throne was 'vacant'.[29] A split soon developed between the Lords and Commons on this point. The Lords, dominated by Tories, viewed James' desertion as an abdication and wished to retain the principle of a hereditary monarchy. By contrast, the Commons, dominated by Whigs, viewed the throne as vacant and, therefore, in the gift of the Convention Parliament. The implications of a finding of a vacancy on the throne would be profound. As the Earl of Nottingham recognised in the Convention's debate, there was concern as to 'whether the Vacancy of the Throne, and filling it again, will not … endanger the turning this hereditary monarchy of ours into an elective one?'[30] Indeed, the Earl of Nottingham went so far as to argue that 'I cannot see by what authority we can … change our ancient constitution, without committing the same fault we have laid upon the King.'[31] Nevertheless, the Lords eventually voted to agree with the Commons that the throne was vacant. It was initially intended that the vacancy would be filled by Mary as Queen, with William as her consort or regent. Such a move would have paid lip service to the line of descent and would have permitted the Tories, in particular, to cling to their favoured ideal of an hereditary monarchy, but William 'refused to be his "wife's gentlemen usher"'[32] and so William and Mary were offered the throne jointly.

By what authority was this offer made? The Convention Parliament was not a legitimate Parliament, for it was not summoned in the King's name but by William and lacked the availability of the royal assent to legislation. Indeed, the Convention Parliament could be regarded as 'a fig-leaf for William's naked power'.[33] This illegitimate Parliament took the throne from the lawful King and gave it to an alien, who subsequently returned the favour by retrospectively declaring the Convention Parliament to be a lawful Parliament.[34] Neither the Convention Parliament nor King William had any legitimacy without the other. In a revolution fought to preserve, rather than overthrow, the law, this was a curious basis for a settlement, but 300 years of Crown and government rest upon this strange turn of events. Of great significance for the future is the fact that the Crown offered to William and Mary was not unlimited. The offer was made immediately after the public reading of the Declaration of Rights, which sought to impose (or, at least, make explicit) a number of limits upon the prerogative powers of the monarch. Such an implied contract has bound the executive power ever since, both in terms of its relationship with the legislature and in its powers over individual subjects.

The relationship between Crown and Parliament and the nature of the executive power had been the source of conflict for much of the seventeenth century.

---

[29] Of course, in theory, a vacant throne is an impossibility in a hereditary monarchy.
[30] 'Conference between Houses on "abdicated" and "vacant"', 6 February 1689, reproduced in Williams, n 13 above, pp 20–26.
[31] *Ibid.*
[32] Williams, n 13 above, p 2.
[33] Kishlansky, n 15 above, p 283.
[34] See Lovell, n 3 above, pp 394–95.

The revolution of 1688 led to a settlement of this issue which has endured, in stark contrast to Cromwellian ideals. Perhaps it is here where the 'glory' of the revolution lies. It is not a glory founded upon a bloodless overthrowing of the principle of divine right monarchy (although this is no small accomplishment). The glory 'lies not in the minimum of violence which was necessary for its success, but in the way of escape from violence which the Revolution Settlement found for future generations of Englishmen.'[35] The glory is not, then, in the revolutionary events themselves, but rather in the settlement which set the foundations for a peaceful kingdom with limited government, individual rights and liberties and an evolutionary constitution.

> The fundamentals [of the 1688 Settlement] have remained to bear the weight of the vast democratic superstructure which the nineteenth and twentieth centuries have raised upon its sure foundations. Here, seen at long range, is 'glory' burning steadily for 250 [sic] years.[36]

The fundamentals of the Revolution Settlement have endured but the spirit of the revolution was never revolutionary. The aim of the revolution was to uphold the law. It was the King who by 1688 was perceived as the 'real revolutionary', who sought to overturn the laws and constitution of his kingdom.[37] He would not be allowed to do so – a fact which has continued to serve as a warning to future governments tempted to exceed the limitations imposed on their powers by the British constitution.

II. Sovereignty under the 1688 Settlement

a) The Changing Relationship between Crown and Parliament

Probably the most fundamental consequence of the 1688 Revolution was the transformation in the relationship between the Crown and Parliament. The

---

[35] Trevelyan, n 1 above, p 9. As Trevelyan notes, 'England has lived at peace within herself ever since' (p 11).

[36] *Ibid*, p 11.

[37] Schama, n 3 above, p 309. See also JR Jones, *The Revolution of 1688 in England* (London, Weidenfeld & Nicolson, 1972), p 328: 'most of those who rallied to William against James were conservative, or conservationist, in their aims. They had been led to resist James because of the kind of changes he was trying to introduce.' Locke's *Two Treatises of Government* (ed P Laslett (Cambridge, Cambridge University Press, 1988)) subsequently provided the theoretical justification for this: 'For Rebellion being an Opposition not to Persons, but Authority, which is founded only in the Constitutions and Laws of the Government; those, whoever they be, who by force break through, and by force justifie their violation of them, are truly and properly Rebels' (ch XIX, para 226). The true 'rebels' were, in Locke's eyes, the Stuart monarchs who had exceeded the powers given to them under the Constitution. See further below on Locke's anticipatory justification for the revolutionary events of 1688.

turbulence of the seventeenth century was largely due to the conflict between these two parts of government, and the enduring outcome of the 1688 Settlement was to award Parliament victory over the Crown.[38] There was, however, little republican fervour by 1688. The parliamentarians were all too aware of the 'fragility of elite control' and determined to avoid any populist threat to the existing social and political order.[39] A constitutional monarchy also remained the preferred form of government for the overwhelming majority of the population. But, from 1688 onwards, it would have to be a limited monarchy. The reason for this was not so much a desire to diminish the powers of the Crown, but rather to ensure that they were not misused (as had been the perception during the reign of James II). The impetus behind the Settlement was 'an exasperated recognition that the only way to ensure that monarchs ruled responsibly was to deprive them of any opportunity to do otherwise.'[40] The Crown offered to William and Mary was therefore an expressly (and no longer impliedly) limited Crown. The Bill of Rights declared certain kingly practices to be illegal, such as the suspension and dispensing of laws, and also included an acknowledgement by William and Mary that Parliament 'should continue to sit.'[41] Furthermore, the Triennial Act 1694 required the calling of Parliament at least every three years,[42] and the Act of Settlement 1701 finally settled all issues of succession by extending the discrimination against Catholics evident in the earlier Bill of Rights.[43] In reality, however, these were not the ties which bound future monarchs. The real sanction of the Revolution Settlement was the new financial system put in place after 1688. The naked truth is that, as Trevelyan states, 'No King after James II has ever been in a financial position even to attempt to break the law or to quarrel seriously with the House of Commons.'[44]

The Bill of Rights stated the now well-established rule that the levying of money for use by the Crown, without the grant of Parliament, is illegal and this was made a genuine limitation in practice due to the new system for funding the Crown. After 1689, parliamentary grants to the Crown were for a single year only.[45] What better guarantee of frequent Parliaments? In addition, the war against France in the 1690s ensured that the Crown was in constant need of

[38] By this period in history the true power of Parliament (particularly in financial matters) rested with the House of Commons rather than the House of Lords. This fact was demonstrated in 1688 by the willingness of the Lords to give way to the Commons on the crucial and divisive issue of a vacancy on the throne.

[39] J Miller, 'Crown, Parliament, and the People' in JR Jones (ed), *Liberty Secured? Britain Before and After 1688* (Stanford, Stanford University Press, 1992), p 77.

[40] *Ibid*, p 56.

[41] Section V, Bill of Rights 1689.

[42] This was justified on the basis that 'frequent and new Parliaments tend very much to the happy union and good agreement of the King and people.'

[43] 'Whosoever shall hereafter come to the possession of this crown, shall join in communion with the Church of England, as by law established' (Act of Settlement 1701).

[44] Trevelyan, n 1 above, p 180.

[45] Lovell, n 3 above, p 397.

money,[46] and the Civil List Act 1697 limited the annual grant to the King to the expenses of civil administration and the royal household. Everything else was henceforth to be in the realm of specific parliamentary grant.[47] The implications of the monarch's reliance on Parliament for funding cannot be overestimated:

> A firmer grip on finance gave Parliament a surer hold on measures and men; and parliamentary influence over the executive was bound to grow as succeeding monarchs came to terms with this truth, as they gradually learned that a ministry and a policy could founder on the rock of supply.[48]

To put it bluntly, 'he who pays the piper, calls the tune,' and after 1688 this was, undoubtedly, Parliament.[49] This new financial pressure on the Crown played an essential role in ensuring that the limitations and obligations imposed on the offer of the Crown to William and Mary proved to be effective.[50]

It was not entirely a one-sided settlement. As stated in the previous section, the Revolution Settlement provided a 'way of escape from violence … for future generations.'[51] A limited monarchy and a supreme (query sovereign?) Parliament have remained the favoured form of government for the United Kingdom ever since. If a monarchy based on the divine right of kings theory had survived the seventeenth century, the United Kingdom may not have escaped with a single, bloodless revolution. As Trevelyan states, 'what the Crown lost in power it gained in security. The Republican movement was buried …'.[52] The crux of the new relationship between the Crown and Parliament post-1688 was that the implied, theoretical limits on the sovereign's powers were made effective by Parliament's control over finances (and, to a lesser extent, by the change in succession which gave the distinct impression that succession was 'subject to legislative modification at any time'[53]). The Crown had to learn to live, and work, with Parliament; Parliament had to learn how best to exercise its new power. This 'settlement' of the unhappy conflict between two parts of government merely raises further difficult questions, however. In particular, this chapter will proceed to consider,

---

[46] J Carter, 'The Revolution and the Constitution' in G Holmes (ed), *Britain after the Glorious Revolution 1689–1714* (London, Macmillan, 1969), p 55. As Carter also notes, the demands of wartime administration also strengthened the position of the executive power in government.

[47] Williams, n 13 above, p 5.

[48] *Ibid.*

[49] As Smith states: 'The Crown's desperate need for tax revenues transformed Parliament from an occasional event into a permanent institution of government. It is a remarkable fact that the English Parliament has met every year since 1689' (Smith, n 17 above, p 313).

[50] For example, as Holdsworth notes, by 1689 it had become redundant to enact that Parliament ought to be held frequently, because it was simply impossible to conduct the business of the state in the absence of Parliament (Holdsworth, n 3 above, p 242).

[51] Trevelyan, n 1 above, p 9.

[52] *Ibid*, p 150. We might perhaps add to this point, 'only to be revived in recent years.'

[53] Lovell, n 3 above, p 396. William and Mary, and later Anne, could (with a little straining of the theory) be regarded as the rightful heirs to the throne, but the next King, George I, became King for no reason other than the Act of Settlement. His successors have continued to base their title solely on this legislative provision (*ibid*).

first, whether the settlement marked the birth of parliamentary sovereignty, as so many writers have claimed and, second, its impact upon individual rights. Most importantly, the following sections will investigate how these implications for sovereignty and liberty have affected our own present-day constitution and government.

b) The Birth of Parliamentary Sovereignty?

The 'forgotten revolution'[54] of 1688 is in fact remembered, at least by constitutional lawyers, for one significant thing: the birth of the doctrine of parliamentary sovereignty,[55] so authoritatively explained by AV Dicey in the nineteenth century.[56] It may be, however, that this is a false memory. The Parliament of 1689 was not 'sovereign', at least not in the sense in which Dicey defines the term. One may wonder, indeed, whether Parliament has ever been sovereign in such a sense.

The characteristic of the Revolution Settlement which has led some commentators to perceive it as the starting point for parliamentary sovereignty is the superiority of statute law over the royal prerogative which dates from this period. The express limitations on the Crown's prerogative powers in the Bill of Rights (and the financial constraints which in practice enforced these) are the clearest indicator of this. The fundamental question under the English constitution in the seventeenth century was whether the King was above the law (as the divine rights theory so beloved by the Stuarts would suggest) or whether the law was above the King and able to impose enforceable limits upon him. The Crown offered to William and Mary was undoubtedly subject to legal limits. The Convention Parliament finally agreed that future monarchs would govern under the law. William and Mary accepted the Crown on this basis, and none of their successors has ever had the political or financial strength to challenge the idea.

The King, then, was subject to the law but, crucially, the law could be changed by the King-in-Parliament. It is this factor which inevitably resulted in Parliament becoming the supreme power in the state. But supremacy is not (necessarily) sovereignty. The fact that statutes enacted by the King-in-Parliament are the highest form of law does not necessarily mean the supreme legislator is unlimited in its powers. The 1689 Settlement made clear that the

---

[54] P Norton, 'The Glorious Revolution of 1688 – Its Continuing Relevance' [1989] *Parliamentary Affairs* 135 at 135.

[55] For example, Hood Phillips' and Jackson's textbook declares: 'The establishment of parliamentary sovereignty was a product of the revolution of 1688' (O Hood Phillips, P Jackson and P Leopold, *Constitutional and Administrative Law*, 8th edn (London, Sweet & Maxwell, 2001), p 39). This statement follows some discussion of constitutional history pre-1688 but there is very little detail provided on why 1688 should be regarded as so significant for parliamentary sovereignty.

[56] See AV Dicey, *Introduction to the Study of the Law of the Constitution*, 10th edn (London, Macmillan, 1959), pp 39–40. Dicey's infamous definition of parliamentary sovereignty is as follows: 'the right to make or unmake any law whatever; and further, that no person or body is recognised by the law of England as having a right to override or set aside the legislation of Parliament.'

King was to operate under the laws of the constitution. There was no suggestion that Parliament should (or could) be elevated above the constitution. A logical issue arising out of this is what the laws of the constitution require of Parliament. A Parliament which is supreme only because of a revolution fought on the basis of endangered rights and liberties might be presumed to be subject to limitations in respect of these. As will be seen below, the Bill of Rights sought to impose such limits. In addition, the idea of liberty meant far more in the seventeenth-century constitution than its modern interpretation of a freedom to do anything not proscribed by Parliament.

The concept of sovereignty in the seventeenth century required supremacy but not necessarily illimitability. The idea of supremacy within a limited jurisdiction – sovereignty *under* the constitution – was much more firmly grasped then than now.[57] And yet it is the most effective of ideas. It explains how the King-in-Parliament of 1689 could be sovereign and yet subject to constitutional limits in relation to natural, or moral, laws, which had been asserted so strongly earlier in the century.[58] It also explains how the modern Parliament of today may retain its sovereignty and yet do so only within a limited jurisdiction, excluding matters covered by the European Communities Act 1972, the Scotland Act 1998, the Northern Ireland Act 1998, and the Human Rights Act 1998, as well as the constitutional limits on its powers which have lingered and developed since 1689.[59] In practical terms, it was obvious in 1689 that if a king could be replaced because he did not abide by the constitutional limits on his sovereignty, the new sovereign body of King-in-Parliament must equally be restricted by such limits, and should abide by them if it wished to survive.

The Parliament of 1689 was, therefore, sovereign in the sense that its laws were thereafter to be superior to the royal prerogative. But there was no suggestion at this period in history that Parliament should be unlimited in its legislative powers. The fundamental principles of the common law constitution, which had sought to bind the Crown in the earlier part of the seventeenth century, remained to bind the King-in-Parliament. The fact that they have not always been effective in doing so does not detract from their existence or their survival to the present day. It is Parliament's legislative supremacy which dates from 1689 and not its alleged omnipotence.

---

[57] In recent years this idea has been asserted by senior members of the judiciary. See, for example, J Laws, 'Is the High Court the Guardian of Fundamental Constitutional Rights?' [1993] *PL* 59 and 'Law and Democracy' [1995] *PL* 72; Lord Woolf, 'Droit Public – English Style' [1995] *PL* 57.

[58] See *Dr Bonham's Case* (1610) 8 Co Rep 107a, in which Coke CJ famously outlined what has become known as Coke's doctrine: 'When an Act of Parliament is against common right or reason, or repugnant, or impossible to be performed, the common law will control it, and adjudge such Act to be void' (p 118). See also *Calvin's case* (1608) 7 Co Rep 1; *Day v Savadge* (1614) Hob 85; and *Lord Sheffield v Ratcliffe* (1615) Hob 334a. Coke may have been outlining little more than a strict statutory interpretation method but, *contra* Dicey, the fundamental nature of certain common law principles certainly endured beyond the 1688 Revolution. See the comments of Holt CJ in *City of London v Wood* (1710) 12 Mod 669 at 687–88.

[59] This argument will be developed more fully in ch 7 below in respect of the European Communities Act 1972. See pp 154–60.

c) Sovereignty of the People?

The concept of popular sovereignty is at the core of many state constitutions. It is the idea of popular sovereignty which serves to legitimise the powers given to government under the founding constitution. This is particularly evident in the two landmark constitutions of the eighteenth century – the United States Constitution 1776 and the French Constitution 1789. Both of these written constitutions followed a bloody revolution in which 'the people', or at least their leaders, secured power from a discredited regime. The English revolution was rather different. The 'people' played a very small role in it and, in addition, the English revolution occurred a century before ideas of popular sovereignty (and its natural companion, democracy) had really surfaced. As Haseler has succinctly noted, 'the British thus missed the democratic boat.'[60] Britain would have to wait a long while for ideas of democracy, popular sovereignty and self-determination to take a firm root in the constitution, but the seeds may have been planted as early as 1689. The enforced change in succession is a prime example of this. As Holdsworth notes, 'the people, through their representatives in Parliament, had assumed the right to make and unmake kings.'[61] On this basis, Keir even goes so far as to argue: 'Sovereignty in 1688 was for practical purposes grasped by the nation.'[62] Such a view can only be accepted, however, if Parliament is regarded as representative of 'the nation'. On modern-day terms, it was clearly not so, but, nevertheless, there is some indication that Parliament sought to be representative according to the standards of the time. The fact is that, in the seventeenth century, neither women nor the poor were regarded as being included in 'the people' with the right to be represented in Parliament.[63] If we judge the 1688 Parliament on these contemporary standards, it may indeed be regarded as representative of this narrower class of 'the people'. The Bill of Rights, for example, is expressed as a declaration by 'the lords spiritual and temporal, and commons, and freely representing all the estates of the people of this realm.' The three estates in the seventeenth century (who were regarded as exclusively comprising 'the people') were clergy, peers and landowners, and these did indeed have considerable power through their representatives in Parliament. Furthermore, the introductory words of the Bill of Rights quoted above sound strikingly reminiscent of later written constitutions. Perhaps, therefore, popular sovereignty was not an alien concept in seventeenth-century England and actually provided a degree of legitimacy to the change in succession and Revolution Settlement similar to that underlying many modern constitutions. England faced a long struggle, however, before such a limited degree of popular sovereignty could

---

[60] S Haseler, 'Britain's *Ancien Regime*' [1990] *Parliamentary Affairs* 415 at 416.
[61] Holdsworth, n 3 above, p 230.
[62] Keir, n 12 above, p 269.
[63] This was not unique to England. 'The people' in the US Declaration of Independence was exclusive of not only women and the poor but also the large slave population.

become more widespread through the growth of democracy in the nineteenth century.

III. Liberty under the 1688 Settlement

a) Liberty as Property

It has been stated that 'the keynote of the Revolution Settlement was personal freedom under the law,' leading to the conclusion that '[t]he most conservative of all revolutions in history was also the most liberal.' [64] The predominance of the idea of liberty in the events of 1688 is evident in the key documents of the time. The invitation to William,[65] William's reply,[66] and, later, the Bill of Rights,[67] all gave unexpected emphasis to the issue of the rights and liberties of the King's subjects. These were described in the Bill of Rights as 'the true, ancient, and indubitable rights and liberties of the people of this kingdom.'[68] The protection of individual rights under the UK constitution is not, therefore, a new idea. It dates from at least the seventeenth century and, in a less formalised manner, from far earlier. The continuing significance of this fact should not be overlooked, for even today, with explicit protection of rights in the Human Rights Act 1998, fundamental (or, in the words of 1688, 'indubitable') constitutional rights may fill important gaps in rights protection, in terms of both coverage and enforcement. The foundation of many modern-day rights can be seen in the Bill of Rights 1689, and this issue will be explored in more detail below, but first it is vital to obtain some clarity on the basis for these rights in the seventeenth century and, in particular, the meaning of the key concept of liberty.

During the seventeenth century, the idea of liberty was transformed. No longer was liberty in the grant of the Crown – it was no longer merely the residual freedom bequeathed to subjects and revocable at any time. Rather, it was a fundamental right of the people[69] and as such was immune from the Crown's recall.[70] This new idea is best illustrated by a phrase from an anonymous

---

[64] Trevelyan, n 1 above, p 12.

[65] '[T]he people are so generally dissatisfied with the present conduct of the government, in relation to their religion, liberties and properties (all of which have been greatly invaded) ...' ('Invitation to William', 30 June 1688, reproduced in Williams, n 13 above, pp 8–10).

[66] 'It is both certain and evident to all men, that the public peace and happiness of any state or kingdom cannot be preserved where the Laws, Liberties and Customs, established by the lawful authority in it, are openly transgressed and annulled ...' ('William's Reply', 30 September 1688, reproduced in Williams, n 13 above, pp 10–16).

[67] 'An act for declaring the rights and liberties of the subject and settling the succession of the crown'(Bill of Rights 1689).

[68] Section VI, Bill of Rights 1689.

[69] There may, perhaps, be early echoes of popular sovereignty here.

[70] Nenner, n 9 above, p 88.

pamphleteer writing in 1689 and quoted by Nenner: 'That power which the people reserveth from the sovereign is called liberty.'[71] This is an idea at the core of Locke's theory: people come together to form societies and entrust limited power to a sovereign to rule on their behalf. If the sovereign exceeds his limited power (in particular by threatening the people's property, defined as including liberties and laws), the people are 'absolved from any further obedience' to the sovereign and the use of force is justified.[72] When viewed in this way, liberty is a hugely significant idea. It demonstrates the error in modern-day assumptions that individuals traditionally only had residual liberty under the constitution. It is often stated that (pre-Human Rights Act) individuals could do anything not prohibited by the law,[73] which embodies a very limited idea of freedom. It seems, however, that 'liberty' circa 1688 meant something far more significant, namely a degree of freedom retained by the people when they bequeathed some limited powers to their sovereign. On this basis, the 'common law constitution' is not as flexible and negative as has recently been assumed. Nenner expresses this point effectively when he describes the security of the subjects' liberties (and law and property[74]) as 'a condition of the monarch's right to rule, the yardstick of the government's right to exist.'[75] He proceeds to argue that '[t]he wish, which had been father to the thought, had come to be an article of constitutional faith.'[76] It still is, and as such should serve as a warning to modern governments that their 'right to exist' relies upon their preservation of their subjects' rights and liberties.

There was, however, a serious limitation on the effectiveness of the idea of liberty in the seventeenth century, and it is not that of 'residual freedom' usually (wrongly) identified. Liberty in the seventeenth century was not founded upon any idea of equality. Nowadays we may find it almost impossible to consider liberty in isolation from equality but, as was shown above, equality played no part in seventeenth-century law or practice. Catholics, as well as the poor and women, suffered the brunt of this inequality during this period. So, although freedom was both a valued, and a valuable, idea in the seventeenth century, there were, according to Miller, 'numerous different types of "freedom" … with people of substantial wealth and high social rank possessing far more "freedom" than the poor and humble.'[77] It was ever thus, we might add, but today there is a

---

[71] *Ibid*, p 89.

[72] Locke, ch XIX, para 222. Locke's *Two Treatises of Government* provides a theoretical justification for the events of 1688–89. The preface makes clear that Locke's intention was to 'establish the Throne' of William. But, as Laslett has pointed out, this was not the original conception of the book, most of which was written prior to the revolutionary events of 1688 (and was actually attacking the misuse of the prerogative by Charles II, rather than James): 'Two Treatises in fact turns out to be a demand for a revolution to be brought about, not the rationalization of a revolution in need of defence.' (P Laslett, Introduction to Locke's *Two Treatises of Government* in Locke, n 37 above, p 47. See also R Ashcraft, *Revolutionary Politics and Locke's Two Treatises of Government* (Princeton, Princeton University Press, 1986), pp 550–51.) In fact, it turned out to be both.

[73] Dicey is particularly influential on this point.

[74] On this link with property, see below.

[75] Nenner, n 9 above, p 88.

[76] *Ibid*.

[77] Miller, n 39 above, p 54.

widespread acceptance that, in theory (if not in practical socio-economic terms), every individual has the same right to freedom. The idea of equality does, after all, underlie the twentieth-century explosion in international human rights protection. In the seventeenth century, in the absence of equality, another concept was linked to liberty – the concept of property.

In the seventeenth century, liberty was regarded as a tangible possession.[78] Locke, for example, describes 'the mutual Preservation of their Lives, Liberties and Estates' as the people's 'property'.[79] He proceeds to argue that 'the power of the society, or Legislature, constituted by them, can never be suppos'd to extend farther than the common good; but is obliged to secure every one's Property.'[80] This seventeenth-century link between liberty and property had three important consequences for the idea of liberty. First, it secured the inapplicability of equality to the issue. In respect of property, we either own something or we do not. It was much the same with liberty. Either a person possessed liberty, in which case this was a strong argument against its removal, or a person did not possess liberty (because of their religion, poverty or other social disadvantage), and any residual freedom could be removed by the government. Second, the linking of liberty with property meant that it became important to prove title to that liberty. It was established by 1688 that a subject's rights and liberties were not in the gift of the Crown – they were 'ancient and indubitable'[81] – but how could such title be proved?

> In a seventeenth century view of basic rights, life, liberty, and estates – all of which were the subject's property – were inherited from an ancestry so remote in time as of necessity to be undocumented … The law, therefore, became everything – the agency by which the inheritance was passed, the weapon by which it was defended from the king, and, not least, an integral part of the inheritance itself. The English had title to their laws; and the laws, in turn, gave them title to all that they valued.[82]

It is for this reason that the terms 'laws' and 'liberties' (as well as 'property') are so often linked in the key documents of 1688–89.[83] The greatest triumph of the Revolution Settlement was, then, the establishment of the Rule of Law.[84] William's reply in 1688 made reference to the subjection of England to 'arbitrary Government'.[85] The Revolution Settlement sought to ensure that this would

---

[78] By the seventeenth century, 'property had become much more than estates or corporeal possessions. The word, highly charged in seventeenth century political usage, had come to mean an Englishmen's vested and unassailable rights' (Nenner, n 9 above, p 94).

[79] Locke, n 37 above, ch IX, para 123.

[80] *Ibid*, para 131. Indeed, Locke's 'central allegation' against James II was his 'direct assault upon a freely chosen legislature.' On this point, see Ashcraft, n 72 above, p 548.

[81] Section VI, Bill of Rights 1689.

[82] Nenner, n 9 above, p 97.

[83] See, for example, the 'Invitation to William', 'William's Reply', and the Bill of Rights.

[84] Trevelyan, n 1 above, p 133.

[85] It proceeded: 'and that not only by secret and indirect ways, but in an open and undisguised manner' (reproduced in Williams, n 13 above, pp 10–16).

never again occur. The supremacy of the law became 'the best of all securities for the liberties of the subject, against both the claims of the royal prerogative and the claims of parliamentary privilege.'[86] The Act of Settlement, a few years later, secured the establishment of the Rule of Law by guaranteeing judicial independence. From then onwards, 'The law was made arbiter of all issues by its own legal standards, without fear of what Government could do either to Judge or to Juries.'[87] Trevelyan goes on to note that it is 'difficult to exaggerate the importance of this as a step towards real justice and civilization.'[88] We continue to reap the benefits and underestimate the fragility of the Rule of Law today.

Both the laws and liberties of the subjects had become their own inherited property and each would safeguard the other for posterity. The third important consequence of the link between liberty and property is simply that the English constitution has been built upon the idea of property. Liberty, when viewed as property, will be soundly protected under the constitution. Property, indeed, is not an entirely inappropriate, or entirely unhelpful, basis for human rights. It is surely inherent in contemporary claims that each individual is entitled to protection of their civil and political rights. But, the absence of an equality basis for liberty in the seventeenth century resulted in the idea of non-property owners in respect of liberty, which may be regarded as both unjust and illogical from today's egalitarian perspective.

b) A Declaration of Rights

The Bill of Rights 1689 is a multi-purpose document, the significance of which remains in dispute. Viewed by some as quasi-contractual in nature, implying constitutional limits on the new monarchs,[89] it is argued by others that it merely documents the concessions granted by William to the English people.[90] The purposes served by the Bill of Rights were equally diverse: it detailed the various means by which James II 'did endeavour to subvert and extirpate the protestant religion, and the laws and liberties of this kingdom';[91] it declared James as having abdicated and the throne vacant; it declared William and Mary as 'King and Queen of England, France and Ireland, and the dominions thereunto belonging';

---

[86] Holdsworth, n 3 above, p 234.

[87] Trevelyan, n 1 above, p 168.

[88] *Ibid.*

[89] 'The Bill of Rights had the appearance of a contract and tacitly implied that William III and his successors were constitutional monarchs' (Kishlansky, n 15 above, p 293).

[90] 'We should see the events of 1689 less as the imposition of terms upon invited rulers than as the granting of concessions to a conquered people by a new William the Conqueror' (J Morrill, 'The Sensible Revolution' in Israel, n 21 above, p 87).

[91] These included, [b]y assuming and exercising a power of dispensing with and suspending of laws, and the execution of laws, without consent of Parliament' and 'by levying money for and to the use of the crown, by pretence of prerogative, for other time, and in other manner, than the same was granted by Parliament.'

it indicated William's and Mary's assent that Parliament would 'continue to sit';[92] and it banned Catholics (and those married to such) from the Crown.[93] But, most significantly and famously, the Bill of Rights listed 13 assertions for the purpose of 'vindicating and asserting … [the subjects'] ancient rights and liberties.' In this key part of the document, it is argued, can be found the basis for many modern civil and political rights. Each will now be considered in turn.

The first point listed in this section is the declaration that the 'pretended' power of suspending laws, without the consent of Parliament, is illegal. This is closely followed by a similar declaration that the dispensing of laws 'as it has been assumed and exercised of late' is also illegal. Together these two prohibitions on arbitrary executive interference with the law comprise the core element of the Rule of Law. Today, the mechanism of judicial review enforces and expands this first tentative attempt to compel the executive power to operate according to, rather than above, the law.[94] The third article raised in this declaration of rights is the illegality of the commission of ecclesiastical courts. The next article plays a further role in securing the Rule of Law by limiting the powers of the executive power. The levying of money for use by the Crown without the grant of Parliament is declared to be illegal. As was discussed above, the financial constraints on the Crown post-1689 represented the most effective assurance of parliamentary supremacy under the constitution and ensured that the executive branch of government was limited by its need to work together with Parliament.

Article five declares the right of subjects to petition the king, and this may be regarded as a precursor of modern access to justice rights. The right of petition also finds direct application in the First Amendment of the US Constitution, where the right to petition the government for a redress of grievances is guaranteed. Article six prohibits the Crown from raising or keeping a standing army in times of peace without the consent of Parliament and this, again, was an effective practical restraint on the Crown's prerogative powers. Indeed, this prohibition is widely regarded as the only novelty in the Declaration of Rights.[95] Article seven may now seem out of place in a self-styled Bill of Rights as it declares a right to bear arms, but only for Protestants. This endemic religious discrimination is a sign of the absence of any established idea of equality. The right to arms itself was later incorporated into the Second Amendment of the US Constitution and

---

[92] Section V, Bill of Rights 1689.

[93] Roman Catholics shall be 'for ever incapable to inherit, possess, or enjoy the crown and government of this realm' (Section IX).

[94] These prohibitions may also be regarded as a very early indicator of the value of equality under the law, an idea expanded upon in this context by Dicey's Rule of Law theory. The second limb of this theory relates to equality before the law and requires that the government be subject to the same laws as every citizen.

[95] See J Miller, *The Glorious Revolution* (London, Longman, 1983), p 37: 'The remainder were largely restatements of what most people regarded as the constitution.' See also Keir, n 12 above, at p 268, where he claims that only this one power 'unquestionably belonging to the Crown' was destroyed by the Bill of Rights.

continues to present seemingly insurmountable problems in a modern state plagued with gun crime.

Article eight in the Declaration of Rights is the first genuinely recognisable modern right, guaranteeing the free election of Members of Parliament. This is an important political right, protected today by Article 3 of the First Protocol to the European Convention on Human Rights (ECHR)[96] and Article 25 of the International Covenant on Civil and Political Rights (ICCPR).[97] It is also an essential foundation for the principle of democratic government. Free elections in the seventeenth century did not, of course, imply universal suffrage, but they did provide a founding principle on which subsequent democratic reforms could be built. Alongside the guarantee of free elections lies a guarantee of freedom of speech within Parliament. This forms article nine of the Bill of Rights' declaration of rights and liberties. Obviously, free speech is regarded as a fundamental civil and political right today, but its appearance in the Bill of Rights was subject to extreme limitations. It was not a general right to freedom of expression but, rather, existed as a complementary political right to the right to free elections and sought to ensure that the proceedings in Parliament would not be impeached or questioned anywhere else, including in a court of law. On this general principle, rests the complicated law of parliamentary privilege, still of considerable practical influence today. The need for a free Parliament was a major goal in the Revolution as is apparent by William's Reply, when he stated that:

> Our expedition is intended for no other design, but to have a free and lawful Parliament assembled as soon as is possible … They shall meet and sit in full freedom, that so the two houses may concur in the preparing of such Laws as they, upon full and free debate, shall judge necessary and convenient ….[98]

This principle has never wavered from the English constitution, and the existence of a free (and now democratic) Parliament is one of the core principles of British government and society.

The tenth article in the Declaration of Rights is '[t]hat excessive bail ought not to be required, nor excessive fines imposed; nor cruel and unusual punishments inflicted.' Here lies the ancestor of modern rights to liberty and dignity of the person. The wording in the Bill of Rights is identical to that used a century later in the Eighth Amendment to the US Constitution, which has been influential throughout many jurisdictions. The prohibition on cruel and unusual punishments has a modern-day equivalent in Article 3 ECHR (now part of domestic law

---

[96] 'The High Contracting Parties undertake to hold free elections at reasonable intervals by secret ballot, under conditions which will ensure the free expression of the opinion of the people in the choice of the legislature.'

[97] The right 'to vote and to be elected at genuine periodic elections which shall be by universal and equal suffrage and shall be held by secret ballot, guaranteeing the free expression of the will of the electors.'

[98] 'William's Reply, 30 September 1688, reproduced in Williams, n 13 above, pp 10–16.

under the Human Rights Act 1998)[99] and Article 7 ICCPR.[100] The original Bill of Rights provision has also seen recent application in domestic courts in the case of *Williams v Home Office (No 2)*,[101] where prison conditions were subject to a challenge on the ground of violation of the 1689 statute, inter alia. The claim was unsuccessful. The regime in the special control unit at Wakefield Prison was held to be neither 'unusual' (when compared to similar units), nor 'cruel' (as it was neither below an irreducible minimum standard nor disproportionate). However, the case stands as an example of the continued application and relevance of the Bill of Rights.[102] The prohibition on excessive bail and fines also continues to serve as a respected principle in criminal and civil justice.

Article eleven in the Declaration of Rights relates to the administration of the courts and requires that juries are 'duly impannelled and returned'. This also clearly retains its influence as a principle of criminal justice. The next article seeks to guarantee judicial independence, the pre-requisite for the preservation of the rule of law and effective protection of individual rights and liberties. All grants and promises of fines and forfeitures before conviction are declared void and illegal. The need and desire for supremacy of the law is again evident here. For the final of the 13 articles in the Declaration of Rights, attention is refocused on Parliament: 'for redress of all grievances, and for the amending, strengthening and preserving of the laws, parliaments ought to be held frequently.' As was noted above, free parliaments are guaranteed in a number of modern treaties and constitutions, and the need for regular elections is expressly referred to in Article 3 of the First Protocol to the ECHR and Article 25 ICCPR. Prior to the 1688 Revolution, the calling of parliaments was at the whim of the monarch. Subsequently, largely because of the practical need to secure finances, Parliament (although in theory still called by the monarch) was continually in session.[103]

The Declaration of Rights, when viewed as a whole, can be seen to contain many important constitutional values – the rule of law, democracy (of a limited form), freedom, human dignity, justice and even, perhaps, a very early tentative move towards equality – all of which continue to form the fundamental basis of the UK constitution. Many of the modern human rights, which now form such a crucial part of the constitution through international treaties, the common law and the Human Rights Act 1998, can trace their ancestry back to the 1689 Bill of Rights. Rights to liberty, dignity, freedom of expression, political rights and equal justice can all be found, albeit in an unsophisticated form, in the 1689 document.

---

[99] 'No one shall be subjected to torture or to inhuman or degrading treatment or punishment.'

[100] 'No one shall be subjected to torture or to cruel, inhuman or degrading treatment or punishment …'.

[101] [1981] 1 All ER 1211.

[102] Admittedly, the need for recourse to the Bill of Rights may have diminished with the coming into force of the Human Rights Act 1998, but this does not detract from the significance of the 1689 document as the ECHR was, to a considerable extent, built upon its early foundations.

[103] Holdsworth goes so far as to state that by 1689 it had become 'quite unnecessary to enact that "Parliament ought to be held frequently", because it was impossible to carry out the business of the state without Parliament' (Holdsworth, n 3 above, p 242).

There are, of course, some noticeable absences, ensuring that this seventeenth-century conception of rights retains a distinctive character. There is no hint, for example, of a right to life.[104] Nor is there any right to privacy, which is particularly surprising given this right's development from seventeenth-century ideas of property.[105] Nevertheless, the Bill of Rights 1689 is the crowning glory of the revolution. It builds upon the key ideas of liberty and property and provides an outline for future human rights development. Its significance in this respect is twofold – it provides the foundations on which future, more detailed and extensive rights could be modelled, and it also continues to serve as a valuable protection for certain rights and liberties as part of the British constitution.[106]

IV. Conclusion

Holdsworth has claimed that '[w]e look in vain for any statement of constitutional principle in the Bill of Rights'[107] and, on this basis, we could query the relevance of this ancient statute (and the events which led to its formation) to our modern-day constitution. Holdsworth's argument overlooks an important consideration, however, namely that, while the Bill of Rights may lack explicit declarations of constitutional principles, it is rife with constitutional significance. Indeed, the lack of any explicit principles – the absence of any 'philosophical strait-jacket'[108] – is advantageous in terms of permitting flexibility and evolutionary development of the constitution. But the constitutional principles do exist – in the 1689 Revolution Settlement and many other sources.[109] Three core ideas were developed as part of the Revolution Settlement and each has taken root in the constitution to such an extent that they remain the fundamental principles of the modern British constitution. The first of these ideas relates to the nature of the monarchy. From 1688 onwards, the monarchy has been severely limited in its prerogative powers. The constitutional limits on the Crown increased over the centuries so that today the monarch is little more than a figurehead, although all government is still done in her name. The royal

---

[104] This right, which is now viewed as the most fundamental of all rights, also assumes a very minor role in the US Constitution of the eighteenth century. It is briefly mentioned in the Fifth Amendment: '[No person shall be] deprived of life, liberty, or property, without due process of law.' Compare its predominant role in Article 2 ECHR and Article 6 ICCPR. or in modern constitutions such as that of South Africa, where it is to be found in Article 11.

[105] The popular slogan that 'An Englishman's home is his castle' clearly links privacy and property interests.

[106] Perhaps, then, it is not to put the case too strongly to claim, as Trevelyan does, that it is 'because Englishmen two and a half centuries ago were set free to worship, to speak and to write as they pleased, that they are free still …' (n 1 above, pp 201–2).

[107] Holdsworth, n 3 above, p 241.

[108] Williams, n 13 above, p 8.

[109] Many of these sources and events will be discussed in subsequent chapters of this book.

prerogative continues to be a controversial source of legal power today,[110] and the relocation of many prerogative powers in the hands of the executive branch of government presents a number of contemporary dangers (as will be discussed in Chapter 3).

The origin of a limited, constitutional monarchy dates from 1688 and is closely linked with its corollary of a supreme Parliament, which forms the second core idea of the Settlement. The 1688 Settlement is often regarded as creating parliamentary sovereignty, but this would be overstating its implications, at least if we accept Dicey's definition of the doctrine. Parliament after 1688 was not unlimited, much less illimitable. The Bill of Rights makes this clear. Parliament was, however, superior to the Crown, and statutes were supreme over the royal prerogative. This parliamentary supremacy was given effect by the acquiescence of the third branch of government – the judiciary. The courts remain at the foundation of Parliament's authority, although today this authority has taken on the illusion of omnipotence. The lessons of 1688 should teach us that such unlimited sovereign power, whether in the hands of Crown or Parliament, is detrimental to the rights, liberties and laws valued so highly by the British constitution and as such is not, and never has been, vested in our supreme Parliament.

The value of the rights and liberties of individuals is the third idea fundamental to the Revolution Settlement. The revolution was fought to protect liberty and the concept takes a central place in the Settlement. The true value of liberty has been forgotten, however, as the plethora of documentation of rights has increased. The liberty which the people reserve from their government is untouchable and encompasses many modern civil and political rights. This idea of liberty is fundamental to the UK constitution and should be recognised as a continuing restraint upon governmental abuse of power. The first true Bill of Rights would be much expanded and improved upon over the centuries but it remains the first clear signal that the constitution must serve to protect the people from sovereign power. The fundamental ideas of a limited constitutional monarchy, a supreme and limited Parliament, and individual rights and liberties were introduced to the English constitution over 300 years ago and, although the legacy is an imperfect one, these ideas still endure in the constitution of today.

---

[110] See the Fourth Report of the Select Committee on Public Administration, Cmnd 200304 (2003).

2

1707 – Union between England and Scotland: Unitary State and Limited Parliament

Eighteen years after the Revolution Settlement, the greatest constitutional event ever known to the British Isles occurred: the two ancient enemies, England and Scotland, united into one kingdom. The legacy of the events of 1707 live on in today's constitution – in the unitary state, the established churches of England and Scotland, the independent Scottish legal system, and much more. The most controversial legacy of the 1707 Acts and Treaty of Union, however, is the nature of the British Parliament constituted in that year. The current British Parliament is the direct heir of the 1707 legislature and, therefore, empowered and limited by its statutory source. The myth of a legally illimitable Parliament, already questioned in the previous chapter, is cast further in doubt by the 1707 origin of the legislative body.

I. The Background to Union: Corruption, Poverty and Fear of Invasion

a) Why Unite?

An essential preliminary question to be addressed in this chapter is: why did England and Scotland choose to unite in 1707? It must first be noted that the union between England and Scotland was not a result of good relations between the two kingdoms, as might have been expected. In fact, it was the direct opposite. Deteriorating relations between the two kingdoms by the early eighteenth century meant that neither could tolerate continuing with the existing state of affairs. Incorporating union was, eventually, seen as the only means to ensure peace and prosperity for, as Kishlansky notes, 'The Scots could not prosper without English trade, nor the English without security on their northern border.'[1] The factors which contributed to this momentous decision were numerous and diverse although the element of fear seems to underlie all of them.

Union between England and Scotland was not entirely unprecedented[2] as there had been previous attempts at integration under James I and Charles II, and short-lived (and controversial) success under Cromwell. Indeed, the two kingdoms had shared a single monarch since the union of crowns in 1603 when James VI of Scotland became simultaneously James I of England.[3] This very union of crowns caused some embarrassment to England in 1700, contributing to the decision to seek union. The infamous Darien episode highlighted the limitations of a mere union of crowns under which Scotland might pursue policies in conflict with those of the King and the English administration. The problem arose when Scotland used funds of the Company of Scotland (trading in opposition to the East India Company) to found a colony in Darien in Central America. Darien was the property of the King of Spain – an ally of William III – and thus the incident proved embarrassing to the Crown. Furthermore, the colony was an unmitigated disaster, and Scotland's economic situation worsened.[4]

The area of foreign policy proved to be a further impetus for union due to England's ongoing conflict with France in the War of Spanish Succession. England feared a 'back-door French assault' through Scotland,[5] and William's deathbed commendation of political union is attributed to this particular fear.[6] Fears were enflamed in 1703 by the Scottish Act Anent Peace and War, which required the consent of the Scottish Parliament before waging war and negotiating peace. Scotland's refusal to supply funds in this year also contributed to English fear. In short, Scotland had 'played its traditional French card',[7] and English concerns about a French invasion from the North were increased. As with the events of 1688, the 1707 union is only explicable within this broader European context.

As if the 'French card' were not enough, Scotland further incensed England by passing the Act of Security and Succession, which endangered a Hanoverian succession by giving the Scottish Parliament the right to decide who should succeed to the throne of Scotland upon Queen Anne's death. The Act set down the conditions under which Scotland would adopt a monarch of England. The

[1] M Kishlansky, *A Monarchy Transformed – Britain 1603–1714* (London, Penguin Books, 1996), p 328.

[2] CA Whatley, *Bought and Sold for English Gold? Explaining the Union of 1707*, 2nd edn (East Lothian, Tuckwell Press, 2001), p 19.

[3] Furthermore, Whatley argues that a union of states was far from anomalous during this period in history: 'Composite or dynastic states … were commonplace phenomena in early-modern Europe' (Whatley, n 2 above, p 20). He states that, between the fourteenth and nineteenth centuries, the number of independent polities in Europe fell from 1000 to only 350 (p 21).

[4] See TC Smout, 'The Road to Union' in G Holmes (ed), *Britain after the Glorious Revolution 1689–1714* (London, Macmillan, 1969), pp 179–80.

[5] Kishlansky, n 1 above, p 325.

[6] *Ibid.*

[7] *Ibid*, p 328.

significance of these two Scottish Acts of 1703–04 should not be underestimated
– the dissolution of the century-old union of crowns and a Scotland free to resur-
rect its old alliance with England's enemy, France, would have been a step too far
for England. It has even been argued that, with these two pieces of legislation,
Scotland 'served notice on the existing constitution.'[8] A new constitutional settlement would now be sought by England – an incorporating union.

The immediate step taken by England in quasi-response to the controversial
Scottish Acts, and a key contributory factor to Scottish assent to union, was the
passing by the English Parliament of the Aliens Act 1705. This Act, which was
only to come into effect if Scotland had not appointed commissioners to negotiate the terms of a union within nine months, declared that all Scottish estates in
England were to be forfeited and laid an embargo on the main imports from
Scotland: cattle, coal and linen. This has been described as 'a measure calculated
to force the Scots into negotiating Union under the threat of economic boycott'[9]
and even as 'a form of economic blackmail'[10] which left Scotland 'virtually no
choice but to discuss union on England's terms.'[11]

The Aliens Act forced Scotland to confront its position of economic weakness.
By the turn of the eighteenth century, Scottish trade was increasingly dependent
upon England, and Scotland needed access to England's markets and those of her
colonies. Smout is a leading proponent of the economic causes of Scotland's
conversion to union with England,[12] although he notes that the eventual support
of the Scottish commissioners and Parliament was never mirrored in the street.
Smout claims that for many Scots the considerable economic reasons supporting
union were not self-evident enough to compensate for the proposed loss of
sovereignty.[13] Even though the economic difficulties of Scottish trade were a
main impetus behind union for the Scottish Parliament, subsequently it became
clear that the union had not produced the anticipated favourable economic
results for Scotland.[14]

Whatever economic advantages were perceived in union with England
pre-1707, there were other more pressing reasons to negotiate a union settlement.
England's fears about Scotland resurrecting its old alliance with France placed the
kingdom north of the border at military risk of invasion by its southern neighbour. As Whatley notes, the possibility of a military solution by England would

---

[8] Smout, n 4 above, p 181.

[9] G Williams and J Ramsden, *Ruling Britannia – A Political History of Britain 1688–1988* (London,
Longman, 1990), p 40.

[10] Whatley, n 2 above, p 67.

[11] *Ibid.*

[12] See Smout, n 4 above. There are opposing views. Riley, for example, plays down the economic
justification for union: 'Trade was hardly more than a propaganda argument for embracing or
opposing a union designed for quite other reasons' (PWJ Riley, *The Union of England and Scotland –
A Study in Anglo-Scottish Politics of the Eighteenth Century* (Manchester, Manchester University Press,
1978), p 8).

[13] Smout, n 4 above, p 188.

[14] Whatley, n 2 above, p 60.

have 'concentrated minds' in Scotland[15] and, when coupled with the economic threat in the Aliens Act, it is perhaps little wonder that Scotland agreed to commence negotiations for a union with its ancient enemy. As Speck writes, 'In the last analysis it was not a choice between Union and independence for Scotland but between the treaty and an English conquest.'[16]

b) Negotiating the Terms of Union

The two kingdoms whose representatives faced each other across the negotiating table had very little in common other, perhaps, than a perceived need to unite. It has been argued that at the beginning of the eighteenth century England and Scotland shared a monarch but little else:

> They differed in religion, in law, government, economic development and in social structure. It was only up to a point that they shared the same language. Between the two peoples, at most levels of society, there was a cordial dislike and occasionally open hostility. To each the other kingdom was the ancient enemy.[17]

From this diverse starting point, the goal of union must have seemed very distant. Negotiations began formally on 16 April 1706. Commissioners from both sides were constrained by their countrymen.[18] In both countries, there was a considerable opposition to the idea of union, both in the respective Parliaments and, on a much broader scale, amongst the two populations. Scottish public opinion, in particular, was, and would remain, opposed to union with the perceived enemy.[19] But, for reasons identified in the previous section, negotiations commenced.

The Scottish commissioners began by proposing a federal union to their English counterparts. This arrangement would have enabled Scotland to retain its independent Parliament and would thus have signalled a very different legacy for the British constitution. However, the English immediately rejected this proposal and argued in favour of an incorporating union under which both national Parliaments would be dissolved.[20] The Scottish commissioners accepted this proposal in return for full freedom of trade and navigation with England.[21] Ultimately, however, the English proposal for incorporating union would be considerably diluted, as Scotland insisted upon retaining a number of

---

[15] *Ibid*, p 87.

[16] WA Speck, *The Birth of Britain – A New Nation 1700–1710* (Oxford, Blackwell, 1994), p 20.

[17] Riley, n 12 above, p xiv.

[18] 'The commissioners on both sides were looking over their shoulders, their antagonists being respectively the Scottish opposition and the English tories rather than the negotiators across the table' (Riley, n 12 above, p 183).

[19] Whatley, n 2 above, pp 79–80. At a later stage in the negotiation process it is likely that the widespread public dislike of union, and consequent public disorder, played some part in shaping the final agreement (Whatley, p 79).

[20] *Ibid*, p 27.

[21] See Riley, n 12 above, p 184.

national institutions, such as its legal system and established church, albeit not its legislature.[22]

Free trade was an important concession to obtain for Scotland. It has been described as justifying 'the concessions in sovereignty' which Scotland would have to make[23] and was the only possibility available as other options such as limitations on the crown or federal union were unacceptable to England.[24] The main elements of the Treaty of Union were soon agreed by both groups of commissioners – a new Parliament, a Hanoverian succession, the largest free trade area in Europe[25] – but there then followed 'serious wrangling' over economic issues and the controversial issue of Scottish representation in the new Parliament.[26] The most serious disagreement during the negotiations occurred over the issue of equality of taxation. The English were keen to retain such equality; the Scottish claimed that their economy could not bear the full weight of equal taxes. The Scottish commissioners requested either tax exemptions or some form of compensation.[27] The English accepted the latter and in 1707 paid compensation to Scotland in the form of the 'Equivalent' (a sum of £398,085 10s).[28] The authority for this is to be found in Article XV of the Treaty of Union and it, together with the many other Articles which enshrine private interests, has been cynically described as the 'price for Scotland'.[29]

Once the terms of the Treaty had been agreed, they were debated by the Scottish Parliament in the form of the Act of Union with England. It is at this stage in the saga at which the 'price for Scotland' issue occurs again, on a more individual basis, as there have been repeated claims since 1707 that bribery formed a key part of the Scottish Parliament's approval of the union with England. It is the apparent lack of consistency and principle on the matter of union amongst the Scottish nobility which, when contrasted with popular disapproval, suggests that bribery and corruption may have played a part in the passage of the Act of Union with England.[30] There is certainly some evidence of the payment of monies to leading opponents to the union.[31] Some commentators are sceptical, however, as to the significance of the claims of bribery. Smout, for example, makes the point that the terms secured by Scotland – free trade, protection of certain industries, preservation of an independent legal system and established church – do not suggest that the Scottish representatives were in the

---

[22] Whatley, n 2 above, p 28. This has led Kishlansky to argue that: 'The first principle established was that union would be incorporative, the creation of Great Britain. The second principle was that there would have to be large exceptions to the first' (Kishlansky, n 1 above, p 328).

[23] Riley, n 12 above, p 178.

[24] *Ibid.*

[25] Smout, n 4 above, p 176.

[26] See Speck, n 16 above, pp 98–100.

[27] Riley, n 12 above, p 184.

[28] *Ibid.*

[29] Whatley, n 2 above, p 48.

[30] Smout, n 4 above, p 191.

[31] See Whatley, n 2 above, pp 35–50.

pockets of England.[32] This argument has been disputed by Riley, who takes the view that the negotiations for the Treaty were never genuine but merely a 'propaganda campaign for the benefit of the Scottish Parliament.'[33] This does not seem a convincing view when the continued significance of the concessions obtained by Scotland – the exceptions to the general principle of incorporating union favoured by England – are considered.

The key provisions of the union were passed with little difficulty. The vital division on the Article providing for a united parliament was passed with a majority of 32 on 4 November 1706, and by 16 January 1707 a majority had agreed to ratification of the entire Treaty. Although it took nearly three months for all of the Articles to be ratified in turn, most of this time was taken up by consideration of the technicalities of the commercial and financial details.[34] A committee was appointed to examine the economic Articles and then suggested amendments. As the Treaty had already been negotiated, these amendments were termed 'explanations'.[35] There was some concern that these amendments might jeopardise the union,[36] but they were, on the whole, insignificant in nature.[37] The presentational impact of the amendments may have been crucial, however. Whatley claims that, without the concessions implicit in the amendments, the union was unlikely to have been peaceful.[38] The high level of public disorder could not be ignored by the Scottish Parliament, nor by the English who moved troops closer to the border.[39] An addition of much broader significance was the Act for Securing the Protestant Religion and Presbyterian Church Government in Scotland. This Act reflected the seriousness with which a sole concern of the opponents to union was taken, namely that, as drafted, the Act of Union with England provided no security for the Scottish Church.[40]

The terms of the Treaty of Union negotiated by England and Scotland, plus the Scottish Parliament's 'explanations' and the Act of Security, were then passed to the English Parliament for similar deliberation. England, as the keener participant of the two, did not delay unduly the passage of the English Act of Union with Scotland. An Act for Security of the Church of England was added to mirror the protection afforded to the Scottish Church and the benefits inherent in the 'explanations' were extended to England. The Tories remained opposed to union

---

[32] Smout, n 4 above, p 192. Smout also claims that the Scottish population was not in reality 'actively hostile' to union, but merely 'apathetic' (p 191).

[33] Riley, n 12 above, p 187.

[34] Speck, n 16 above, p 109.

[35] Riley, n 12 above, p 290.

[36] Speck, n 16 above, p 109.

[37] Riley, n 12 above, p 290.

[38] Whatley, n 2 above, p 80.

[39] *Ibid*, p 79.

[40] Speck quotes a key opposition speech by Lord Belhaven: 'I think I see a free and independent kingdom delivering up that which all the world hath been fighting for since the days of Nimrod ... to wit, a power to manage their own affairs by themselves without the assistance and counsel of any other' (Speck, n 16 above, pp 107–8). The essence of these, perfectly understandable, sentiments was 'ridiculed' in Parliament (p 108), but one of Lord Belhaven's key objections to union – the lack of security for the Church of Scotland – was alone taken seriously.

but a Whig majority comfortably passed the Acts. There now existed three documents of similar, but not identical, content: the original Treaty of Union drafted by the commissioners; the Act passed by the Scottish Parliament entitled the Act of Union with England; and the Act passed by the English Parliament entitled the Act of Union with Scotland. To complicate matters further, the latter two were not, in fact, single Acts but two related Acts establishing union and protecting the established church respectively. It is the combination of these three documents which forms the 'union' and bequeaths a legacy to the modern-day state of the United Kingdom.

The process which led to union was, of necessity, complex; the impetus for it born of fear and distrust rather than high ideal or national convergence. It was, it has been claimed, 'an instance of early modern *real politik*, a practical arrangement between inequal partners, born and made of political, economic and strategic necessity.'[41] What is remarkable is that it has endured for so long.[42] The remainder of this chapter seeks to identify the core elements of the union agreement of 1707, analyse their role in the evolution of the British constitution and evaluate their continuing significance as constitutional values at the heart of our modern-day state and government. From humble, and somewhat shabby, beginnings has grown an enduring union which could so nearly have bequeathed a very different constitution to Britons of today.

II. The Terms of Union and their Legacy

a) A Union of Kingdoms

The union of England and Scotland, it has been claimed, 'was far from being the outcome of sweeping vision. What mattered to contemporaries were its more mundane and even sordid by-products.'[43] This criticism is given some support by the express terms of the Acts and Treaty of Union. Very few of the 25 Articles incorporate what could be termed as the broad ethos of union. The remainder are so specific and narrow as to merit the derogatory label 'mundane'. But is it possible that the same criticism could be levelled at all constitutional documents? Constitutional documents have as their purpose the conveyance of rules relating to the governmental system within a state and, while the framework of the system is a good starting point, it can be nothing more until supplemented by more specific guidance on the day-to-day operation of the system. What does, undoubtedly, distinguish the Acts and Treaty of Union from other constitutional

---

[41] Whatley, n 2 above, p 89.
[42] *Ibid.*
[43] Riley, n 12 above, p 311.

documents is the predominance of trade-related Articles but, as freedom of trade was one of the core aims of the union, this again is not surprising.

The most fundamental aspect of the union of England and Scotland is the very fact of union, and this is outlined in Article I of the Acts and Treaty of Union: 'That the two kingdoms of England and Scotland shall upon the first day of May, which shall be in the year of one thousand seven hundred and seven, and for ever after, be united into one kingdom by the name of Great Britain.' The Article then continues by declaring the new flag of this new kingdom.[44] Having established a new state, its name and ensigns, the Acts and Treaty of Union proceed in much the same way as more modern written constitutions by outlining the executive power (in Article II) and the legislative power (in Article III). Article IV then deals with freedom of trade, and the allocation of the judicial power of government (in Scotland alone) is postponed until Articles XVIII and XIX.

The key issue arising out of the first Article – and indeed the key issue in the entire Treaty – is whether the union of two previously independent kingdoms resulted in an entirely new state or merely an absorption of one by the other. The dominance of England, in terms of economic and military strength, created an illusion of a take-over. The creation of a 'new' Parliament which sat in the same building, with the same English MPs, abiding by the same rules and procedures, as the old English Parliament, only added to this perception. This, together with the very real threat of an English military conquest of Scotland as an alternative to (and impetus for) the Treaty of Union, has led some commentators to view the union of the kingdoms as 'a quasi-union at best,'[45] representing 'absorption rather than partnership.'[46] The reality is rather more complex. For example, O'Gorman writes that 'The Act of Union of 1707 provided for the political incorporation of Scotland into England. It created a new unitary state.'[47] There is clearly a contradiction inherent in this view. If Scotland was merely incorporated into England – and so an expanded version of England emerged – a 'new unitary state' would not have been created. This outcome would never have been accepted by Scotland, at least not without an armed struggle, and is not evident in the Acts and Treaty of Union. Article I, as quoted above, makes clear that England and Scotland were to be 'united into one kingdom by the name of Great Britain.' This kingdom of Great Britain was new. It required a new Parliament to legislate for it (Article II) and a new flag to represent it (Article I). It was a

[44] '[T]he crosses of St George and St Andrew be conjoined in such manner as her Majesty shall think fit.'

[45] M Lynch, *Scotland – A New History* (London, Pimlico, 1991), p 326.

[46] Williams and Ramsden, n 9 above, p 41. In fact, these authors write that '*the Act* represented absorption rather than partnership' (emphasis added). The simplification of the complex series of negotiations and documents (including an international treaty) into a single *Act* of Parliament (presumably that passed by the English Parliament) is a telling approach to the issue, destined to result in a one-sided picture of the agreement.

[47] F O'Gorman, *The Long Eighteenth Century – British Political and Social History 1688–1832* (London, Arnold, 1997), p 57. Note again here the identification of a single Act of Parliament.

coming together unprecedented in contemporary Europe because the two previously existing states were extinguished. As I have argued elsewhere,[48] this is best
understood (in international law terms) as two distinct events: the dissolution of
both England and Scotland, and the creation of Great Britain. The root of title
for this new state can only be cession – that is, a transfer of sovereignty by agreement. Both England and Scotland, through the international Treaty of Union,
conditionally renounced title to their territory in favour of a new state yet to
come into existence. It is in this context in which the distinction between the
international Treaty of Union between England and Scotland, and the two
domestic Acts of Parliament, becomes useful. Upton illuminates this point clearly
when he argues that the two domestic Acts created a new Parliament for the new
state which had been created by the international treaty.[49] Indeed, it is *only* the
international agreement between England and Scotland which could have
resulted in a new state to replace the two ancient kingdoms. While this is legally
possible (if exceptional), it has been queried whether such a surrender of sovereignty by both kingdoms was legitimate without popular support. In Scotland,
particularly, the anti-unionists argued that the Scottish Parliament had no right
to create a union without consulting the people.[50] One can only imagine the
outcry today if a similar action was attempted by the Westminster Parliament
(even given its more representative nature). Any move towards closer union
within the European Union (EU), for example, heralds demands for a referendum (and, in most other countries, requires one). Was the 1707 surrender of
sovereignty by the Scottish (and English) Parliament legitimate?

The most effective way to answer this question seems to be to consider, first,
whether such a surrender actually occurred before then addressing the issue of its
constitutional legitimacy. On the first point, an important distinction can be
made between national sovereignty and state sovereignty. State sovereignty is
inextricably linked to the existence of an independent state. It requires a defined
territory and permanent population, together with a social organisation and
political structure, an internal body with authority to rule, and a degree of
freedom of action and decision on the international plane.[51] Post 1707, neither
Scotland nor England retained state sovereignty. However, national sovereignty
may have endured. This form of sovereignty relates more closely to the Scottish
and English people, their close ties of nationhood and ongoing distinctive
national identity and culture. In this sense, both ancient kingdoms retained
national, but not state, sovereignty. Kidd has expressed a similar view by arguing
that Scotland did not surrender its national sovereignty in 1707 but 'merely

[48] E Wicks, 'A New Constitution for a New State? The 1707 Union of England and Scotland' (2001)
117 *LQR* 109 at 109–13.

[49] M Upton, 'Marriage Vows of the Elephant: the Constitution of 1707' (1989) 105 *LQR* 79 at 82.
The fact that the Treaty and the Acts share much of the same text – ie the Articles of Union – is also
noted as a complicating factor by Upton.

[50] Riley, n 12 above, pp 220–21.

[51] See E Wicks, 'State Sovereignty – Towards a Refined Legal Conceptualisation' (2000) 29
Anglo-Am LR 282 for more detail on the author's view of state sovereignty.

agreed to pool it with England in a new entity.'[52] This idea of pooled sovereignty is of modern-day significance in relation to the EU. Can national sovereignty be pooled to form a larger entity? The clearest way of viewing this issue is to regard national sovereignty as an element which can exist without independent statehood, which attaches itself to a people and which can be pooled with the national sovereignty of other peoples on a temporary basis to create a new sovereignty, which nevertheless does not extinguish that previously existing. State sovereignty, on the other hand, cannot be so pooled. If a state's independence and freedom of action is diminished (for example, by closer co-operation and/or integration with other states or international entities), so too is its sovereignty. Thus, in 1707 both England and Scotland surrendered the entirety of their state sovereignty to a new entity entitled Great Britain, but their respective national sovereignty continued in existence, undiminished by its new home within a larger state.

This concept of a distinction between state and national sovereignty helps to settle the issue of the lack of constitutional legitimacy of the surrender of sovereignty in 1707. While national sovereignty belongs to the people and any attempt to extinguish it by a branch of government would be ineffective, state sovereignty can be legitimately surrendered by a government on behalf of its people. A merger of states, while perhaps requiring popular support for political reasons, would not be legally illegitimate in the absence of such support, although it may result in a revolution in constitutional terms. The Scottish union with England (and vice versa) was a worrying exercise of unrepresentative power – a union with another country against the wishes of the people should never be condoned – and the national sovereignty of the Scottish people was not (and could not be) diminished, but it did, nevertheless, amount to an effective surrender of state sovereignty to a new entity. A new state was born.

What is the continuing significance, if any, of this most fundamental term of the union between England and Scotland? The answer is, to some extent, obvious. The modern-day British constitution has as one of its core defining features the existence of a unitary state.[53] The changes to this state since 1707 (most significantly the 1800 union with Ireland and the 1922 partial dissolution of this union) have never threatened the value of unitary statehood which is at the very essence of British government and society. Recent devolution to Scotland, as well as to Wales and Northern Ireland, has come as close as anything since 1707 to threatening the continued existence of the unitary state. But it is, crucially, an attempt by the British government to preserve the unitary state while conceding to increasing demands for recognition of national sovereignty. Devolution, thus understood, is in fact evidence of the continuing relevance of the fundamental basis of the 1707 Acts and Treaty of Union. The two kingdoms of

---

[52] C Kidd, *Subverting Scotland's Past – Scottish Whig History and the Creation of an Anglo-British Identity 1689–c1830* (Cambridge, Cambridge University Press, 1993), p 71.

[53] Chapter 8, on devolution in 1998, considers the unitary nature of the United Kingdom and proposes 'union' as a more accurate description of the modern state than 'unitary'. See pp 167–70.

England and Scotland do remain 'united into one kingdom by the name of Great Britain', and the modern constitution has been constructed around this assumption of unity. Any moves towards independence for Scotland, or a federal arrangement for Britain, would not only breach Article I of the Acts and Treaty of Union but would also undermine the entirety of the modern British constitution. The 'for ever after' phrase in Article I is increasingly appearing to be accurate. Whether it is also obligatory is another question (to be considered below).

b) The Economic Provisions: Freedom of Trade and Equality of Rights

The majority of the Articles of Union secure freedom of trade within the new state. This, for Scotland, was the raison d'etre of union. The general principle, agreed by the commissioners for both kingdoms during negotiations, is declared in Article IV: 'That all the subjects of the united kingdom of Great Britain shall, from and after the union, have full freedom and intercourse of trade and navigation to and from any port or place within the said united kingdom, and the dominions and plantations thereunto belonging.' This latter point was especially crucial for Scotland as access to England's colonial markets was seen as an essential element of union. Article IV thus created the largest free trade area in contemporary Europe: 'the creation of a British common market embracing almost seven million people.'[54] The principle of freedom of trade was supplemented in Article IV by a general rule that there be 'communication of all other rights, privileges, and advantage, which do or may belong to the subjects of either kingdom,' but this rule is undermined by the exceptions contained in succeeding Articles, which permitted many commercial interests to be protected. For example, the malt (Article XIII) and paper (Article X) industries gained exemptions, and specific (and very detailed) provisions are included in relation to grain (Article VI), salt (Article VIII), and land (Article IX).[55]

The general rule in Article IV that taxes be equal throughout the whole of Great Britain has relatively recently been the subject of a legal challenge to the community charge (or 'poll tax'). This controversial tax was introduced in Scotland one year before it was to be introduced in England. This led to a number of challenges on the basis of the Acts and Treaty of Union. The most common cause for complaint related to Article XVIII, which will be considered in the legal system section below. One complainant, however, produced an argument under Article IV. In *Pringle, Petitioner*[56] it was argued that the imposition of the poll tax

[54] Smout, n 4 above, p 176.
[55] Note that the economic provisions also include the two key issues of the payment of the 'Equivalent' to offset losses incurred by Scotland (Article XV), and monetary union (Article XVI) which is, interestingly, on the terms of England: 'the coin shall be the same standard and value throughout the united kingdom, as now in England …'.
[56] 1991 SLT 330.

in Scotland contravened the requirement in Article IV that 'there be communication of all other rights, privileges, and advantages, which do *or may* belong to the subjects of either kingdom' (emphasis added). The case was decided on the basis of a lack of competence on the part of the court to relieve the petitioner of liability imposed by statute. Lord President Hope accepted that the court had power in the exercise of its *nobile officium* to grant relief in cases where no provision had been made by statute but denied the possibility that this power could be invoked to override the express provisions of a statute (in this case, the Abolition of Domestic Rates (Scotland) Act 1987, section 8(1)).[57] On the issue of substance, the Lord President chose to reserve his opinion although he did state, obiter, that it was not self-evident that being obliged to pay the community charge rather than domestic rates was a 'disadvantage' or even that a difference in 'methods of raising finance for local government in the two parts of the United Kingdom' would contravene Article IV.[58] Although this may have been disappointing for the petititioner, it has been argued that, on a broader level, *Pringle* suggests a potential continuing effect for Article IV.[59] It does so merely by the Lord President's refusal 'to close the door once and for all'[60] on Lord Cooper's obiter remarks in *MacCormick v Lord Advocate*.[61] In this earlier case, Lord Cooper had suggested modern-day justiciability of the Articles of Union. While it is true, as Edwards claims, that 'the court took great care' not to close the door on this possibility, the most that can be said in respect of *Pringle* is that it does not rule out continuing application for the economic provisions of the Articles of Union. Considerable obstacles remain for any claimant seeking to rely on these provisions, not least the broader issues of justiciability.

c) The Scottish Legal System

A significant concession obtained by Scotland during negotiations, and perhaps the largest exception to the English-favoured principle of incorporating union, was the preservation of an independent Scottish legal system. This is achieved in Articles XVIII and XIX of the Acts and Treaty of Union. The starting point in Article XVIII is that all laws in Scotland 'do after the union, and notwithstanding thereof, remain in the same force as before.'[62] The general principle that laws in Scotland should remain in force is subject to exceptions in respect of those laws

---

[57] *Ibid*, at 332.

[58] *Ibid*, at 333.

[59] DJ Edwards, 'The Treaty of Union: More Hints at Constitutionalism' (1992) 12 *Legal Studies* 34 at 36.

[60] *Ibid*, at 41.

[61] 1953 SC 396.

[62] It is interesting to note that the same protection is not afforded to the laws of England. On this point, Scott notes that: 'It is eloquent of the nature of the Union, more a take-over than a merger, that it was not thought necessary to state that the laws of England would continue in force' (PH Scott, *Andrew Fletcher and the Treaty of Union* (Edinburgh, John Donald, 1992), p 155). The dominance of England in the negotiated union is revealed by this omission.

which are contrary to the union itself. This exception clearly indicates that the protection afforded to the laws of Scotland is limited in nature and dependent upon the Acts and Treaty of Union for authority. In the hierarchy of laws, there is no doubt that the Articles of Union are superior to the entirety of the Scottish (and therefore, by necessity, English) legal system.

Having afforded a degree of protection to the laws of Scotland, Article XVIII then proceeds further to clarify the relative inferiority of the Scottish legal system by stating that the laws of Scotland currently in force are 'alterable by the parliament of Great Britain.' The new Parliament established under Article III of the Acts and Treaty of Union thus has the legislative competence to alter pre-existing laws. A vital distinction is made in Article XVIII, however, between laws of 'public right, policy, and civil government, and those which concern private right.' The former 'may be made the same throughout the whole united kingdom' but no alteration may be made to the latter 'except for evident utility of the subjects within Scotland.' It is this aspect of Article XVIII which causes considerable debate and complexity. It has been subject to interpretation by Scottish courts in more recent years in a number of cases.

The legal claims relating to the introduction of the community charge in Scotland included challenges on the basis of Article XVIII. In *Murray v Rogers*,[63] for example, it was argued that the requirement to pay the community charge was a matter of private right and, as such, was contrary to Article XVIII of the Acts and Treaty of Union because it was not for the 'evident utility' of the subjects of Scotland. The argument was ultimately unsuccessful because the court held that a challenge to the validity of an Act of Parliament (namely the Abolition of Domestic Rates Etc (Scotland) Act 1987) could not constitute a reasonable excuse for non-compliance with the Act's requirements, and thus the appellant could not be excused from his liability to pay the community charge. In other words, the form of proceedings was inappropriate to require consideration of the substantive issue. The First Division refused to consider the issue of whether the introduction of the community charge was for the evident utility of the Scottish people.

A similar approach was adopted in the earlier case of *Gibson v Lord Advocate*.[64] This case concerned a challenge to section 2(1) of the European Communities Act 1972 on the basis that this provision had the effect of rendering non-exclusive to Scottish citizens the right to fish in Scottish coastal waters (by virtue of incorporating Article 2 of EEC Regulation No 2141/70 into domestic law), which was not, it was argued, for the 'evident utility' of Scottish subjects. In this case, the Outer House first considered whether the law relating to fishing in territorial waters was a branch of public or private law. It was decided that the law in question operated solely in the field of public law and did not alter the private law of

[63] 1992 SLT 221.
[64] 1975 SLT 134.

Scotland.[65] It was thus not necessary for the court to consider whether the restriction on exclusive fishing rights for Scottish subjects was for their evident utility. As it was a matter of public law, it was alterable by the British Parliament without further restriction, by virtue of Article XVIII. Nor was it necessary for the court to decide the broader, and even more problematic, issue of jurisdiction to declare an Act of Parliament void.

In one case, however, a Scottish court has grappled with the issue of evident utility, demonstrating that it is not immune from contemporary application and interpretation. This case is *Laughland v Wansborough Paper Co Ltd*,[66] in which it was argued that a requirement to submit to the jurisdiction of an English court was in contravention of the evident utility rule in Article XVIII. Lord Ashmore considered the issue in some depth before concluding that there was no sufficient ground for deciding that the procedural rules contravened Article XVIII.[67] This judgment is of huge significance for it demonstrates that the judiciary will, in the appropriate circumstances, contemplate adjudicating on whether alteration of the private rights of Scottish subjects is for their evident utility and, it seems, if it is not, the courts may consider declaring an Act of Parliament void.[68] It is obvious, therefore, that the provisions of the Acts and Treaty of Union relating to the preservation of the Scottish legal system continue to provide the courts with a potentially live issue today.

In addition to the protection afforded to Scottish laws in Article XVIII, Article XIX seeks to protect the Scottish court system itself. It is stated in Article XIX that both the court of session and the court of justiciary 'do after the union, and notwithstanding thereof, remain in all time coming within Scotland, as it is now constituted by the laws of that kingdom, and with the same authority and privileges as before the union.' The dual protection afforded to the laws and courts of Scotland has proved to be one of the most significant concessions obtained by the eighteenth-century Scottish negotiators. The continued, and guaranteed, existence of an independent Scottish legal system has helped to preserve Scotland's national identity and has even served as an element in the forging of a national desire for greater devolution from England. The independent Scottish legal system is, from the opposing point of view, the greatest weakness in the union agreement because it represents such an important exception to the general principle of incorporating union.

The protection afforded to the Scottish legal system has a further characteristic. It is a core element of the union because it (along with the established churches and the union of kingdoms itself) is unchangeable within the terms of the union. The Scottish courts, it is said, must continue 'in all time coming' and

[65] On this point, see Lord Keith at 136.

[66] 1921 SLT 341.

[67] See pp 345–46 of his judgment. Lord Ashmore concludes that there is insufficient evidence that the procedural rule, under which an English court had jurisdiction over the complainant, 'is not calculated on the whole to meet the convenience of the people at both ends of the island' (p 346).

[68] This latter point will be considered in more depth in the following section.

no modern-day court (or politician) has ever suggested that this provision is not just as binding on the British Parliament today as it was in 1707. Indeed, it has even been hinted by a few judges that, contrary to the dominant view of parliamentary sovereignty usually expressed by the judiciary, Parliament lacks the legal competence to abolish the Scottish legal system.[69] Is the Parliament created by the Acts and Treaty of Union omnicompetent or does it still operate within the jurisdictional limits imposed by the documents which created it?

d) The British Parliament and its Limits

One of the most significant elements of the 1707 Union of England and Scotland, and certainly the one which has caused the most legal debate in recent years, is the creation of a new British Parliament. Article III allocates the legislative power of government in the following way: 'the united kingdom of Great Britain be represented by one and the same parliament, to be stiled the Parliament of Great Britain.' Despite the apparent simplicity of this provision, debate still rages today as to whether a new British Parliament was in fact established or whether, alternatively, the pre-existing English Parliament continued to legislate, albeit for a new territorial entity.[70] Three related issues form the basis for consideration of this question. The first issue concerns the composition of the 'new' Parliament post-1707; the second issue concerns the legal status of this Parliament; and the final issue, and by far the most important, relates to the consequences of the establishment of a new Parliament, in particular for its sovereign status. It is this final issue which will illuminate the importance of the preceding discussion.

First, however, attention must focus on the question of composition. Article XXII of the Acts and Treaty of Union purports to settle the composition of the new legislature by declaring that 'by virtue of this Treaty, of the peers of Scotland, at the time of union, sixteen shall be the number to sit and vote in the House of Lords, and forty five the number of the representatives of Scotland in the House of Commons of the parliament of Great Britain.' By contrast, it is stated that, subject to the Queen's declaration, 'it may be expedient that the lords of parliament of England, and commons of the present parliament of England, should be the members of the respective houses of the first parliament of Great Britain, for and on the part of England.' In other words, the new Parliament established under the Acts and Treaty of Union was to comprise the existing members of the English Parliament plus 16 Scottish peers and 45 Scottish MPs. This has, understandably, led to accusations that the post-1707 Parliament was merely the

---

[69] See *MacCormick v Lord Advocate* (1953 SC 39b) for a concession by the Lord Advocate that parts of the Acts and Treaty of Union are fundamental law and for Lord Cooper's comments at 411-412. See also *Gibson v Lord Advocate* ((1975) SLT.134 at 137), in which Lord Keith expressly reserves his opinion on the issue of a purported contravention of expressly unalterable provisions in the Acts and Treaty of Union.

[70] Munro takes the latter view: CR Munro, *Studies in Constitutional Law*, 1st edn (London, Butterworths, 1987). See, by way of contrast, Upton, n 49 above, at 88–90.

pre-1707 English Parliament with a few Scottish additions.[71] Closer investigation of the reasoning underlying this provision may suggest otherwise, however. Although Scottish representation in the new Parliament was disproportionate to the Scottish population within the new state, this was not the sole criteria for representation in the early eighteenth century. A more relevant factor at this time has been identified as the proportion of taxation paid to the government.[72] On this basis, Scottish representation in the House of Commons would have amounted to only 28 – far fewer than the 45 allocated by Article XXII. During negotiations for the Treaty, English commissioners proposed a number of 38; Scottish commissioners proposed 50. The final total of 45 was, hence, a compromise.[73] Scottish representation in Parliament, although disproportionate in terms of population, was overly generous in terms of proportion of taxation and was thus appropriate by contemporary standards.

There remains for discussion, however, the second issue which casts doubt upon the creation of a new Parliament in 1707. This is the fact the English Parliament seemed to continue in a new form by, for example, sitting in the same building as the previous English Parliament and adopting the same privileges and procedures. Perhaps most significantly, elections for the new Parliament were held not in 1707 but in 1708, when elections to the English Parliament would have been due. There was some disagreement on this issue even in 1707. Marlborough argued at the time that if a new Parliament had been created, it would have a full three years of life beginning in 1707, while Harley claimed that the so-called new Parliament was merely a continuance of the English Parliament elected in 1705 and thus would be due for new elections in 1708.[74] The latter argument won and elections were indeed held in 1708. This does not, however, prove that the new Parliament was merely the old English Parliament in an amended form, for one vital reason which is often overlooked: the authority for the 1708 elections is to be found in the Articles of Union themselves. Article XXII clearly states that the new British Parliament 'may continue for such time only as the present parliament of England might have continued if the union of the two kingdoms had not been made.' Thus, the constituting document itself determines the time span of the new Parliament. While it is possible to interpret this provision as seeking to connect the new Parliament with the old English Parliament (and thus fuel arguments that they are one and the same), a better view is that the new Parliament depends upon its constituting document, rather than its English predecessor, for authority.[75] Perhaps it is Upton who provides the most

---

[71] See MK Addo and VM Smith, 'The Relevance of Historical Fact to Certain Arrangements Relating to the Legal Significance of the Acts of Union' [1998] *Juridical Review* 37 at 51; Munro, n 70 above, p 66.

[72] Speck, n 16 above, p 100.

[73] *Ibid.*

[74] Riley, n 12 above, p 310. There was, of course, a party political background to this dispute over the timing of the next election.

[75] Upton, n 49 above, at 89.

convincing solution to this whole dilemma. He argues that a new Parliament was constituted in 1707 in law, even if not in fact.[76] This law/fact distinction is useful because it focuses attention upon the legal consequences of Articles III and XXII. A new Parliament was given legislative authority by the Articles of Union, albeit that the new Parliament was to be similar, in many ways, to its English predecessor. Even if the two Parliaments – British and English – had been identical in every way, they would not, indeed could not, have been the same body for the simple reason that the English Parliament had no legal authority to legislate for Great Britain. At its most basic, the issue can thus be stated as follows: a new state of Great Britain was, undoubtedly, created in 1707 and this necessitated the creation of a new Parliament to legislate for it. While an element of continuity was ensured by Article XXII, the statutory basis for the new legislature fundamentally transformed the legislative branch of government.

It is this realisation which has led to considerable debate on the issue of the sovereign status of the new Parliament. The commonly accepted premise for this debate is that the pre-1707 English Parliament was sovereign in the sense of legally illimitable. This view relies upon the 1689 Revolution Settlement as the source of legislative sovereignty, and yet this proposition was firmly rejected in the previous chapter due to the lack of historical evidence supporting the creation of such an illimitable legislature. Even if this argument is erroneous and the 1689–1707 English Parliament was indeed sovereign in the sense in which Dicey defined it in the nineteenth century, this will only be of negligible relevance to the post-1707 British Parliament. It was not, as has been discussed above, a mere continuation of the previous English Parliament.[77] The crucial distinction is that the new Parliament depends upon its constituting document for legislative authority. And there is no mention within the Acts and Treaty of Union of Parliament being sovereign in the sense of unlimited. Indeed, all evidence suggests the exact opposite. As has been seen, the union documents purport to impose limits upon the new Parliament, for example in relation to the Scottish legal system and established church. Furthermore, there was no discussion during negotiations for the Treaty on this important issue of Parliament's illimitability. While this fact has been used by Addo and Smith to indicate that the new Parliament must be sovereign by implication because the principle of parliamentary sovereignty 'was too entrenched in English constitutional law to be abandoned without discussion,'[78] this is unconvincing. Even if the English Parliament was sovereign, it could only have been so for less than

---

[76] *Ibid*, at 90.

[77] See Lord Cooper's famous comments in *MacCormick v Lord Advocate*: 'Considering that the Union legislation extinguished the Parliaments of Scotland and England and replaced them by a new Parliament, I have difficulty in seeing why it should have been supposed that the new Parliament of Great Britain must inherit all the peculiar characteristics of the English Parliament but none of the Scottish Parliament, as if all that happened in 1707 was that Scottish representatives were admitted to the Parliament of England. That is not what was done' (1953 SC 396 at 411).

[78] Addo and Smith, n 71 above, at 47.

two decades. It was, at most, a new and relatively untested principle, and so the suggestion that it was so obviously vital to the English constitution as to not warrant any discussion is unrealistic. In fact, the English Parliament, as was argued in the previous chapter, was only sovereign post-1689 in the sense of being the supreme law-maker, not in the sense of being unlimited. On this definition, the English Parliament was not so very different in nature from the Scottish Parliament. While it is well documented that until the 1690s, the Scottish Parliament was not 'anything like the equal of its English sister,'[79] post-1689, and with the abolition of the Lords of the Articles (which had previously decided the agenda for Parliament), the Scottish Parliament discovered a new independence and, arguably, superiority of legislative function. It was far from being sovereign in the Diceyian sense but then, it has been argued, so was the English Parliament.

The key issue remains the creation of a new Parliament in 1707 which derived its authority from the Acts and Treaty of Union. The fact that these documents do not appear to envisage an unlimited legislature is strong evidence that one was not created. It is without doubt that the Parliament created was intended by the drafters of the union to be limited. This is self-evident in the terms of the union. Dicey himself has even conceded the point that those who created the new Parliament in 1707 envisaged a very different type of Parliament to the one Dicey subsequently claimed was created: 'The statesmen of 1707, though giving full sovereign power to the Parliament of Great Britain, clearly believed in the possibility of creating an absolutely sovereign legislature which should yet be bound by unalterable laws.'[80] Dicey viewed this as 'something like a contradiction of ideas'[81] although he did accept that there was some value in seeking to impose limits on the new Parliament.[82] Dicey does not, however, give sufficient weight to the intention of the drafters of the union documents for, when this is coupled with the clear terms of the union which can only be read as seeking to impose limits on Parliament's legislative competence, there is very convincing evidence that Parliament was thus limited.

Furthermore, the mere fact of a constituting document immediately imposes a higher authority over the legislature created. This was a fact well understood at the time:

> as the Parliaments of Britain are founded, not upon the original right of the people, as the separate Parliaments of England and Scotland were before, but upon the treaty which is prior to the said Parliament, and consequently superior; so, for that reason, it

---

[79] Kidd, n 52 above, p 71. It was 'but one of a group of bodies vying for legal and representative authority' and was controlled by the Lords of the Articles.

[80] AV Dicey and RS Rait, *Thoughts on the Union Between England and Scotland* (London, Macmillan & Co, 1920), p 252.

[81] *Ibid.*

[82] This point is discussed further in the following section.

cannot have power to alter its own foundation, or act against the power which formed it, since all constituted power is subordinate, and inferior to the power constituting.[83]

This argument seems entirely logical, and it is, surely, significant that it was an argument in circulation at the time of the union. This issue can, therefore, be summarised in the following terms: a constituting document created a new Parliament and purported to impose limits upon it, and its drafters intended those limits to be effective. There is no reason to believe that the new Parliament took on an entirely different (and, I would argue, previously unknown) characteristic of legal illimitability.

e) Are the Acts and Treaty of Union Entrenched as Fundamental Law?

Legal and academic debate in recent years has queried whether the Articles and Treaty of Union amount to a constitution.[84] It will be argued below that a better view is that certain core values of the union agreement amount to constitutional values entrenched within a modern-day constitution. First, however, it will be useful to ascertain the intention at the time of the union. Was it really intended to be 'for ever after'? Despite the many such references within the terms of the union, some commentators have discerned a lack of permanence in contemporary intentions. For example, Ferguson writes that 'at the time the union was passed few politicians seem to have regarded it as permanent,'[85] and Lynch states that 'both novelty and the half-baked appearance of the proto-British state led many in 1707 to believe that they had embarked on an experiment which might well be reversed.'[86] These are interesting sentiments because they are in apparent contradiction to the terms of the Acts and Treaty of Union. Their genuine nature is proven, however, by the extraordinary attempts in 1713 to dissolve the union.

What has been described as the 'first gesture of secession'[87] occurred when the government tried to extend the duty on malt to Scotland at the English rate, contrary to Article XIII of the Acts and Treaty of Union.[88] A motion for dissolution of the union was moved in the House of Lords by Seafield.[89] It failed by only

---

[83] D Defoe, 'The History of the Union between England and Scotland' (London, 1786), quoted by PH Scott (ed), *1707 – The Union of Scotland and England in Contemporary Documents with Commentary* (Edinburgh, W & R Chambers, 1979), p 62. Scott does note, however, that Defoe was a famous propagandist and had also argued the opposing view.

[84] See especially, TB Smith, 'The Union of 1707 as Fundamental Law' [1957] *PL* 99; N MacCormick, 'Does the United Kingdom have a Constitution? Reflections on *MacCormick v Lord Advocate*' (1978) 29 *NILQ* 1; and Upton, n 49 above.

[85] W Ferguson, *Scotland's Relations with England: A Summary to 1707* (Edinburgh, John Donald Publishers, 1977), p 273.

[86] Lynch, n 45 above, p 317.

[87] *Ibid*, p 322.

[88] See Lynch, *ibid*, pp 322–23.

[89] *Ibid*.

four votes.[90] This attempt at dissolution clearly suggests that the union was not regarded as entrenched as of 1713. Is this conclusive evidence that it was not, in fact, entrenched? The answer must be negative. Despite the apparent willingness to initiate dissolution, capacity to dissolve the union is an entirely separate matter. Logic dictates that a legislature cannot repeal its constituent document. There is, of course, an essential distinction here between what a Parliament can do in reality and what it can do in law. It is undeniable that, with four more votes, the union of England and Scotland could have been dissolved in 1713 (heralding a very different future for the British Isles) but, in law, under the existing constitution, the British Parliament was not authorised to repeal its constituent document. If it had done so, a constitutional revolution would have occurred (as it did in 1922 when the Irish political situation forced a re-evaluation of Anglo-Irish relations). The influential legal commentator, TB Smith, has expressed this very view in the following terms: 'the entrenched provisions could only be superseded by revolution – in the sense of a fundamental reconstruction of the British Constitution.'[91]

What of the Acts and Treaty of Union today? Do they remain as constituent documents removable only by means of constitutional revolution? There is an argument (albeit a rather unconvincing one) that the union documents have lost their binding force subsequent to 1707. Addo and Smith argue that 'the Acts of Union have progressed from potentially effective instruments of legal restraint on government activity to political and historical documents of interest.'[92] How can this be so? The union agreement retains its role as constituent of the state and Parliament of Great Britain (albeit with the later amendment in respect of Ireland). If this was once sufficient to serve as 'potentially effective ... of legal restraint', why should it cease to do so merely by the passage of time? Of course, Addo and Smith's argument might be alluding to the reality of the enforcement of the Articles of Union which, it has to be acknowledged, has been patchy at best. Whatley describes it as 'a moveable feast, upheld on occasion, but more often ignored in the details.'[93] For example, while the preservation of the Scottish legal system, established church and principle of free trade have been respected over the centuries, other less fundamental provisions do appear to have been breached.[94] Despite some arguments to the contrary,[95] it is clear that public support does not excuse, or lessen, a breach of a fundamental law.[96] The only explanation is that, while some provisions of the Acts and Treaty of Union are entrenched as fundamental law, the Acts are not, as a whole, so entrenched. This

---

[90] Scott, n 83 above, p 67.
[91] TB Smith, n 84 above, at 113.
[92] Addo and Smith, n 71 above, at 62.
[93] Whatley, n 2 above, p 89.
[94] See Upton, n 49 above, at 93.
[95] See, eg, Smith, n 84 above, at 121, and Upton, n 49 above, at 93.
[96] See Wicks, n 48 above, at 119.

explains why, despite breaches of minor Articles, the core values of the union have never been under threat.

Dicey, although often assumed to deny all validity to purported entrenchment, actually adopts a very subtle argument on this issue. In *Thoughts on the Treaty of Union*, Dicey and Rait state:

> A sovereign Parliament, in short, though it cannot be logically bound to abstain from changing any given law, may, by the fact that an Act when it was passed had been declared to be unchangeable, receive a warning that it cannot be changed without grave danger to the Constitution of the country.[97]

To reiterate, Dicey accepts that 'the enactment of laws which are described as unchangeable, immutable, or the like, is not necessarily futile' because it represents the conviction that those provisions 'ought to be morally or constitutionally unchangeable.'[98] It is clear from this that Dicey does not, unsurprisingly, regard the Acts or Treaty of Union as a 'constitution' in itself, but he does consider that violating the union's core values (which are described as unchangeable) would cause 'grave danger' to the British constitution. Why is this so? The most likely answer is that Dicey regarded those core values as inherent within the constitution. To claim that these values ought to be constitutionally unchangeable is merely to reiterate the argument outlined above that they are only changeable as an intrinsic part of a constitutional revolution.

III. Conclusion

Could the Acts and Treaty of Union have ever amounted to a constitution for the new state of Great Britain? As undoubtedly constituent documents, the Acts and Treaty of Union constitute a new state. In addition, Articles II, III, and XVIII allocate the powers of government. Fundamental values are expressly identified and protected: the Scottish legal system in Articles XVIII and XIX; the established churches of England and Scotland in the two adjoined Acts; monetary union in Article XVI; and the principle of freedom of trade and navigation in Article IV. The foundations of a constitution seem to be provided here, although it lacks the type of detailed rules relating to day-to-day government usually found in more modern written constitutions. The key characteristic of a constitution, however, is its higher law status. A constitution must be prescriptive and must be binding upon the organs of government. It is on this key point that the Acts and Treaty of Union fail as a constitution. Quite simply, despite their potential to be regarded

---

[97] Dicey and Rait, n 80 above, pp 253–54.
[98] *Ibid*, p 253.

as binding, the organs of government have not treated these 1707 documents as a constitution. Breaches of certain Articles of Union have undoubtedly occurred since 1707 and, most significantly, the British constitution has continued to evolve. New laws, conventions and constitutional practices have evolved to supplement those existing in the eighteenth century, such as in the fields of executive power, individual rights and democratic representation. The potential constitution of 1707 was never treated as such. As was seen above, even as early as 1713, attempts were made to dissolve the Acts and Treaty of Union as a whole.

Does this mean, therefore, that the 1707 Acts and Treaty of Union are merely documents of historical interest? This cannot be correct. The core values of the union remain at the very heart of our modern-day constitution – unchanged and unchangeable since 1707. The nature of Great Britain as a unitary state, the independence of the Scottish legal system, the two established churches, freedom of trade throughout the united kingdom, and the 'evident utility' protection of private rights in Scottish law are constitutional values. As such, they are entrenched as fundamental law within the modern (uncodified) constitution. As Dicey noted, breach of these fundamental values, although clearly possible, would cause grave danger to the constitution. Nothing is impossible in factual terms but, legally, the Parliament constituted by the 1707 Acts and Treaty of Union was expressly prohibited the competence to repeal these core values of the union agreement. If the predecessor of that same Parliament, even today, sought to exceed its original legal competence, it could do so only at the cost of the existing constitutional order.

3

1721 – The First Prime Minister? Executive Power and Its Journey from Monarch to Prime Minister

Today the office of Prime Minister is a core, if conventional, part of the British constitution, but its development has been gradual rather than revolutionary. Before the eighteenth century, 'kings were their own prime ministers.'[1] The development of the position of Prime Minister radically transformed the nature of the executive power under the UK constitution. Although it remained legally unchanged, the constitution was transformed through convention to the extent that even its key players changed roles. Sir Robert Walpole's Whig ministry of 1721–42 laid the foundations for this transfer of executive power from the monarch to a leading Cabinet minister. It would be a mistake to believe that the transfer was complete by 1742, but the journey had undoubtedly begun and could not be reversed. The position was to develop incrementally over centuries rather than over years, but its impetus – its foundation – was the Walpole ministry of 1721–42. This chapter will consider the defining characteristics of Walpole's ministry, before moving on to analyse the power shift it heralded.

I. Walpole as the First Prime Minister?

What started as a term of abuse became the ultimate political goal. As Hennessy has noted, 'the man upon whom history has laid the mantle of Britain's first Prime Minister spent his entire career denying he was any such thing.'[2] The reason for this denial is that, for much of the eighteenth century, 'Prime Minister'

---

[1] GW Jones, 'The Office of Prime Minister' in H Van Thal (ed), *The Prime Ministers, Vol 1: Sir Robert Walpole to Sir Robert Peel* (London, Allen & Unwin, 1974), p 15.

[2] P Hennessy, *The Prime Minister: The Office and its Holders Since 1945* (London, Allen Lane, 2000), p 38. For example, when the Protest of Dissentient Peers demanded Walpole's removal on the basis that he was a Prime Minister and no such office existed under the constitution, Walpole replied that 'as one of his Majesty's council I have but one voice'. (See BE Carter, *The Office of Prime Minister* (London, Faber, 1956), p 24.)

was merely a term of abuse with 'connotations of unjustified royal favouritism.'[3] During Queen Anne's reign both Godolphin and Harley faced this accusation, but it was Walpole to whom the phrase stuck.[4] Executive power was moving away from the King and towards a member of his Cabinet who would no longer be called Prime Minister as an insult, but as the ultimate political accolade. A brief overview of Walpole's life and ministry will now be provided before the ministry's defining characteristics are explored in more detail.

a) Walpole's Ministry: An Overview

Robert Walpole was born in 1676 in Houghton, Norfolk. After an education at Eton and King's College, Cambridge, he joined the House of Commons in 1701 as Whig member for Castle Rising. He switched seats to King's Lynn the following year and continued to represent this constituency until 1742. In 1708, Walpole was appointed Secretary of War and, in 1710, he was appointed to the more lucrative post of Treasurer of the Navy. Walpole's rapid rise was halted when he was dismissed from office in 1711 by the new Tory ministry and subsequently committed to the Tower for corruption. But he was soon released and, with his brother-in-law Townshend now appointed Secretary of State for the Northern Department in the incoming Whig ministry, Walpole was on the rise again. In 1714 he was appointed Paymaster-General of the Forces, and he also became a Privy Councillor. When Townshend fell in 1717 over the issue of foreign policy, Walpole resigned in support, but his political power was by now significant.[5] After a prolonged period in opposition, Walpole returned to the government in 1720 as Paymaster-General and it was from this post that he was able to save the day when the South Sea Bubble scandal arose. This scandal concerned a financial scheme which was opposed by Walpole (although he profited from it). When the scheme crashed in 1720, it led to the ruin of many ministers, both financially and politically. Walpole produced a complex plan to deal with the financial scandal and defended it expertly in the Commons. He was seen as the major beneficiary of the crisis,[6] and on 2 April 1721 he was appointed First Lord of the Treasury and Chancellor of the Exchequer. From that date until 1742, Walpole was the King's leading minister. He used bribery and propaganda, as well as more traditional parliamentary skills, to retain power for over two decades. His main political goal in this time was to keep the country at peace (and thus prosperous) which he did until 1739. By the late 1730s, the King favoured war and he was not alone. Walpole's policy of peace faced influential opposition in Parliament and in the City. In 1739, Walpole reluctantly declared

---

[3] F O'Gorman, *The Long Eighteenth Century – British Political and Social History 1688–1832* (London, Arnold, 1997), p 132.

[4] As Blake notes, 'whether or not he deserves the title, no one before him does' (R Blake, *The Office of Prime Minister* (London, Oxford University Press, 1975), p 5).

[5] See J Black, *Walpole in Power* (Stroud, Sutton Publishing, 2001), pp 9–11.

[6] *Ibid*, p 19.

war on Spain but by now his parliamentary majority was rapidly decreasing. In February 1742 he lost a vote in the House of Commons and resigned. He was succeeded by Spencer Compton (Lord Wilmington), who survived as leading minister for only one year. Walpole (now the Earl of Orford) died in 1745.

Was Walpole a 'Prime Minister'? How are we to identify the defining characteristics of this potential first Prime Minister when the subject himself categorically denied the title? As Holmes has queried, 'how does one define a "Prime Minister" in an age when no such office was legally recognised and the term itself, more often than not, was used pejoratively?'[7] Perhaps the answer is that we can not define a 'Prime Minister' at this stage in our constitutional history, but we can now proceed in the ensuing pages to describe and subject to analysis the defining characteristics of Walpole's ministry. This can be followed by consideration of what it is about those defining characteristics that has led commentators to place Walpole at the top of the list of British Prime Ministers. Why does his portrait 'hang on the wall behind the Prime Minister's seat in the Cabinet Room as the de facto father of the breed'?[8]

b) Defining Characteristics of Walpole's Ministry

The first innovation of Walpole's ministry was to combine the offices of First Lord of the Treasury and Chief Minister. Even today, this link continues, although it is now the secondary position in the Treasury – the Chancellor of the Exchequer – that carries with it day-to-day responsibility for the Treasury. In Walpole's era, supremacy over the Treasury was significant as it indicated control over fiscal policy and thus over all aspects of government.[9] Since the eighteenth century it has become clear that whoever exercises control over government income and expenditure will be able to determine the government's broader policies, and thus the Treasury continues to supply the bedrock for a Prime Minister's power.

The second important innovation initiated by Walpole was to sit within the House of Commons. This simple decision transformed the course of history. The Commons was the future. In order to rule through Parliament (as the 1689 Settlement had decreed), the head of the executive would need to sustain majority support within the Commons. Walpole's decision to retain his seat in the Commons was significant because of the way in which it united the Treasury – of which he was head – with the political leadership in the Commons.[10] By the eighteenth century the House of Commons had established itself as the dominant House of Parliament for financial matters, and its dominance on all other

---

[7] G Holmes, 'Sir Robert Walpole' in Van Thal, n 1 above, p 29.

[8] Hennessy, n 2 above, p 39.

[9] Lord Chancellor Hardwicke recognised this in 1755: 'the head of his Treasury was indeed an employment of great business, very extensive, which always went beyond the bare management of the revenue ...' (EN Williams, *The Eighteenth Century Constitution, 1688–1815 – Documents and Commentary* (Cambridge, Cambridge University Press, 1960), p 131.

[10] O'Gorman, n 3 above, p 74.

matters would soon follow. Thus the presence of the King's Chief Minister and First Lord of the Treasury within that chamber was fitting. It was not a precedent which would be followed by all of Walpole's successors. Indeed, even into the twentieth century, some Prime Ministers chose to sit in the House of Lords rather than the Commons,[11] but today it would be inconceivable for the de facto head of the executive[12] to sit anywhere but in the lower (and, significantly now, elected) chamber. Walpole was the first to foresee the advantage of sitting within the House of Commons and, as Holmes has noted, 'it cannot be overstressed how much Walpole was an innovation in this respect … and how important in the long term his innovation was …'.[13] From a twenty-first century perspective, the Prime Minister's presence in the House of Commons is inevitable. Electoral reform, the growth of political parties and the personalisation of politics have all contributed to this, as has the transformation in the relationship between the two chambers of Parliament in the early twentieth century. But Walpole's presence in the Commons preceded, and may even have encouraged, these factors. He certainly foresaw the potential of party organisation in a way which was unprecedented in the eighteenth century. Thus it was not only his presence in the lower chamber, but his astute political management of it, which left a legacy for future Prime Ministers.

Walpole has been described as 'one of the greatest parliamentarians who ever lived,'[14] which would be an unlikely accolade for any Prime Minister of recent years. The need to manage Parliament had become critical since the 1689 Revolution Settlement in which the need for the King to govern through Parliament had been firmly established for the final time. As the power of Parliament grew, so did its desire to be critical of the King's government, and thus it needed managing by a representative of the government. As the influence of the House of Lords reduced, the government's need to retain support in the Commons became (and would continue to become) all the more pressing. Infamously, patronage played its part. Walpole is criticised for his expertise in this respect and it is a part of eighteenth-century politics which is impossible to ignore. Walpole's control of the Commons was not solely owed to patronage, however. He also relied upon more traditional parliamentary skills: he attended the Commons 'assiduously, intervened in debate constantly and patiently, and in simple language explained ministerial policy.'[15] He also relied upon party politics, seeking to conciliate opponents in his own (Whig) party. This use of party – novel then, ubiquitous now – also extended to Cabinet, where Walpole sought to have his supporters appointed. He foresaw that Cabinet government rests upon the party system and thus, despite George III's efforts to restore practical power to himself by

---

[11] The last Prime Minister to sit in the House of Lords was Lord Salisbury during his ministry of 1895–1902.

[12] The monarch remains the de jure head of the executive.

[13] Holmes, n 7 above, p 31.

[14] *Ibid*, p 45.

[15] O'Gorman, n 3 above, p 74.

appointing his personal friends (both Whig and Tory) to Cabinet,[16] single-party government was given (an albeit faltering) birth. Many of the modern Prime Minister's means of controlling Cabinet remained far in the future – indeed the King himself continued to sit in Cabinet until 1781[17] – but the foundations for future dominance had been laid with Walpole's use of the party system to bolster the strength and unity of both Cabinet and Commons.

Walpole's ministry was unique in its time because, for the first time, support of the King, although still crucial, was not sufficient to retain power. The continued support of both Crown and Commons was essential. When Walpole finally lost the support of the latter in 1742, even the King's support was not enough to save him. It was Walpole's recognition of this new state of affairs that caused him to appreciate the significance of his presence in, and management of, the House of Commons. Walpole played a dual role: as minister for the King in the House of Commons; and as minister for the House of Commons in the King's closet.[18] He provided the link between Crown and Parliament that heralded a new form of government under the British constitution. The executive and legislative branches of government were drawing closer together so that by the twentieth century their close relationship was perceived as a new threat to the effective working of the constitution. In Walpole's age, however, the embodiment of the new link between Crown and Parliament faced dual threats. Not only must the Commons be kept in line but also the support of the King continued to be vital. When he first came to power, Walpole won over George II, who was not initially favourably predisposed to him. A timely increase in the civil list undoubtedly played a part in the King's change of heart.[19] By 1733–34 Walpole's efforts to win the favour of the King paid off. During this period, Walpole's attempts to extend excise duties to wine and tobacco caused a major political storm.[20] Walpole faced opposition in the Commons and in his ministry, and his leadership itself became under threat. Eventually, Walpole withdrew the Excise Bill in order to avoid defeat. Significantly, Walpole's dependence upon the King became evident during this crisis, as he relied upon the King's dismissals, promotions and peerages to help him survive this challenge to his leadership.[21] This first 'Prime Minister' thus depended greatly upon the de jure head of the executive for survival in a way which seems anachronistic today. But it was also a reciprocal relationship – the King needed his Prime Minister. As noted above, George II did not initially favour Walpole and would have preferred Compton as his leading minister. The usual practice in the early eighteenth century would have been for the King to appoint his favourite, but he did not do so. Why? The pay-off of the increased civil list may have played its part but, more significantly, it has been

---

[16] Carter, n 2 above, p 26.
[17] Hennessy, n 2 above, p 45.
[18] Holmes, n 7 above, p 46.
[19] O'Gorman, n 3 above, p 73.
[20] Black, n 5 above, p 36.
[21] O'Gorman, n 3 above, p 81.

argued that the King knew Walpole commanded a parliamentary majority and it was this which made him 'indispensable to the crown.'[22] Today, by convention, the monarch will appoint as Prime Minister whoever can rely upon a majority in Parliament. This is now seen as an aspect of the democratisation of the constitution but, as we have seen, it stems from the monarch's need to be able to rely upon the support of Parliament for his ministers' policies. And this in turn stems from the Revolution Settlement of 1688, which continues to underlie all aspects of the relationship between Crown and Parliament.

As was seen in chapter 1, the Revolution Settlement created the constitutional basis for a parliamentary monarchy: the King would continue to rule but would henceforth be legally required to do so through the legislative body. It has been suggested that, while 1688 created the constitutional basis for this new type of government, political instability in the years 1689 to 1721 prevented the system operating in an effective manner.[23] A suitable political environment did not yet exist:

> A parliamentary monarchy could not simply be legislated into existence. It required the development of conventions and patterns of political behaviour that would permit a constructive resolution of contrary opinions within a system where there was no single source of dominant power.[24]

Under a constitution in which Crown and Parliament shared supreme legislative power, new conventions would need to be developed and the emergence of the office of Prime Minister is one such convention.

As noted above, Walpole provided a strong link between Crown and Parliament and, as a consequence of this, the longevity of his ministry is unparalleled in British history. Twenty-one years in power is inconceivable in today's political society[25] and was similarly unique in the eighteenth century. It is this very characteristic of Walpole's ministry which leads some commentators to herald him as the first Prime Minister. For example, Black is sceptical of the view that Walpole was the first Prime Minister because he takes the view that his power was not unique when compared to previous leading ministers such as Godolphin and Harley (who were also in their time labelled 'Prime Ministers' as a term of personal abuse). But he defines Walpole's longevity as the key distinguishing feature of the ministry (together with his decision to sit in the Commons).[26] For two whole decades, Walpole was the architect of stability, and this set him apart from his contemporaries and lit the way for the effective operation of a genuine parliamentary monarchy. Longevity, and the political stability which it provided, is indeed an important feature of Walpole's ministry but it would be a mistake to

---

[22] Black, n 5 above, p 53.

[23] *Ibid*, p 51.

[24] *Ibid*.

[25] Compared to this, Thatcher's 11 years in power pale into insignificance and yet even this is unlikely to be repeated on a frequent basis.

[26] Black, n 5 above, p 59.

view this as a defining characteristic of Britain's first Prime Minister. The longevity (and hence the stability) was due to the other unique elements of Walpole's ministry: his decision to sit in the Commons, and to combine this with his role as First Lord of the Treasury, and his ability to manage the Commons in a way unprecedented at the time involving, as it did, an appreciation of the potential role of the party system in parliamentary government. It was because of these key factors that Walpole's grip on power endured for so long. The British governmental system needed an executive focus in the Commons and a strong parliamentary leader in the King's closet. When Walpole created and served as both he ensured his own political success. It is not that Walpole is the first Prime Minister because he was in power for 21 years; he remained in power for that unprecedented period because he was a Prime Minister. And a Prime Minister was just what the new British parliamentary monarchy needed.

II. The Power Shift from Monarch to Prime Minister

a) Transference of Executive Power

From a historical perspective, the main significance of Walpole's long ministry in the eighteenth century is that it gave added impetus to the slow process of a power shift under the British constitution. The locale of executive power has shifted over the centuries from its origin in the person of the Crown to its present-day location in the Cabinet and its leading, or prime, minister. The moveable object of executive power was subjected to the irresistible forces of the post-1688 constitution and its later additional concept of democracy. From today's perspective it is clear to see that the real power once exercised by the monarch now lies in the hands of his or her Prime Minister: the formation of government policy; its presentation to Parliament and the public; control over all aspects of fiscal and other government business. However, it would be misleading to present this displacement of executive power as a simple, and complete, journey from monarch to Prime Minister, because the matter is rather more complex for two very important reasons. First, in strictly legal terms, there has been no power shift at all: the monarch remains the head of the executive branch of government. Even today, 'Her Majesty's Government' carries out Her policies as introduced in the Queen's speech at the State Opening of Parliament. Furthermore, it is Her Majesty's Government in more than just name, for the monarch retains a number of significant legal powers under the royal prerogative.[27] The extent of these prerogative powers has been severely curtailed by constitutional conventions, and many are now in practice exercised by government ministers

---

[27] For example, the monarch's power of dissolution of Parliament could prove decisive in the context of a hung Parliament following a General Election.

rather than the monarch in person. The existence and exercise of executive powers under the royal prerogative is today an extremely controversial issue, as evidenced by a recent Select Committee Report on prerogative powers.[28] The Committee was concerned that the power shift from monarch to ministers under the guise of the prerogative excludes Parliament from effective scrutiny of executive powers. This led the Committee to recommend legislation to provide greater parliamentary control over the prerogative: 'This is unfinished constitutional business. The prerogative has allowed powers to move from Monarch to Ministers without Parliament having a say in how they are exercised. This should no longer be acceptable to Parliament or the people.'[29]

There is also a second reason why the power shift from monarch to Prime Minister is more complex than it may at first appear: the Prime Minister has no executive powers vested in him. Therefore, as Jones has noted, 'to achieve anything he must work with and through his ministers who have executive power vested in them.'[30] Would it be more accurate, therefore, to refer to a power shift from King to Cabinet? This is certainly how the journey towards prime ministerial government began. The origins of the Cabinet can be seen in the ancient institution of the Privy Council. By the 1690s the most important members of the Privy Council were being described as the full Cabinet.[31] However, Walpole's ministry foretold the decline in the influence of the Cabinet which would occur over the next couple of centuries. The idea of Cabinet government, at its peak in Bagehot's era when he famously described it as 'the hyphen which joins, the buckle which fastens, the legislative part of the state to the executive part,'[32] has been receding from this high ever since, although its decline, it has been argued, 'has been concealed from the public eye even more successfully than its rise to power.'[33] In the twentieth century, the phrase 'prime ministerial government' assumed an accusatory tone reminiscent of the first uses of 'Prime Minister' in the early eighteenth century. While it is certainly true that 'ultimately the Prime Minister is only as strong as his colleagues let him be'[34] (as indicated by Thatcher's downfall[35]), provided the Prime Minister retains the support of his Cabinet colleagues, his power is untrammelled. In a very real sense, Crown sovereignty has become prime ministerial sovereignty.

[28] Fourth Report of the Select Committee on Public Administration, Cmnd 200304 (2003).

[29] *Ibid*, at para 61.

[30] GW Jones, 'The Prime Minister's Power' in A King (ed), *The British Prime Minister*, 2nd edn (London, Macmillan, 1985), p 215.

[31] P Hennessy, *The Cabinet* (Oxford, Basil Blackwell, 1986), p 1.

[32] W Bagehot, *The English Constitution* (London, Fontana Library, 1963 edn), p 68. Note that Crossman regards this function as now being exercised by a single person: the Prime Minister (RHS Crossman, 'Prime Ministerial Government' in King, n.30 above, p 189).

[33] Crossman, *ibid*, p 191.

[34] Jones, n 30 above, p 206.

[35] Hennessy's words, written in 1986, were strangely prescient: 'Cabinet government remains a putty-like concept. A Prime Minister can make of it very largely what he or she will, provided colleagues do not baulk at their treatment' (Hennessy, *The Cabinet*, n 31 above, p 4).

Such a state of affairs did not exist in Walpole's era. Two serious restraints upon his power and influence remained: the King continued as an 'active executive figure'[36] and the constitutional principle of collective responsibility had not yet arisen. This latter point meant that when Walpole resigned in 1742, his Cabinet colleagues did not follow suit. These two factors both derive in part from the fact that in the eighteenth century each minister remained individually responsible to the King, rather than to each other or to the Prime Minister. While this remained true, the leading minister could not be regarded as a Prime Minister in the modern sense. Gradually, however, Walpole's successors acquired more power and influence over their colleagues, which freed them from his eighteenth-century restraints.

b) The Development of Prime Ministerial Power

The vital notion of collective responsibility first developed during the 1780s. By 1782–83, it was recognised by the monarch that all members of the inner Cabinet would fall with the Prime Minister.[37] This followed closely on the heels of the last appearance of the monarch in Cabinet in 1781 and was an important step on the road towards modern-style Cabinet government, allowing Pitt to act more recognisably like a modern Prime Minister during the 1790s than Walpole had been able to do.[38] Other significant changes in the Prime Minister's role stemmed from the 1832 Reform Act, the significance of which cannot be overestimated. As will be discussed in the next chapter, the 1832 Reform Act transformed British politics and government and signified that a genuine democratisation process had begun. With it came increased party influence that was to colour the political process up to the present day.[39] Within a few years of the 1832 Act, a constitutional convention had been established that ministers would be drawn from Parliament. During the early twentieth century, it was further established that a Prime Minister was able to remove ministers (Balfour, 1903); a request to the monarch for a dissolution of Parliament would come from the Prime Minister alone (Lloyd George, 1918); the first permanent standing committee of Cabinet was established (the Home Affairs Committee, 1918); and the 'mediafication' of the premiership began when Baldwin delivered the first political radio broadcast during the General Election campaign of 1924.[40]

Many of these advances towards a modern-style Prime Minister and Cabinet

---

[36] Blake, n 4 above, p 24.

[37] Hennessy, n 2 above, p 45.

[38] By the 1790s, it has been noted, Pitt was 'behaving like a Prime Minister in his determination to centralise power in his own person and to reserve to himself key decisions about the personnel of his Cabinet' (O'Gorman, n 3 above, p 278).

[39] As Jones has stated, the 1832 Reform Act 'finally shattered the capacity of the Crown to win elections' (in Van Thal, n 1 above, p 19), as was proved only two years later when the King was forced to reinstate Lord Melbourne as Prime Minister following a failed attempt to impose Sir Robert Peel on an unwilling House of Commons and electorate (see Carter, n 2 above, p 31).

[40] See Hennessy, n 2 above, pp 45–51.

were due to significant changes in the British political system. For example, the democratisation of Parliament, the growth of the party system, the expansion of the state, and the personalisation of politics have all contributed to the development of the office of Prime Minister. Without these factors, the Prime Minister would be a very different role but it remains clear that the foundations of the office were laid by Walpole. Hennessy explains that 'in the Walpole years the enduring DNA-like strands were spun which continue to determine the strength and scope, as well as the vulnerabilities, of the job.'[41] But he goes on to note that 'as in any living organism, there is more than one strand of DNA.'[42] The subsequent strands have shaped the 'living organism' in a way unforeseen in Walpole's day. It is now necessary to examine in more detail the nature of this 'living organism' and its position under the similarly evolving constitution.

c) The Conventional Nature of the Job

The office of Prime Minister does not exist in law, despite a few mentions in twentieth-century statutes.[43] The role of Prime Minister is a creature of convention and as such is neither a fixed nor a certain position. It has been claimed that 'the office is what the holder makes of it' and that it is 'sufficiently unstructured for different men with different personalities to make entirely different use of it.'[44] It is shaped by both personal and political factors,[45] and thus we can contrast Thatcher and Major, Blair and Callaghan, not just on their politics but also on the nature of the prime ministerial position they created.[46]

Jennings famously said of conventions that 'they provide the flesh which clothes the dry bones of the law; they make the legal constitution work; they keep it in touch with the growth of ideas.'[47] Conventions are distinct from laws in that they are not enforceable in a court of law,[48] but they are, nevertheless, binding upon those to whom they are addressed. Indeed, it is their binding character which defines them as conventions. Conventions are thus elusive elements of the constitution, but even if we cannot see them directly, we can see their shadows in the form of their effect upon the institutions and practices of government. So, for example, collective responsibility of Cabinet, the monarch's inability to refuse royal assent to a Bill, and the appointment of the leader of the majority party in

---

[41] *Ibid*, p 41.

[42] *Ibid.*

[43] Examples include Chequers Estate Act 1917, Ministers of the Crown Act 1937, Parliamentary and Other Pensions Act 1972, House of Commons Disqualification Act 1975, and the Ministerial and Other Pensions and Salaries Act 1991.

[44] Jones, in Van Thal, n 1 above, p 13.

[45] *Ibid.*

[46] See Hennessy, n 2 above, for discussion of the differing styles of modern Prime Ministers.

[47] I Jennings, *The Law of the Constitution*, 5th edn (London, Hodder & Stoughton., 1959), pp 81–82.

[48] This consequence can be avoided, however, by the discovery of a parallel law co-existing with the convention, as in *Attorney-General v Jonathan Cape* [1976] QB 752.

the House of Commons as Prime Minister are all conventional in nature. These conventions (together with many others) also share a further defining characteristic: they limit the powers of the monarch.[49] A strictly legal view of the modern British constitution would portray a powerful monarch with real influence over her government of the day (and no leading, or prime, minister to dominate his colleagues), but when the constitution is viewed through the spectrum of convention, the monarch is revealed as a mere figurehead and the Prime Minister as the effective head of government. In this context, the emergence and growth of the office of Prime Minister can be seen as part of a broader conventional movement towards restricting the power of the monarch. Such a movement is entirely at home – indeed may be inevitable – within a constitution based upon the fundamental value of democracy. In Walpole's era this would not have been evident (although its foundations had been laid in 1688) but, as the next chapter will show, democratisation of the constitution was soon to begin. The relocation of executive power in the hands of the Prime Minister and Cabinet did not, however, prevent misuse of that power. An elected politician is as capable of abusing his powers as a hereditary monarch, and conventions provide little security for the citizens against such abuse.

III. Conclusion

Imagine a Prime Minister adept at party management, reliant upon an inner Cabinet of close colleagues, accused of borrowing policies from other sources and of reshaping his party's ideology, unable to rely upon all elements of his party, and charged of cronyism, patronage and manipulation. The similarities between the first and most recent premiership are striking and have led Black to compare the two, concluding that Walpole was 'far more impressive in a number of respects.'[50] Most significantly, Black concludes that Walpole was 'far better able to handle the Commons and understood its importance'[51] and, of course, it is this very factor that laid the foundations for the powerful role Blair was to acquire over two centuries later. Walpole's recognition that the future lie in the Commons was prescient. His reliance upon party management, cronyism and patronage were less desirable characteristics, but ones which are now often linked with the premiership. A Prime Minister must be pragmatic: his entire existence depends upon the support of a majority in the Commons (which the party and whip system should, in normal circumstances, be able to assure) and the support

---

[49] Indeed, Dicey defined conventions as 'rules intended to regulate the exercise of the whole of the remaining discretionary powers of the Crown' (AV Dicey, *Introduction to the Study of the Law of the Constitution*, 10th edn (London, Macmillan, 1959), p 426). However, the category of conventions is now broader than this.

[50] Black, n 5 above, p 182.

[51] *Ibid.*

of his Cabinet colleagues, for which pragmatism, patronage and manipulation are invaluable. Crossman has argued that the only remaining distinction between a Prime Minister and a President is that a Prime Minister can be removed by his colleagues before the end of his term in office,[52] as was proved by Thatcher's downfall. Provided that a Prime Minister can avoid this fate, his power is untrammelled, and Walpole's legacy is thus a poisoned chalice for the British constitution.

On the one hand, the emergence of the office of Prime Minister provided a conventional counter-balance to the monarch's dwindling political authority. A Prime Minister provides a link between Crown and Parliament which has ensured that there has been no repetition of the seventeenth-century power struggles between these two sources of authority. In addition, as an electorally accountable Member of Parliament, the Prime Minister can rely upon democratic legitimacy as a justification for the imposition of his policies upon the citizenry. On the other hand, the emergence of a Prime Minister has presented real danger to the delicate balance of power under the British constitution. In providing a link between Crown and Parliament, the Prime Minister bridges the separation of powers between executive and legislative branches of government (along with all ministers sitting in Parliament). Today's Prime Minister has inherited the power of a seventeenth-century monarch coupled with the democratic legitimacy of the twentieth-century Parliament, resulting in an office of unprecedented political power. As the office is one of convention there is no legal limitation, and little legal accountability, upon the office of Prime Minister. In short, the office of Prime Minister is an effective and necessary addition to the British democratic constitution but it is also a potential threat to the very principle upon which the constitution is based. Democracy is not assured by the mere existence of electoral support for the Prime Minister and his government (even if that support were majority support, which it never is). The dominance of the party system in Parliament means that the legislative branch of government is dominated by the executive branch led by the Prime Minister. The potential for misuse is very real. Walpole's legacy is a mixed blessing for the constitution, but one without which British government would be unrecognisable.

---

[52] Crossman, n 32 above, p 191.

4

1832 – The Great Reform Act: A First Step towards Democratic Representation?

The previous chapter discussed an important development in the form and identity of the executive branch of government. This chapter identifies an equally significant development in relation to the legislative branch. The Great Reform Act of 1832 is, without doubt, a landmark constitutional statute. It radically transformed the system of representation to the Westminster Parliament and opened the door to further incremental reform on this issue. Whether it can be regarded as a first step towards democracy is more debatable, but it will be the argument of this chapter that its implications for Parliament, constitution, and country were significant. The 1832 Act did not create a democratic state, but it was the key constitutional moment from which subsequent reforms can be traced. Perhaps most significantly, it is not only the content of the Act but its controversial passage which created important precedents for the future evolution of the constitution.

I. The Reform Act 1832

a) The Need for Reform

The Great Reform Act of 1832 – 'an Act to amend the Representation of the People in England and Wales'[1] – has a place in history as the first in a series of Reform Acts, spread over more than a century, which culminated in a system of democratic representation for the Westminster Parliament. It was to be a long and bumpy road. The first step, taken in 1831–32 by the Whig coalition ministry of Earl Grey, was controversial and divisive despite its limited ambition. As will

---

[1] There were in fact three Reform Acts of 1832: one each for England and Wales, Scotland, and Ireland. This chapter, however, will focus solely upon the first.

be seen, it was a reform wedded to existing priorities: property, the representation of interests, and deference to the aristocracy. But the pre-1832 system was so corrupt that change, in whatever form, was needed.

In 1831, there were 489 representatives of English constituencies. Apart from 82 returned from the counties and four from Oxbridge, the remainder were all sent by boroughs, with most boroughs sending two members. Only approximately 13 per cent of adult men in England and Wales (and 0 per cent of adult women) had the vote.[2] They usually derived this vote from land ownership although, under an extremely complex system with no uniform franchise, there were exceptions. These included the 'scot-and-lot boroughs' in which any man who paid poor rates could vote, and the 'potwalloper boroughs' in which any man resident for six months who 'boiled a pot there' (ie possessed a house and hearth) and was not a charge on the poor rate could vote. In such boroughs, described as 'open' as opposed to the infamous 'nomination' or 'pocket' boroughs, there was a degree to which an election was genuine,[3] but even here there was widespread corruption, as a voter might regard his vote as a rare commodity and sell it to the highest bidder.[4] In other boroughs, the situation was far worse. Elections would be controlled by a single individual, hence the name 'nomination borough'. This individual would often be a peer, which thus undermined the growing dominance of the House of Commons over the House of Lords. As Brock has argued, it 'was not a system based on property, but the caricature of one.'[5] Furthermore, the distribution of seats bore no relation to population. Major industrial towns such as Manchester, Birmingham and Leeds had no representatives, whereas there were over 100 so-called 'rotten boroughs' with fewer than 100 voters, such as Old Sarum which, in 1831, had just seven voters.[6] Therefore, as of 1831, a number of problems with the system of representation in Britain were notorious, prominent amongst which were the very limited and non-uniform franchise, the existence of nomination boroughs, the lack of representation for major industrial towns, the existence of rotten boroughs with only a handful of voters, and the widespread corruption, bribery and intimidation which was an integral part of every election. Something had to be done.

By 1830 reform had become such an important issue within, and outside of, Westminster that, when the Duke of Wellington set himself against any form of, even moderate, parliamentary reform, he made inevitable the fall of his Tory government, the formation of a Whig ministry under Grey, and an extensive, rather than moderate, Bill of Reform. Even so, when Lord John Russell

---

[2] H Cunningham, *The Challenge of Democracy: Britain 1832–1918* (Harlow, Pearson, 2001), p 30. The figure was even lower in Scotland at less than 1%.

[3] For example, the radical reformer Henry Hunt was elected by the cotton weavers of industrialised Preston who, ironically, would be disfranchised when the 1832 Act introduced a uniform franchise (E Pearce, *Reform! The Fight for the 1832 Reform Act* (London, Jonathan Cape, 2003), p 30.)

[4] *Ibid*, pp 30–31. See M Brock, *The Great Reform Act* (London, Hutchinson & Co, 1973), ch 1, for more details on an old system in decline.

[5] Brock, *ibid*, p 26.

[6] *Ibid*, p 32.

introduced the Whig Bill to the House of Commons in March 1831, it was far more sweeping than had been expected: 'A well-kept secret, its extent and audacity now came as a bombshell.'[7] The Bill sought to achieve three main goals: to introduce a uniform franchise; to disfranchise the nomination boroughs; and to enfranchise the new, industrialised towns. It was, perhaps surprisingly, the extensive redistribution of seats, rather than the limited extension of the franchise, which was to have the greatest impact at the time, as well as in hindsight.[8] When Russell read out the long list of boroughs to be disfranchised, the House of Commons was in uproar.[9] The slow and controversial passage of the Bill through both Houses of Parliament was to take over a year and comprise 'griefs, hesitations, asininity in the monarch, loss of nerve in government, exaltations in opposition and ... real fears of a civil war involving an angry people and unsure troops.'[10] Of constitutional significance, there would also be a stalemate between the two Houses of Parliament, ministerial resignations, and threats of a mass creation of peers to pass the Bill. There would also be modification and amendments as two further Bills replaced Russell's original March 1831 Bill but, through this parliamentary and public turmoil, the key principles of a uniform franchise and redistribution of seats remained.

b) The Reform Act 1832

The Bill which finally became law in June 1832 had the effect of doubling the electorate, mainly by giving the vote to lower middle-class townsmen. A uniform franchise was introduced in section XXVII: 'every Male Person of full Age, and not subject to any legal Incapacity, who shall occupy ... as Owner or Tenant, any House ... or other Building ... of the clear yearly value of not less than Ten Pounds, shall, if duly registered ... be entitled to vote.' While on paper this is a uniform franchise, in reality its effect was anything but uniform. Property prices varied across the country so that in London, where prices were high, enfranchisement penetrated much further down the social scale than in other areas. It was, as Cunningham notes, a crude measure,[11] and one which was exacerbated by the principle that no pre-existing voter should be disfranchised by the reforms. Thus the actual impact of the 1832 Act was, for example, to produce an electorate

---

[7] JCD Clark, *English Society 1660–1832: Religion, Ideology and Politics During the Ancien Regime*, 2nd edn (Cambridge, Cambridge University Press, 2000), p 541. The Tory Lord Ellenborough made the following note in his diary: 'The Reform proposed is much more extensive than was expected. Parts of it were very absurd. There was no little laughter as they were detailed. The feeling in the Gallery was against it, as absurd ... The feeling ... is that the Bill cannot pass ...' (Ellenborough's Diary, 2 March 1831, in A Aspinall, *Three Early Nineteenth Century Diaries* (London, Williams & Norgate, 1952), at pp 61–62).

[8] Cunningham, n 2 above, p 33.

[9] See Pearce, n 3 above, pp 72–74.

[10] *Ibid*, p 301. The difficult passage of the Bill through Parliament will be discussed in detail in the following section.

[11] Cunningham, n 2 above, p 33.

of 11 per cent in the newly enfranchised town of Birmingham as compared to an 88 per cent electorate in Preston.[12] Such inconsistencies ensured that fairness and equality (and hence democracy) remained excluded from the system of representation until well into the twentieth century.

Although the extension of the franchise to (some of) the middle class was controversial at the time, especially amongst the aristocracy, who feared their period of predominance was ending, it was the radicalism of the Bill's redistribution of seats which proved most significant. Fifty-six boroughs were disfranchised in section I (and Schedule A), and a further 30 boroughs lost one of their two members under section II (and Schedule B). The new boroughs which benefited were listed in sections III and IV (and Schedules C and D). Twenty-two new boroughs received two members, including representation for the first time for Birmingham, Manchester, Leeds, Sheffield, Oldham and Sunderland, and a further twenty boroughs, including Huddersfield, Walsall and Gateshead, gained one member. The boroughs disfranchised were selected by means of their population. This in itself was a novel concept. From early on in the drafting process of the first Bill, the idea for Schedules A and B emerged. Lord Durham relied upon the 1821 census to identify towns with a population of fewer than 2,000, which would lose both of their members, and those with a population of fewer than 4,000, which would lose one member. The figures were misleading and outdated,[13] and the government was to amend the Schedules throughout the Bill's progress through Parliament, but the principle of a link between representation and population was evident throughout. This was heretical even to most Whigs[14] and is not prominent enough in the Act to displace the old rationale of property as the measure of fitness to vote: 'The rationale of the old constitution, something which would spill into the final new draft, was that it was property (definable) and the intelligence (more problematic) of the nation which should be represented in the Commons.'[15] Thus, although population was a factor in the selection of boroughs to be disfranchised, in general the redistribution of seats in the Act was motivated by a desire to secure representation of certain interests.[16] As well as the traditional landed interest, these now included the new manufacturing interests such as wool, cotton and coal, represented by the new boroughs in Schedules C and D.

That the redistribution of seats and widening of the franchise was significant is evident from the battle which ensued within Parliament during the passage of the Act and which even, at times, spilled over into the country. However, the fact remains that both the intentions and the effects of the 1832 Reform Act were extremely conservative. The nomination boroughs, although reduced in number,

---

[12] *Ibid*, p 34. The electorate in Preston would dwindle as the pre-existing voters died.

[13] Pearce describes the 'rough and ready, back-of-an-envelope methods' by which the government defined qualification for borough status, and the anomalies later exposed by the opposition (Pearce, n 3 above, p 101).

[14] *Ibid*, p 70.

[15] *Ibid*.

[16] N Gash, *Politics in the Age of Peel* (London, Longmans, 1953), p 23.

were not entirely extinguished; bribery and corruption continued; and, perhaps most significantly, the male working class (as well as all women) remained disfranchised:

> If the Whigs ever intended calling into being a democracy, then they made a signal mess of it. The total franchise probably expanded by about 300,000 or 80 per cent. This provided for a reformed electorate of just over 650,000 people, most of them still in England, out of a population of over 16 million.[17]

There was, contrary to anti-reformers' fears, no large-scale transfer of power from one class to another, and certainly no direct benefit to the working class. In effect, as Gash notes, 'privileged wealth was being asked to admit unprivileged wealth to the close circle of the ruling class.'[18]

Furthermore, the Whigs made no attempt in the 1832 Act to tackle the root cause of much corruption: the absence of a secret ballot. This was one of the major demands of the Reform movement (and, indeed, had been recommended by the committee of ministers which first drafted the Bill), but was opposed by Grey and most of his Cabinet. The problem was that a secret ballot remained extremely controversial at this time. Far from being recognised as a guarantee of fair elections, a ballot was widely viewed as likely to increase corruption by enabling voters to accept bribes from both sides, rather than just one.[19] It was also commonly regarded as a 'low, sneaking thing, the act of a cad' to keep one's vote secret.[20] Thus the secret ballot would not be introduced for another 40 years until the Ballot Act of 1872 was passed.

Demands for a secret ballot, together with other radical ideas such as universal adult suffrage (for men only, of course), equal voter numbers in each constituency, annually elected Parliaments, abolition of property qualifications for MPs, and payment of MPs, formed the Charter, first published in 1837, from which the Chartism movement gained its name. Such demands, so soon after the 1832 Act, represented a direct challenge to the contents of the Act. Perversely, this dissatisfaction indicates the success of the 1832 Act in achieving its aims. The Act was always intended to be a compromise, representing 'the most that could be pushed through Parliament and the least that would satisfy the country at large. That the Tories regarded it as revolutionary and the more extreme radicals as a betrayal was a reasonable indication of its value as a rational solution.'[21] It is this

---

[17] M Bentley, *Politics Without Democracy 1815–1914: Perception and Preoccupation in British Government*, 2nd edn (Oxford, Blackwell, 1996), p 55.

[18] Gash, n 16 above, p 18.

[19] Brock, n 4 above, p 141.

[20] Pearce, n 3 above, p 70.

[21] Gash, n 16 above, p 10. When introducing the Bill to the House of Commons, Lord John Russell acknowledged the Whigs' desire to provide a compromise: 'We wish to place ourselves between the two hostile parties. Neither agreeing with the bigotry of the one, that no Reform is necessary, nor agreeing with the fanaticism of the other, that only some particular kind of Reform can by any means be satisfactory to the people; we place ourselves between the two, and fix ourselves on what is, I hope,

issue of the context in which the Act was passed to which attention will now be turned.

II. The Passage of the Act

a) The House of Commons

Earl Grey, a man 'both aristocratic and intermittently radical, if soft-spoken about it,'[22] came to office in 1830 at the head of a coalition of Whigs, Canningites and Ultras. As parliamentary reform was the only issue on which they all agreed, it was no surprise when it became an early priority for the government.[23] In December 1830, Grey appointed a committee of four ministers to prepare reform proposals and, by March 1831, the government was ready to introduce its newly drafted Bill to Parliament. When Russell introduced the Bill to the House of Commons on 1 March 1831, it was to a 'stunned and derisory' House.[24] Few had expected such a radical and sweeping Bill. Russell explained that ministers thought that:

> it would not be sufficient to bring forward a measure which should merely lop off some disgusting excrescences, or cure some notorious defects: but would still leave the battle to be fought again with renewed and strengthened discontent. They have thought that no half measures would be sufficient – that no trifling, no paltering, with so great a question could give stability to the Throne – or satisfaction to the Country.[25]

As Russell proceeded to read out the long list of boroughs in Schedules A and B which were to lose members, the reaction of the House made it clear that the Bill's passage would not be as straightforward as Grey appears to have assumed.[26]

Hysteria was dominant during the long days (and nights) of debate. Many opposition members argued that such a reformed House of Commons would dispose of both the King and the House of Lords within 10 years.[27] Belatedly realising that some reform was now unavoidable, the Tories decided to oppose

---

firm and steadfast ground, between the abuses we wish to amend, and the convulsions we hope to avert' (HC Deb, 3rd Series, Vol 2, col 1062, 1 March 1831).

[22] Pearce, n 3 above, p 71.
[23] Clark, n 7 above, pp 539–40.
[24] Bentley, n 17 above, p 47.
[25] HC Deb, 3rd Series, Vol 2, col 1065, 1 March 1831.
[26] See Brock, n 4 above, pp 152–53.
[27] Pearce, n 3 above, p 87. See, for example, Sir Robert Inglis, who began his response to Russell by acknowledging his 'sensation of awe at the contemplation of the abyss, on the brink of which we stand, and into which the motion of the noble Lord will, if successful, hurl us' (HC Deb, 3rd Series, Vol 2, col 1090, 1 March 1831).

the Bill but propose more moderate reform: disfranchising the most objectionable of boroughs and enfranchising Leeds and Birmingham. However, as Pearce notes, this was 'the day before yesterday's advanced thinking, yesterday's moderation, today's impossible nostalgia.'[28] When the second reading division came, it was dramatic: the Commons was fuller than anyone had ever known and the final vote was 302 in favour of the Bill, with 301 opposed to it.[29] The battle was far from over, however. A one-vote majority was never going to be sufficient to push through such a significant piece of legislation. During the long committee stage, General Isaac Gascoyne moved what was, in effect, a wrecking amendment: to maintain the exact percentage of English members in a reformed House of Commons. The government declared that this would be a decisive issue for the Bill and suffered 'a not unexpected defeat'.[30] Grey asked the King for a dissolution of Parliament and, after a short delay, William IV was persuaded to come in person to prorogue Parliament.[31]

A General Election now turned upon the issue of reform. Unsurprisingly, the country (or, at least, those privileged members of it who currently had a vote) returned a decidedly pro-reform House.[32] Some doubt has been cast over the 1831 elections, in which intimidation and violence were rife. This was not unusual, but does appear to have been unusually one-sided (in favour of reform).[33] There is no doubt, however, that the most significant factor in the elections was the popularity of the Reform Bill.[34] It might be assumed that this would create a mandate for the Bill but this was not strictly so: 'there was an element within the Cabinet, best represented by Palmerston, which would still have favoured wholesale concession to the people who had lost the election.'[35] The second Reform Bill was introduced to the House of Commons by Russell on 24 June 1831, and 'everything conspired towards tedium'[36] as the argument shifted from 'end of the world talk to niggling practicalities.'[37] On 22 September 1831, the House of Commons passed the Reform Bill by a majority of 109. The House of Lords now 'stood at the end of a long, unshaded and sticky constitutional road along which the new Bill had to be carried.'[38]

---

[28] Pearce, n 3 above, p 120.

[29] Interestingly, amongst the English members there was a majority against reform (241:238); Scottish members were also opposed (26:13); but the Irish members voted in favour (56:36) (Pearce, n 3 above, p 128).

[30] *Ibid*, p 140. The vote was lost by 299 votes to 291.

[31] *Ibid*, pp 144–45.

[32] Pearce estimates a majority of 130–140 for reform in the newly constituted House (*ibid*, p 151).

[33] See Brock, n 4 above, pp 197–98.

[34] *Ibid*, p 198.

[35] Pearce, n 3 above, p 154.

[36] *Ibid*, p 157.

[37] *Ibid*, p 158.

[38] *Ibid*, p 154.

b) The House of Lords

The debate in the House of Lords on the Reform Bill began on 3 October 1831. Grey himself introduced the Bill, imploring the Lords to 'avoid those dangers which inevitably arise from your rejection of this measure.'[39] Grey reiterated to the Lords that 'It is not quite so great a sacrifice as some would represent that you are now called upon to make. You are asked only to give up that which is odious, unjust, and unconstitutional, and by retaining which the security of this House may be shaken.'[40] The Lords were unconvinced and, on 8 October, rejected the Bill by 199 votes to 158. This defeat, by a majority of 41, was worse than the government had expected and caused serious concern. While the King may have been prevailed upon to create a number of new peers to push through the Bill, he would baulk at the figures that were now needed.[41] Indeed, ministers themselves, including Grey, were reluctant to rely upon such a mass creation of peers. But the country was behind the Bill, and retreat for the government was to prove impossible. Political unions, such as that founded in Birmingham by Thomas Attwood, campaigned peacefully for reform, but the Bill's defeat in the House of Lords not only stimulated the growth of such organisations, but also presented leaders such as Attwood with 'problems of control.'[42] The House of Lords defeat ignited riots in Bristol, Nottingham and Derby.[43] A further consequence was to force the unions to drop their more radical reform objectives and instead focus upon supporting the government's Reform Bill, regardless of its shortcomings.[44] Given that one of the Bill's shortcomings, from the point of view of the unions, was a failure to enfranchise their working-class members, their support for the Bill could be viewed as generous.

During a five-hour Cabinet meeting, it was decided to recall Parliament (against Grey's wishes, as he favoured delay)[45] and not to dilute the Bill in any significant way. Some minor modifications, such as new criteria for disfranchisement and a reduction in single-member constituencies, were introduced. It was, Pearce has argued, 'a version delicately adjusted to provide excuses for a Tory retreat.'[46] The Bill quickly passed through the House of Commons for a second time, with 324 votes in favour and only 162 against on the second reading. At about this time, Lord Althorp, a key government spokesman whose great expertise did much to further the case for reform, wrote to Grey threatening to resign unless new peers were immediately created. Grey refused, and Althorp surrendered

---

[39] HC Deb, 3rd Series, Vol 7, col 969, 3 October 1831.
[40] HL Deb, 3rd Series, Vol 7, col 956, 3 October 1831.
[41] Brock, n 4 above, p 244.
[42] *Ibid*, p 249.
[43] See Pearce, n 3 above, p 203.
[44] ND LoPatin, *Political Unions, Popular Politics and the Great Reform Act* (London, Macmillan, 1999), p 129.
[45] Pearce, n 3 above, p 211.
[46] *Ibid*, p 217.

on the issue, knowing that to force the issue would lead to Grey's own resignation and the destruction of the government.[47] So the Bill returned to the House of Lords with no guarantee of the government being able, or wishing, to create pro-reform peers to ease its passage. Amidst much controversy and debate on the issue, the Bill passed its second reading on 14 April 1832, due to the support of the so-called 'waverers'. One hundred and eighty-four peers voted in favour of the Bill, with 175 voting against. However, the waverers' continued support could not be relied upon. The first clause of the Bill listed each of the 56 boroughs to be disfranchised. The Tories realised that postponement of discussion of this clause was essential if the Bill were to be defeated: 'If we get into battles on details we are lost, for our own people will not stay and theirs will. So we must postpone the first clause.'[48] Thus on 7 May 1832, Lord Lyndhurst proposed an amendment to postpone consideration of clause 1. The waverers, contrary to government expectations, deserted the Bill, and the amendment was carried by a majority of 35.[49] Grey obtained an adjournment in order to consider what to do but, 'for once, all the Cabinet knew what they had to do and they did it'[50]: they immediately agreed, unanimously, to offer their resignations if William IV did not now create sufficient peers to ensure the Bill's passage. It was now obvious that as many as 50 to 60 new peers would be required.[51] William could not accede to this. The ministerial resignations were duly accepted. The process of reform had ground to a halt.

Amidst public demonstrations and agitation, William asked the Duke of Wellington to form a government. In one of the great political U-turns, Wellington agreed to support a reform Bill in order to gain personal power. The irony did not escape his contemporaries:

> The Duke of Wellington who ... in November 1830 declared he knew nothing more perfect than the Constitution of the House of Commons, and who has since opposed every principle of Lord Grey's Reform Bill, kissed hands this day at 1 o'clock at St. James' Palace, and is to bring in very nearly the same Bill.[52]

It was not, however, to be this easy. The political unions campaigned against Wellington, using the power of public opinion to frustrate his efforts to form a government.[53] In addition, the senior Tory in the House of Commons, Sir Robert

---

[47] See Brock, n 4 above, p 278.

[48] Ellenborough's Diary, 30 April 1832, in Aspinall, n 7 above, p 234.

[49] One hundred and fifty-one voted in favour of the amendment; 116 against. Le Marchant admitted in his diary that the government 'went down to the Lords on Monday wholly unconscious of our fate' (Le Marchant's Diary, 7 May 1832, in Aspinall, n 7 above, p 240).

[50] Pearce, n 3 above, p. 276.

[51] *Ibid.*

[52] Littleton's Diary, 12 May 1832, in Aspinall, n 7 above, p 249.

[53] See LoPatin, n 44 above, p 158: 'Their threats to boycott payment of taxes and stage a run on the Tory Bank of England, as well as rumours of arming and revolutionary activity among the Unions, all added credence to Grey's claims that the people would not tolerate a Tory government and the emasculation of the Reform Bill.'

Peel, refused to be part of any government which proceeded with reform.[54] Many followed his principled example,[55] and the prospects of Wellington leading a government diminished. When, on 10 May 1832, Lord Ebrington introduced a motion in the House of Lords in favour of a ministry which would carry the Reform Bill into effect unimpaired, there was a majority of 80 in favour. Following a bitter debate on 14 May in the House of Commons, during which the Tories admitted that the Reform Bill 'should pass and pass by the hands of those who had initiated it,'[56] Wellington admitted to the King that he was unable to form a ministry.

Grey was reluctant to return to government without a guarantee that the necessary peers would be created in order to ensure the Bill's passage. William now had little choice and, on 18 May, Grey and the Cabinet received the guarantee that they sought. Althorp told the House of Commons that ministers had received 'sufficient guarantee for being able to pass the Reform Bill unimpaired.'[57] When the same was confirmed by Grey in the House of Lords, Wellington and 50 to 60 other Tory peers walked out of the chamber: 'Historically, with however ill a grace, the walkout was surrender.'[58] These anti-reformers stayed away throughout the Bill's progress through the House of Lords (negating the need for a creation of new pro-reform peers). On 4 June 1832, the Bill passed its third reading by 106 votes to 21 and, on 7 June, the Bill finally received the Royal Assent. The surrender of the Lords marked an important change in the relationship between the two Houses. It established a principle, to be echoed even more loudly in 1911, that 'the House of Lords were never to carry resistance to any measure coming from the Commons beyond a certain point – beyond the time when it became unmistakably evident that the Commons were in earnest.'[59] Indeed, it may be that it was the passage of the Reform Act, rather than its limited contents, which heralded a new concept of democracy.

c) The Role of Public Opinion

The role of the political unions, and more broadly public opinion, in facilitating the passage of the Reform Act was unique. It was an indication of the power of the electorate and also, perhaps, a reminder that the real power of the people is not dependent upon the ability to participate in elections. Although the middle and working classes joined together to campaign for the Reform Bill, the working

---

[54] Pearce, n 3 above, p 287.

[55] *Ibid*, p 291.

[56] *Ibid*, p 298.

[57] HC Deb, 3rd Series, Vol 12, col 1072: 'His Majesty's Ministers conceive they have secured for the passing of the Reform Bill such an arrangement as they deem sufficient, and, therefore, that we continue to hold the offices we are now in possession of.'

[58] Pearce, n 3 above, p 300.

[59] J McCarthy, 'Important Constitutional Principles Established' in WH Maehl, *The Reform Bill of 1832 – Why Not Revolution?* (New York, Holt, Rinehart & Winston, 1967), p 94. Note this passage was written in 1882, three decades before the 1909–11 constitutional crisis.

class (and later the suffragette movement) would have to fight on for the right to vote. However, it became increasingly obvious in 1832 that no government could hope to rule effectively without a genuine commitment to parliamentary reform. That the reform was limited is not really the point. The fact that reform was essential in order to appease a dissatisfied mass of the people restrained the freedom of Parliament. When Grey warned of 'the just discontent of a vast majority of the people of this country'[60] and cautioned that the continuance of such discontent and political dissatisfaction 'threatens all those disastrous consequences which must arise when ill feeling is engendered in the people towards the Government of the country,'[61] he was not, contrary to opposition claims, exaggerating. Some commentators have even claimed that a revolution threatened; certainly the means of direct action – public demonstrations, raising barricades, mobilising the public by placards, initiation of a run on the Bank of England, and non-payment of taxes – were activities which 'could form the foundations of revolution.'[62] For Grey's government to enact the Reform Act by peaceful means was, therefore, undoubtedly ' a great and beneficent feat of statesmanship.'[63] Not only did a majority of members of the House of Commons feel compelled, either by their own consciences or by fears as to electoral repercussions, to support reform, but also both the House of Lords and the monarch eventually voluntarily stepped aside to permit the controversial legislation to be passed. The Lords ultimately yielded when it became clear that the Commons would not support any anti-reform (or even moderate reform) government, and the King, after some delay, promised to do all in his power – including creating peers – to enable the Bill to pass. As McCarthy states, by William giving way 'to the advice of his ministers on a matter of vital importance to the nation, and on which his opinions were opposed to those of the majority … it became thereby settled that the personal will of the sovereign was no longer to be a decisive authority in our scheme of Government.'[64] However, despite these undoubted precursors of democratic government, it must never be overlooked that the Reform Bill was not, and was never intended to be, democratic: it was designed to prevent democracy; to put a stop to the people's dissatisfaction; to preserve government by deference. No one, least of all Grey, had foreseen the use of democratic means to pass such a Bill.

---

[60] HL Deb, 3rd Series, Vol 7, col 935, 3 October 1831.
[61] *Ibid*, col 929.
[62] Pearce, n 3 above, p 280.
[63] Brock, n 4 above, p 336.
[64] McCarthy, n 59 above, p 95.

III. Towards Democracy?

a) Further Steps to Reform

The limitations of the 'Great' Reform Act were most effectively illustrated by the radical Henry Hunt, during a parliamentary debate when he responded to Russell's claim that the Bill was about 'representation of the people' by noting that nine-tenths of the male adult population (and, we might add, the entire female adult population) were to remain excluded.[65] It was to be another 96 years before Britain achieved (something approaching) universal suffrage. Opposition fears in 1831–32 that the Act would open the door to further, more radical, reform were, thus, accurate in principle, but in error on the fundamental issue of timescale. The move towards democratic representation would be by small, incremental steps. When Peel warned the Whigs in the House of Commons that 'others will outbid you, not now, but at no remote period – they will offer votes and power to a million men, will quote your precedent for the concession, and will carry your principles to their legitimate and natural consequence,'[66] he was, as Pearce notes, 'not quite as prophetic as this suggests,'[67] because the essence of his prophecies lay in the timescale.[68] Crucially, the reformed electorate was to prove not to be as radical as expected.

Tensions between the working and middle class increased after 1832, as those who had the vote and now wanted stability were pitted against those who did not yet have the vote and wanted further reform.[69] In the 35 years before the second Reform Act of 1867, the idea of democracy was simultaneously a threat (to the upper and middle classes) and a hope (to the working class):

> democracy was, for most of the upper and middle classes, a bogey: a threat, but a threat at a distance, to be held up as a sign of how things could go wrong. For the politically aware of the working classes it might be a hope, but one frustratingly out of reach. After the passage of the second reform Act in 1867, democracy was a much more immediate threat or hope ....[70]

The main effect of the 1867 Act was to give the vote (in boroughs only) to all adult male owners and occupiers of dwelling-houses, and to lodgers in lodgings worth £10 per annum. The electorate was thus increased to approximately 36 per cent of the adult male population. This was a significant advance although, as Cunningham notes, it still left two thirds of men and all women without a vote.[71]

---

[65] See Pearce, n 3 above, p 216.
[66] HC Deb, 3rd Series, Vol 2, col 1353, 3 March 1831.
[67] Pearce, n 3 above, p 98.
[68] Brock, n 4 above, p 206.
[69] LoPatin, n 44 above, p 173.
[70] Cunningham, n 2 above, p 103.
[71] *Ibid*, p 104.

Between the second and third Reform Acts there were two significant legislative attacks on corruption in the form of the Ballot Act 1872 (which finally introduced a secret ballot) and the Corrupt Practices Act 1883 (which specified the amount of money that could be spent on elections). The Third Reform Act of 1884 then extended male household suffrage to the counties and thus extended the electorate to approximately two thirds of adult males. The next year, the Redistribution Act 1885 created single-member constituencies. However, although contemporaries might, by the late nineteenth century, have regarded themselves as living in a democracy, 'to historians it is the limitations of democracy even after the Third Reform Act that are most striking.'[72] Perhaps most significantly, there remained a perception that a vote was not a right, but rather a privilege which had to be earned. It was thus not until 1918 that women first earned the privilege to vote (along with the remaining disfranchised men), and not until 1928 that they could vote on the same basis as men.[73] So, through this long process of reform, how significant was the original 1832 Act in producing a democracy? To answer this question, a brief investigation of the concept of democracy may be helpful.

b) The Meaning of Democracy

A superficial definition of democracy would be 'rule by the people' as the word, first used in the fifth century BC, combines the Greek words of *demos* (the people) and *kratein* (to rule).[74] However, this rule by the people is no longer literal.[75] Democracy has now evolved to require rule by the people's representatives. As we have seen, much debate has centred upon who comprises the people and, even now, some are excluded within the United Kingdom, such as those aged under 18, and convicted prisoners. In addition, UK electoral law imposes residence conditions. This latter factor requires that citizens be included on the electoral register in their constituency before they are permitted to vote. In the past, this had the effect of disenfranchising the homeless, who failed to meet the residence requirement.[76]

---

[72] *Ibid*, p 128.

[73] Under the Representation of the People Acts 1918 and 1928, respectively.

[74] See B Holden, *Understanding Liberal Democracy* (Oxford, Philip Allan, 1988), p 5.

[75] In classical antiquity, and elsewhere, democracy was associated with large gatherings of citizens, but an arrangement that worked efficiently in the city-states of ancient Greece is inconceivable in modern industrial societies (although it is possible that the internet may provide new opportunities in this direction). See D Held, *Models of Democracy*, 2nd edn (Cambridge, Polity Press, 1996), p 338.

[76] The Representation of the People Act 2000 seeks to avoid this situation by introducing the concept of 'notional residence' (Representation of the People Act 1983, s 7B, inserted by Representation of the People Act 2000, s 6). A homeless person can make a declaration of local connection, giving an address of a place where he 'commonly spends a substantial part of his time' including, if necessary, a shop doorway. (See H Lardy, 'Democracy by Default: The Representation of the People Act 2000' (2001) 64 *MLR* 63, at 68–71.) Nevertheless, residence (whether notional or real) remains the foundation of the right to vote in the United Kingdom.

Under these restrictions, it is clear that not all of 'the people' will be entitled to choose representatives to rule them. Furthermore, there remains the issue of the conditions under which elections are held. The voting system is perhaps the most controversial aspect of UK elections. The traditional first-past-the-post system contributes significantly towards dual goals of strong government and local representation. But it does not produce fair results.[77] It favours the two main parties, thus producing strong governments and opposition, but discriminating against third, and minor, parties, particularly those with support spread throughout the country. Democracy has to be founded upon the idea of equality: each member of the people having an equal say about who is to be elected. Whatever its benefits, the first-past-the-post system does not provide this equal say. Electors in safe seats (the overwhelming majority) have little say, while those in marginals can change the face of the government. A citizen who does not vote for the winning candidate in his constituency has, in effect, wasted his vote. Proportional representation, in its many forms, aims to alleviate this problem and, despite posing its own dangers (such as the greater weight given to minor parties holding the balance of power), comes closer to ensuring equal value for each vote.

The United Kingdom thus continues to face some difficulties in satisfying the requirements of a genuinely representative government.[78] Even this, however, cannot in itself guarantee a democratic form of government. The government must also be limited. Human rights will play a key role here, ensuring that an elected government is not unlimited in its power to impinge upon the lives of its citizens. Effective legal protection of rights will ensure that a majoritarian, representative government does not arbitrarily infringe the rights of the minority within society. Furthermore, certain rights, such as freedom of expression, are pre-requisites for the provision of political choice to the electorate. The UK government, although long subject to legal limits on its powers at the international level, has been reluctant to acknowledge domestic legal limits. The Diceyian tradition of negative liberty and illimitable legislative sovereignty has overshadowed any constitutional limits on the government's legislative power. The tide is turning, however, and the Human Rights Act 1998, although retaining Parliament's ability lawfully to violate individual rights, marks an overdue acceptance of the legitimate role of human rights in preserving democracy. Lord Irvine of Lairg, has explained this role as follows:

> I am convinced that incorporation of the European convention into our domestic law will deliver a modern reconciliation of the inevitable tension between the democratic

---

[77] The famous example of the 1983 Election results is worth repeating here, since it never fails to shock: Conservative: 42.4% of the votes = 397 seats; Labour: 27.6% of the votes = 209 seats; Liberal–SDP Alliance: 25.4% of the votes = 23 seats.

[78] Other requirements of a representative government, such as the existence of a multi-party system, are self-evidently satisfied in the United Kingdom.

right of the majority to exercise political power and the democratic need of individuals and minorities to have their human rights secured.[79]

This overstates the conflict, however, since, although democracy does require both the majority to exercise political power and the protection of individual rights, the first requirement is unachievable without the second. How is the majority to be identified without genuine free elections? How is the majority's political choice to be realised without freedom of expression and association? Human rights are not an optional extra in a secure democratic society: they are the only means by which it can be attained.

c) The Significance of the 1832 Act

It may be impossible to identify when the United Kingdom can first be regarded as becoming a democratic state, but it is far easier to assess when it did not do so. The Reform Act of 1832, although a significant piece of legislation, did not create a democracy. Perhaps the more interesting question is whether it made one inevitable in the future. As Gash has argued, 'Unlock the door and not only could it never be closed again but inexorably, it would be shifted more and more open as the pressure from without increased.'[80] The 1832 Act unlocked the door to democratic representation by attempting a fairer solution to the problem of who was entitled to be represented in Parliament, by extending the interests represented beyond land to new commercial interests, and by recognising that the middle class (if not yet the working class) were entitled to have a say in the governing of their country. The passage of the Act also unlocked the door to democracy by serving as a response to a public demand. Thus it was 'not necessary that the first generation of politicians bred by the new system should themselves be anxious to introduce fresh measures of democratisation. It was enough that they had proclaimed the principle that government must follow the popular voice.'[81] It was not merely the Grey ministry which launched the country on the path, or at least towards the path, of political democracy but also, crucially, the people, through the political unions' extra-parliamentary reform campaign.[82] The Act 'was a recognition of an altered social balance. The agitation which accompanied its passage diffused political awareness. It was a precedent for further changes. In these ways its tendency was democratic.'[83]

Furthermore, when the further changes came, they were carried out peacefully, 'in near tranquillity.'[84] The passage of the 1832 Act was the closest that

---

[79] HL Deb, Vol 582, col 1234, 3 November 1997. See further on this, ch 6.
[80] Gash, n 16 above, p 7.
[81] *Ibid*, p 8.
[82] LoPatin, n 44 above, p 170.
[83] Brock, n 4 above, p 335.
[84] I Newbould, *Whiggery and Reform 1830–41: The Politics of Government* (London, Macmillan, 1990), p 77.

Britain has ever come to a popular revolution on the issue of representation. That such an outcome was avoided is one of the Act's greatest triumphs: 'Whether the authors of the Act unwittingly quickened Britain's progress to democracy cannot be determined. What can be said is that they helped to make this an orderly progress, uninterrupted by revolution or episodes of dictatorship.'[85] As with so many constitutional reforms discussed in this book, such as the 1688 Revolution and Scottish devolution, the reform was a compromise, essential within a constitution that is to evolve peacefully. Such a reform needs to ensure that the existing principles of the constitution are maintained but also to appease popular demands for more radical change. In serving these dual purposes, whilst also opening a door to further reform in the future, the 1832 Act was a success. If the tendency of the Act was democratic, however, it is worth noting that less than two centuries later democracy is increasingly being regarded as an outdated notion.

There are two main allegations against democracy as an accurate reflection of modern government. The first of these asserts that democracy does not represent a realistic explanation of national governments in an increasingly globalised world. Sovereign statehood is still valued highly by the international community, but it is no longer worshipped to the exclusion of all other ideals. From the moment states looked outside their borders for trade partners, political allies and military enemies, sovereignty has only had meaning as a relative term. States enjoy varying degrees of sovereignty in inverse proportion to their involvement in international organisations, treaties, agreements, ideals and conflicts. As Held recognises, globalisation – the increasing inter-connectedness of states – has implications for all the 'key ideas of democracy' such as 'the nature of a constituency, the meaning of representation, the proper form and scope of political participation, and the relevance of the democratic nation-state as the guarantor of the rights, duties and welfare of subjects.'[86] These implications need not be devastating, however. The idea of democracy is not inextricably linked with the idea of state. This has been merely a partnership of convenience, reflecting the predominance of sovereign statehood in recent centuries. Democracy – rule by a government both representative of the people and limited in its actions – is desirable and, significantly, achievable at any level of government, from local government to national, regional and even international government. The continued emphasis on the democratic state is unsurprising as sovereign statehood, and even more so, the perception of its value, still dominates the international scene, but the need for so-called 'cosmopolitan democracy' – the idea of 'deepening and extending democracy across nations, regions and global networks'[87] – is gaining in recognition.[88]

---

[85] Brock, n 4 above, p 335.
[86] Held, n 75 above, p 338.
[87] *Ibid*, p 353.
[88] This is not to claim, however, that regional or international organs are satisfactorily democratic at this early stage in their development. Indeed, the perceived democratic deficit in such organisations is a major cause of mistrust. Euro-sceptics in the United Kingdom, for example,

The disintegration in the power of the state, in a different context, also poses the second challenge to democracy. The centralised state is not only diminishing in significance because of the growing influence of supra-national factors, but also as a result of the changing locale of power within the state. The formalised allocation of governmental powers within a state's constitution merely provides 'a framework which legitimises and hides real power relationships.'[89] Government may be both representative and limited, but this only has significance to the extent that it is government which wields the real power over its citizens' lives. The issue now at the crux of democratic theory is what types of powers – and what sort of decisions – are by their nature properly exercised by elected governments?

> Whereas in the nineteenth century there was argument about who should vote, in the twentieth century there is argument about what is properly subject to voting. Thus a trade union official must be seen to be elected, but not the chairman of a nationalised industry, not the manager of a factory, not the proprietor of a newspaper. This qualified and selective democracy is an inevitable liberal position while it is tied to economic individualism and private property in the means of production. It is on strong ground in the means of opposing bureaucratic collectivism, but on very weak ground in the matter of any serious general democracy.[90]

This argument is closely linked to the perennial problem of the public/private divide. The subjective nature of this divide (if such a divide is even logically necessary) is a fact which is widely accepted. There will inevitably be people and organisations within society who exert great, perhaps unwelcome, influence over their fellow citizens' lives without ever facing the obstacle of electoral accountability. However, the right to vote, for a government which will be both representative and limited, is no less important because power is dispersed (both within and outside the state). It is the elected government, after all, which consents to such a dispersal. Thus, despite operating within a globalised world of disintegrated states and diverse vestiges of power, democracy remains relevant today and, within the United Kingdom, the development of a democratic form of government can be traced back to the 1832 Act – and a very different world.

---

perceive the 'Brussels bureaucrats' as the core danger in European integration. The proposed EU constitution is a direct attempt to confront this perception.

[89] A Hunt, 'Evaluating Constitutions: The Irish Constitution and the Limits of Constitutionalism' in T Murphy and P Twomey (eds), *Ireland's Evolving Constitution 1937–1997* (Oxford, Hart Publishing, 1998), p 321. See also J Morison, 'Models of Democracy: From Representation to Participation?' in J Jowell and D Oliver, *The Changing Constitution*, 5th edn (Oxford, Oxford University Press, 2004), pp 151–53.

[90] See I Harden and N Lewis, *The Noble Lie: The British Constitution and the Rule of Law* (London: Hutchinson, 1986), p 73, quoting R Williams, writing in the *Guardian*, 10 October 1984.

IV. Conclusion

The 1832 Reform Act was the first of a series of Reform Acts passed during the nineteenth and twentieth centuries. As the first, it 'predicated all the increments which would follow,'[91] but it was a limited reform. It did not, in any real way, benefit the people.[92] It may be, however, that it is the change in perceptions, rather than reality, which proved crucial. Although the opposition's fears of a disintegration of the state and constitution proved exaggerated, perceptions of the main characteristics of society did change.[93] As Clark states, 'the world before 1832 was pictured as a lost world, to which (for good or ill) there could be no return.'[94] Future evolution of the constitution owes much to this change in perception.

The fact that our constitution bends, but does not break, in response to society's changing perceptions and priorities is one common theme of this book which is particularly highlighted in this chapter. A further common theme, highlighted here, is the controversial circumstances in which constitutional reform is often enacted. In respect of the 1832 Act we have seen the role played by public agitation, political unions and a threat to create new peers. We have also seen the stand-off between the two Houses of Parliament, and the disputes between the King and his ministers. Such circumstances can be compared with the passage of other significant constitutional reforms. For example, in 1911 (as will be seen in the next chapter), a monarch was again forced to threaten the creation of new peers in order to ensure a controversial constitutional Bill's passage through the House of Lords. In 1707, we encountered allegations of bribery; and, in modern-day reforms, a Prime Minister recently sought (unsuccessfully) to abolish the ancient constitutional position of Lord Chancellor as part of a Cabinet reshuffle. Constitutional reform deserves better. It is in the nature of our evolving constitution, however, that reform is subject to the common political processes of its day. 1832 was no exception. The fact that it heralded such political upheaval only alerts us to the significance of its terms and the new world to which it was opening the door.

---

[91] Pearce, n 3 above, p 301.

[92] As Pearce notes, 'How much "the people" would actually benefit from a reform programme best suited to an urban middle class which employed and feared them is a large and melancholy question' (*ibid*, p 33).

[93] Clark, n 7 above, p 554.

[94] *Ibid.*

5

1911 – The Parliament Act: Guaranteeing the Legislative Superiority of the House of Commons

This chapter considers the first major constitutional event of the twentieth century. The Parliament Act 1911 fundamentally changed the nature of the sovereign legislature. Whilst the supremacy of the House of Commons may have been assumed before this date (especially, although not exclusively, since the 1832 Reform Act), from 1911 onwards it was expressed unambiguously in an Act of Parliament. The House of Lords was denied any power to veto legislation (except for an Act to extend the lifetime of a Parliament) and was left with a consolation prize of a delaying power over ordinary legislation (although not money Bills) of two years (subsequently reduced, in 1949, to one year). This statutory approval of a delaying power could have had the effect of legitimising the use of it, but it soon became apparent after 1911 that the House of Lords had been left in an extremely weakened condition. Not only had it lost its power to veto Bills but also, due to its outdated and undemocratic composition, it lacked the legitimacy to even delay Bills:

> The replacement of its powers to veto with the suspensory veto was more than just a technical adjustment. It was an assertion of the primacy of the Commons in legislative matters and a source of very great demoralisation of the upper house. A chamber of veto was forced to reinvent itself as a chamber of scrutiny.[1]

The dominance of the parliamentary executive today owes much to the unchallenged supremacy of the House of Commons established in such a conclusive manner in 1911. The House of Lords as a 'chamber of scrutiny' serves an important role, but it is no longer a coequal partner in the legislature. With greater legitimacy ensured by recent composition reforms, the Upper House may yet become more active in delaying primary legislation but, to understand its role in today's constitution, we must examine the events which led to the curbing of its

---

[1] R Walters, 'The House of Lords' in V Bogdanor, *The British Constitution in the Twentieth Century* (Oxford, Oxford University Press, 2003), p 192.

ancient powers. This chapter will seek to explain the background to the Parliament Act 1911, before proceeding to discussion of its passage through Parliament, and its subsequent impact upon Parliament and the British constitution.

I. Background: The People's Budget

Following a landslide election victory in 1906, a Liberal government (initially led by Campbell-Bannerman and later by Asquith) took office. In addition to a total of 377 Liberal MPs, the government could rely upon 53 Labour and 83 Irish Nationalist votes to support it against the Unionist party. This translated into a huge majority of 357 for the government in the House of Commons.[2] In stark contrast, the House of Lords contained a nominal Unionist majority of 391.[3] The parliamentary stage was thus set for conflict between the two Houses. Given the discrepancy between political affiliations in the two Houses, it was not surprising that the leader of the opposition, Arthur Balfour, should seek to manipulate the Unionist majority in the House of Lords. This first became obvious when the government's much heralded Education Bill reached the House of Lords in 1906.[4] Balfour instructed Unionist peers to pass the Bill, but to accept extensive amendments drafted by Balfour himself. The peers acquiesced and the Bill returned to the Commons in 'a quite unrecognisable form.'[5] The House of Commons rejected the Lords' amendments but, when these were insisted upon by the Lords, the government was forced to abandon the Bill. This was not a single instance of defeat for the government. Over the next three parliamentary sessions every Bill which was opposed by Balfour and the Unionists in the House of Commons was rejected or amended out of all recognition by the House of Lords. As Jenkins states, 'For three years the smallest opposition within living memory had effectively decided what could, and what could not, be passed through Parliament.'[6] As Lloyd George (the Chancellor of the Exchequer) was later to say, the House of Lords was not acting as the watchdog of the constitution but as 'Mr Balfour's poodle. It fetches and carries for him. It barks for him. It bites anybody that he sets it on to.'[7] A House of Parliament seeming to be

---

[2] R Jenkins, *Mr Balfour's Poodle* (London, Collins, 1954). p 19.

[3] *Ibid*, p 24. This excessive Tory dominance of the Upper House was a relatively recent development. Many Liberal peers defected from the Liberal party during the 1886 Home Rule controversy, hence the use of the name 'Unionist' throughout this chapter for the official opposition. (See *ibid*, p 27.)

[4] This Bill is described by Jenkins as 'the much-canvassed, first major measure of a Government elected by a huge majority' (*ibid*, p 44).

[5] *Ibid*, p 42.

[6] *Ibid*, p 63.

[7] Quoted in D Butler and G Butler, *Twentieth Century British Political Facts 1900–2000*, 8th edn (London, Macmillan, 2000), at p 286.

permanently in the pocket of one political party was a major constitutional, as well as political, problem, which the government would have to confront. The opportunity for such a confrontation occurred as a result of Lloyd George's radical 1909 Budget.

It has been argued that Asquith chose Lloyd George as his Chancellor of the Exchequer 'knowing full well that this did not mean a quiet life.'[8] In 1909 the Chancellor was facing huge fiscal debts and yet he sought to use the Budget to turn these into political assets.[9] The fiscal problems arose from two factors. First, the Liberal government had been elected on the promise of extensive social reforms, and one such measure which had successfully passed through the second chamber was the creation of old age pensions. Lloyd George had originally hoped to fund this new expense by cutting the military budget. However, by 1909 Britain was competing with Germany in a rearmament race. More specifically, the 'Dreadnought', 'a state-of-the-art battleship rightly renowned for its mighty armour and, not least, its mighty expense,'[10] became a must-have purchase. Thus, the bills for social reform combined with this second factor of a naval race with Germany to create a pressing need for extra funding. Lloyd George's response was to raise revenue by increasing direct taxation. The 1909 Budget included seven entirely new taxes, comprising a so-called 'super-tax' on the rich,[11] four new land taxes and the first taxes on motor cars and petrol. Lloyd George also sought to increase tobacco and liquor duties, death duties and stamp duties, as well as raising income tax. Furthermore, and in many ways most controversially, the Budget's new scheme for taxing land necessitated a valuation of all land. This was widely perceived as facilitating further land taxes in the future.[12]

Blewett has argued that the taxes 'were as much designed to "stop the electoral rot" as to meet the financial deficit faced by the Government.'[13] The licence duties and land taxes were popular with Liberal supporters, while the income tax rise would appeal to working-class voters. But the Budget was also controversial and a variety of powerful interests (the land interest, tariff reformers and the licensed trade) were united in opposition to it, thus raising a suspicion that Lloyd George and the government may have designed the Budget to be rejected by the House of Lords and thereby to force a resolution of the ongoing battle between the two Houses. The weight of academic opinion no longer supports this argument, however. While Owen regards the Budget as 'deliberate political provocation',[14]

---

[8] P Clarke, *Hope and Glory: Britain 1900–1990* (London, Penguin Books, 1996), p 54.

[9] N Blewett, *The Peers, The Parties and the People: The General Elections of 1910* (London, Macmillan, 1972), p 68.

[10] Clarke, n 8 above, p 56.

[11] This was charged at six pence in the pound on the amount by which all incomes of over £5,000 exceeded £3,000.

[12] The land taxes introduced in the 1909 Budget were at a very low rate and never even recouped the costs of collection, but the widespread valuation did open the door to further taxes in the future (C Cross, *The Liberals in Power 1905–1914* (Westport, Greenwood Press, 1963), p 103).

[13] Blewett, n 9 above, p 69.

[14] F Owen, *Tempestuous Journey: Lloyd George – His Life and Times* (London, Hutchinson, 1954), p 170.

Jenkins, Blewett and Grigg all argue that the government genuinely wanted the Budget to pass. As Grigg notes, Lloyd George was 'above all interested in constructive achievement'[15] and it would have been out of character for him to be willing to sacrifice his radical taxation plans. Furthermore, the government would have been aware that a rejection of the Budget by the House of Lords would necessitate a General Election in which the Liberals' 1906 landslide would inevitably be diminished. It seems, therefore, that, when Lloyd George introduced his 1909 Budget, he and the government hoped that its radical terms would be passed by the House of Lords. They had good reason for such hope as the dominance of the House of Commons over finance was long established. Indeed, this has led Cross to claim that Asquith and Lloyd George 'intended the budget to be a means of by-passing the Lords' veto, not of smashing it.'[16] Nevertheless, there was much speculation as to the response of the House of Lords: would it reject the Finance Bill? And, if it did, what would be the constitutional consequences of such unprecedented action?

The progress of the Budget through the House of Commons served as an indicator of future developments when Balfour's Unionists opposed its terms at every possible stage. By the autumn of 1909, it was becoming obvious that rejection by the House of Lords was a real possibility. Lloyd George delivered a number of strong speeches, including his famous Limehouse speech,[17] which had the effect of moving many Unionists (probably including Balfour) towards rejection. In October, Lloyd George gave a further speech which, in the words of Jenkins, was 'designed to inject the maximum amount of heat into the already torrid controversy.'[18] Lloyd George accused the Lords of 'forcing revolution,' but continued by warning that 'the Lords may declare a revolution which the people will direct.'[19] Ominously for the future the Chancellor warned that 'issues will be raised that they little dream of.' Specifically, he asked: 'Should 500 men, ordinary men chosen accidentally from among the unemployed, override the judgement – the deliberate judgement – of millions of people who are engaged in the industry which makes the wealth of the country?'[20] Such a direct attack on the Lords was unprecedented and the 'unemployed' jibe was particularly controversial. It was clear by this stage that Lloyd George was prepared for rejection and the constitutional controversy which would follow.

By November the opposition leader in the House of Lords, Lord Lansdowne, affirmed that he would move that 'this House is not justified in giving its assent to the Bill until it has been submitted to the judgement of the country.'[21] It was,

---

[15] J Grigg, *Lloyd George: The People's Champion 1902–1911* (London, HarperCollins, 1978), p 180.

[16] Cross, n 12 above, pp 101–2.

[17] 30 July 1909. See (1909) *The Times*, 31 July, and Jenkins, n 2 above, pp 87–89.

[18] Jenkins, n 2 above, p 93.

[19] Speech at Newcastle-on-Tyne, quoted in (1909) *The Times*, 11 October, and Jenkins, n 2 above, p 94.

[20] *Ibid.*

[21] HL Deb, Vol IV, col 731, 22 November 1909.

in effect, a declaration of war on the House of Commons but, as Jenkins has argued, it was predictable by any intelligent observer that such a course of action would not ultimately defeat the Budget and would make inevitable the destruction of the Lords' legislative veto.[22] So why did the House of Lords begin a fight which it could only lose? The answer lies in the internal politics of the Unionist party and Balfour's need to unite his party. Egremont goes so far as to claim that Balfour believed 'there was no other way to enter the next election united.'[23] Furthermore, it was not inevitable that the Unionists would lose the election which would follow the House of Lords' rejection of the Budget. The Liberal government had lost much popularity since its landslide victory in 1906. As Cross states, 'the actions of both Liberals and Conservatives in 1909 make sense only in the light of the fact that the Conservatives had every hope of winning a general election.'[24] Perhaps ultimately Clarke identifies the dominant reason for the House of Lords' actions when he claims that the Unionist majority blocked the Budget 'because they thought they could get away with it.'[25]

After much speculation, the House of Lords finally rejected the Budget by 350 votes to 75. It has been argued, including by the government of the day,[26] that this was a violation of a 200-year-old constitutional convention. It has to be noted however that the idea of a 'Budget' – that is, an omnibus Bill including all revenue measures for the year – was a relatively new concept in 1909. Balfour made this very point in the House of Commons on 2 December 1909:

> The right hon Gentleman [Asquith] tells us that there is an unbroken tradition under which the House of Lords has never rejected the financial provisions of the year … How long has that unbroken tradition continued? It evidently could not go back before the period when all our provisions for taxation were embodied in one Bill, and that is within the memory of men living … It is quite true that the Budget embodying the taxes of the year was never rejected, because there never was a Budget Bill embodying them: it is an entirely modern invention …[27]

However, this is somewhat misleading because, in rejecting the Budget, the House of Lords was challenging the House of Commons' control over financial measures for the year. As Blewett notes, although the House of Lords possessed the legal right to reject a money Bill (and had last exercised this power in 1860 when it rejected Gladstone's Paper Duties Bill), it had not attempted to challenge the House of Commons' control over the general financial provisions of the year since the seventeenth century.[28] Thus, what the House of Lords did in 1909 was, contrary to Balfour, significant in terms of constitutional history: the House of

---

[22] Jenkins, n 2 above, p 95.
[23] M Egremont, *Balfour: A Life of Arthur James Balfour* (London, Collins, 1980), p 219.
[24] Cross, n 12 above, p 102.
[25] Clarke, n 8 above, p 61.
[26] See Asquith in *Hansard*, HC Deb, 5th Series, Vol 13, col 552, 2 December 1909.
[27] *Ibid*, at col 562.
[28] Blewett, n 9 above, p 98.

Lords had refused supply. As Jenkins says, 'in these circumstances no government could carry on.'[29]

On 2 December Asquith moved that the House of Lords' action was a 'breach of the Constitution and an usurpation of the rights of the Commons.'[30] He argued that, in rejecting a Finance Bill, the Lords had acted unconstitutionally, and he rejected the Unionists' argument that the broad terms of the Budget meant that it was not solely a Finance Bill[31] and thus that it required reference to the electorate.[32] Asquith mocked the idea that 'the people require to be protected against their own elected representatives, especially – may I not say exclusively? – when the majority of those representatives happen to belong to the Liberal party.'[33] Asquith echoed Lloyd George in noting that in their rejection of the Budget the Lords had 'opened out a wider and more far-reaching issue', namely 'whether when the Tory Party is in power the House of Commons shall be omnipotent, and whether when the Liberal Party is in power the House of Lords shall be omnipotent.'[34] It was, he claimed, 'a system of false balances and loaded dice.'[35] Balfour responded by reiterating the existence of a doctrine of the mandate which authorised the House of Lords' actions and by mocking the government for seeking 'to persuade the people of this country that they are suffering some wrong, some terrible indignity, by having their opinion asked about the Budget.'[36] So it was to the voting booths that the conflict adjourned. Although Asquith clarified during the campaign that limitation of the legislative powers of the House of Lords was an issue for the electorate, the main focus of the voters remained on the merits of the Budget itself.[37]

During the January 1910 election, the Liberals held their position in the North but suffered losses in the Midlands and, especially, in the South.[38] The results of the election were as follows: Liberals 275; Unionists 273; Labour 40; Irish Nationalists 82.[39] Curiously, this result was seen as a victory for both main parties, when it could more accurately be described as a defeat for both. The Liberals lost their absolute majority and were reduced to relying upon Irish support. The Irish, however, disliked the 1909 Budget, specifically the increase in whiskey duties, and thus their support was far from guaranteed. Indeed, while the election result guaranteed the passage of the Budget through the House of Lords, its passage

---

[29] R Jenkins, *Asquith* (London, Collins, 1964), p 202.

[30] *Hansard*, HC Deb, 5th Series, Vol 13, col 546, 2 December 1909.

[31] *Ibid*, col 555.

[32] *Ibid*, col 556. See below for discussion of the 'doctrine of the mandate' and its role in the events of 1909–11.

[33] *Ibid*.

[34] *Ibid*, col 558.

[35] *Ibid*.

[36] *Ibid*, col 569.

[37] Although members of Asquith's Cabinet were all in agreement that the House of Lords could have no veto over finance, beyond that obvious issue there was little agreement, as would become evident after the election (Blewett, n 9 above, pp 92–93).

[38] *Ibid*, p 135.

[39] See Blewett, n 9 above, ch 7 for analysis.

through the House of Commons might now prove more problematic as the Unionists would be justified in opposing it there and the Irish would hold the key to success. Perhaps it was for this reason that, despite losing the election in dramatic fashion, 'many Unionists seemed not to appreciate that they had been beaten.'[40] As Blewett has accurately described:

> It is not surprising that in this confused situation, with the Unionists defeated but convinced of the immediate frustration of their opponents, and the Liberals victorious but apparently unable to utilise their victory, the most common reaction of all to the election results was the expectation of a second election.[41]

It was certainly an interesting electoral outcome. There was a sense in which the people did not support the so-called 'People's Budget'. Grigg makes an important point, however, when he argues that the reason that the people did not vote overwhelmingly for their Budget was because most of 'the people' remained disfranchised.[42]

The people did eventually receive their Budget. After one year's delay the Finance Bill 1909 passed into law with very little debate in the House of Lords. By then, the focus of conflict had moved on. The focus was now on how the Liberal government would curb the Unionist dominated House of Lords. The answer was that they would be able to do so only after political deals, a further election, and the direct involvement of the monarch. The ramifications of the 1909 Budget were certainly extensive. As Murray notes, the modernisation of the British system of taxation, the financing of the social service state, and the defeat of tariff reform, as well as the destruction of the absolute veto of the Lords and the slide towards civil war in Ireland, all flowed from Lloyd George's radical Liberal plans for raising revenue.[43]

II. Reform of the House of Lords

a) How to reform?

Cross has argued that 'after their experiences from 1906 onwards the Liberals would be abdicating the right to govern if they did not curb the upper house.'[44] By the beginning of 1910 this had become obvious. However, the government

---

[40] *Ibid*, p 141.

[41] *Ibid*, pp 143–44.

[42] Grigg, n 15 above, p 240: 'Only 58 per cent of adult males had the vote, and it is a fair assumption that the remaining 42 per cent would, if enfranchised, have voted in very large numbers for Liberal or Labour candidates.'

[43] BK Murray, *The People's Budget 1909–1910: Lloyd George and Liberal Politics* (Oxford, Clarendon Press, 1980), p 290.

[44] Cross, n 12 above, p 114.

lacked any clear plans on how to proceed. As early as 1907 the Camp-bell-Bannerman plan had laid the groundwork for what was later to become the Parliament Act 1911. The former Prime Minister proposed the replacement of the Lords' absolute veto with a suspensory veto, and the House of Commons passed (by 432 to 147 votes) a government resolution that:

> in order to give effect to the will of the people as expressed by their elected representa-tives, it is necessary that the power of the other House should be so restricted by law as to secure within the limits of a single Parliament the final decision of the Commons must prevail.[45]

In 1907 no further progress was made to achieve this end, but by 1910 the government had added incentive to succeed. On 21 March 1910, a series of reso-lutions were introduced into the House of Commons. In essence these resolutions comprised what was to become the Parliament Act: the House of Lords would not be able to amend or reject money Bills; it would only be able to delay other Bills for two sessions; and the maximum duration of Parliament would be reduced from seven years to five years. These principles were very similar to the Campbell-Bannerman scheme but with one significant exception. In 1907, nobody had thought it necessary to legislate that the House of Lords had no power to amend or reject money Bills but, by 1910, recent events meant that such a convention could not be taken for granted. It was thus included at the core of the government's legislative plans.

By March 1910 even some members of the House of Lords recognised the need for change. In an attempt to retain the veto of the House of Lords, some peers sought to reform the composition of the Upper House so as to make the exercise of its powers more legitimate in the eyes of the public. As the Earl of Rosebery said during a House of Lords debate on his proposed resolutions to reform the House: 'there has long been a body of opinion in this House that has been profoundly conscious of some imperfections in its structure, which it would be well in the interest of this House to remove without delay.'[46] The implication here is clear: if we do not reform ourselves, we will be destroyed by others.

> What is the alternative? The alternative is to cling with enfeebled grasp to privileges which have become obsolete, shrinking and shrinking until at last, under the unsparing hands of the advocates of single-Chamber Government, there may arise a demand for your own extinction, and the Second Chamber, the ancient House of Lords, may be found waiting in decrepitude for its doom.[47]

Rosebery recognised that the hereditary principle was the feature of the House most easy to attack and most difficult to defend,[48] and he thus moved that the

---

[45] *Hansard*, HC Deb, 4th Series, Vol 176, cols 929–30, 24 June 1907.
[46] *Hansard*, HL Deb, 5th Series, Vol 5, col 141, 14 March 1910.
[47] *Ibid*, col 168 (the Earl of Rosebery).
[48] *Ibid*, col 164.

possession of a peerage should no longer of itself give the right to sit and vote in the House of Lords.[49] Perhaps surprisingly the Rosebery Resolutions were passed by the House of Lords which recognised the truth of Rosebery's claim that the government faced a choice between reforming the composition of the second chamber so as to make the exercise of its powers more legitimate or retaining the current discredited composition and removing its powers.[50] This was indeed the stark choice facing Asquith's government. Unfortunately, the Cabinet was divided on the issue.

Since returning to power in January, a serious split had arisen within Cabinet between those who wanted reform and those who wanted to curb powers by enacting the suspensory veto plan. The compromise solution at which the Cabinet eventually arrived was a scheme under which the absolute veto would be replaced by a suspensory veto, but only as a means whereby composition reform could subsequently be pursued.[51] Therefore, a preamble was inserted into the newly drafted Parliament Act which infamously declared that 'it is intended to substitute for the House of Lords as it at present exists, a Second Chamber constituted on a popular instead of a hereditary basis.' This was seen as a means of appeasing the pro-reform members of Asquith's Cabinet but, with the benefit of hindsight, we can see that the Parliament Act scheme was a very one-sided compromise. Those in favour of reforming the composition of the House of Lords lost the Cabinet battle, and it was to be a very long wait before the hereditary principle was removed from the Upper House.[52] The intention to constitute the Upper House on a popular basis remains unachieved almost a century later.

The indecision in Cabinet was not helped by the complicating factor of the Irish Nationalists. Their votes would be essential, both for acting on the House of Lords and for the delayed passage of the 1909 Budget. Unfortunately, the Irish, led by Redmond, remained opposed to the Budget and sought concessions on the whiskey duties before they would support it. At a Cabinet meeting on 13 April, a crucial decision was taken to refuse to permit any concessions on the Budget.[53] This meant that, in order to secure the votes of the Irish members for the Budget, the Cabinet would have to accede to the other demand of the Irish: to request a guarantee from the King before another election that he would ensure the passage of a Bill to curb the powers of the House of Lords, if necessary by swamping the House with newly created Liberal peers. The removal of the veto from the House of Lords was vitally important to Irish Nationalists who regarded

[49] In full, the Rosebery Resolutions were as follows: '(1) That a strong and efficient Second Chamber is not merely an integral part of the British Constitution but is necessary to the well-being of the State and to the balance of Parliament. (2) That such a Chamber can best be obtained by the reform and reconstitution of the House of Lords. (3) That a necessary preliminary of such reform and reconstitution is the acceptance of the principle that the possession of a Peerage should no longer of itself give the right to sit and vote in the House of Lords' (*ibid*).

[50] *Ibid*, col 148.

[51] Blewett, n 9 above, p 152.

[52] House of Lords Act 1999.

[53] See Grigg, n 15 above, p 253.

the Lords as the obstacle to their desired goal of home rule. Asquith agreed to the Irish demand in order to preserve the 1909 Budget. However, nature was to inter- vene tragically at this stage in the saga when King Edward VII died suddenly on 6 May 1910. Asquith's response to this event is telling. He wrote of his concern that, at the very moment when the country was 'nearing the verge of a crisis without example in our constitutional history', a successor with no political experience would accede to the throne.[54] In order to prevent the new, politically inexperi- enced sovereign, George V, from immediately facing a momentous decision concerning the use of his prerogative powers, the Liberal and Unionist parties agreed to participate in a constitutional conference in an attempt to reach a compromise solution.[55] Thus 'for six months the constitutional struggle retired behind closed doors.'[56]

b) Constitutional Conference and the Home Rule Stumbling Block

The constitutional conference comprised Asquith, Lloyd George, Crewe and Birrell for the government, and Balfour, Lansdowne, Chamberlain and Cawdor for the opposition. They held 21 sessions between June and November 1910 but, in the words of Grigg, 'the parties never came really close to agreement'[57] because it was 'an essentially futile exercise, tediously prolonged and more or less doomed to fail.'[58] The factor which may be regarded as dooming the conference to failure was the old Irish question. The Unionists proposed that legislation be divided into three categories: financial, ordinary and constitutional.[59] They were willing to agree with the government to end the Lords' veto over financial Bills, although the Unionists emphasised that 'tacking' (the inclusion of broader social measures into purported financial legislation) should be prevented by the scrutiny of a joint committee working with the Speaker. The Unionists proposed that ordinary legislation rejected twice by the Lords should be submitted to a joint session of both Houses. Constitutional questions should, in the view of the Unionists, be submitted to a referendum of the people if both Houses could not agree upon them.

 Ultimately, the conference broke down over two issues. First, no agreement could be reached upon the composition of the proposed joint sittings. The Liberals were willing to agree to an in-built Unionist majority of 45 (reflecting their dominance in the Upper House), but this was not a substantial enough

---

[54] Oxford and Asquith, *Fifty Years of Parliament*, pp 86–88, quoted in Jenkins, n 2 above, at pp 145–46.

[55] Jenkins is less charitable of Asquith's motives and claims that he 'found procrastination given a new lease of life by the accession of King George' (Jenkins, n 2 above, p 147).

[56] *Ibid*, p 148.

[57] Grigg, n 15 above, p 263.

[58] *Ibid*, p 261.

[59] See Jenkins, n 2 above, p 151.

majority for the Unionists to accept.[60] Second, and the major stumbling block, the government refused to include home rule in the Unionist's excepted category of 'constitutional legislation'. The government knew that a referendum of the British people would not support home rule, and they were unwilling to subject this policy to the need for public approval. For both parties this was a deal-breaker. The Unionists' primary concern now was to prevent home rule. When the government refused to have its hands permanently tied on this issue, negotiations broke down: 'The government would not countenance any arrangement that precluded home rule, the Unionists any that facilitated it.'[61] Jenkins regards Lord Lansdowne, the Unionist leader in the House of Lords, as primarily responsible, as he believes that Asquith and Balfour both genuinely sought a resolution of the conflict.[62] Lloyd George was also keen for the conference to succeed and indeed, for a brief time, there emerged a 'play within a play'[63] as Lloyd George initiated discussions on a coalition government.[64] There was some prospect of success for this plan as Balfour had some sympathy with it,[65] but ultimately it failed, as with the narrower search for consensus on House of Lords reform, on the home rule question.[66]

c) Another Election and a Guarantee from the King

When the attempt at negotiation in the constitutional conference failed, the government resorted to another appeal to the country. Nearly one year earlier, the deceased King Edward VII had made clear to Asquith that he would not use his personal prerogative to create peers to force through House of Lords reform before a second election directly on that issue. Now, Asquith asked the new King George V for a pre-election guarantee that he would create peers should the government be returned to power and make such a request. George V had serious reservations about such a guarantee, but he was eventually persuaded to acquiesce by a well-timed misleading piece of advice from one of his advisers, Lord Knollys. George V's two advisers gave conflicting advice,[67] but Knollys's view was decisive when he told the King, probably knowing that it was not true, that

---

[60] Egremont, n 23 above, p 229.

[61] Clarke, n 8 above, p 65.

[62] Jenkins, n 29 above, p 215.

[63] Grigg, n 15 above, p 272.

[64] As Cross writes, 'party mattered little to Lloyd George compared with the opportunity of translating his ideas into practical action' (Cross, n 12 above, p 118). The People's Budget saga highlighted to Lloyd George that party politics could hinder, rather than facilitate, social change and thus he believed that a coalition government might be the way to remedy this. His plans for such a government were well developed. See the appendix in Grigg, n 15 above.

[65] Jenkins, n 2 above, p 165.

[66] See Grigg, n 15 above, p 272.

[67] Douglas-Home says they 'engaged in a struggle for the new King's soul' (C Douglas-Home (and S Kelly), *Dignified and Efficient: The British Monarchy in the Twentieth Century* (Wiltshire, Claridge Press, 2000), p 17).

Balfour would refuse to form a government.[68] This was significant because the King's only other option to agreeing to create peers would be to accept Asquith's resignation and invite Balfour to form a government. The King seriously considered this course of action[69] but, had he taken this option only for Balfour to refuse, the King would have been in an intolerable situation: forced to recall Asquith having 'fallen into the arena of party politics.'[70] Thus, Cross argues that 'Knollys saved the monarchy by deceiving the monarch.'[71] It is certainly true that the alternative course of action would have left the King looking more partisan.[72] The King thus agreed to the Cabinet's demand: 'I agreed most reluctantly to give the Cabinet a secret understanding that in the event of the Government being returned with a majority at the General Election, I should use my prerogative to make peers if asked for.'[73] With this guarantee in place, Parliament was dissolved and a general election was called for December 1910.

A large number of seats changed hands in the December election but overall the result was remarkably similar to that of the January election. The Liberals lost 24 seats to the Unionists but the Unionists also lost 23 seats to the Liberals.[74] The net result was that the Liberals and Unionists were both down by 2; the Irish Nationalists and Labour both up by 2. Jenkins concludes that the government 'became marginally stronger vis-à-vis the Opposition and marginally weaker vis-à-vis the more independent parts of its own majority.'[75] Jenkins also argues that, by December, the electorate were bored with being asked to vote again on similar issues and that this apathy caused the total poll to fall from January by more than one million votes.[76] This is a significant argument because, if true, it suggests that the people had no real interest in the constitutional struggle which was igniting in Parliament and were unconcerned about the Lords' battle with those whom they had elected to represent them. Given that both Houses of Parliament (and both political parties) were claiming to be acting to uphold the will of the people, this casts a different light upon the conflict. However, Blewett has convincingly countered Jenkins's argument by pointing out that, although as noted above 'the people' as a whole could not vote, the proportion of registered voters who did vote has never been surpassed. In January 1910, 86.7 per cent of

---

[68] Jenkins, n 2 above, p. 179.

[69] Cross, n 12 above, p 120.

[70] *Ibid.*

[71] *Ibid.* Douglas-Home takes a rather different view, describing Knollys's misleading statement as 'at best, a gross piece of incompetence, at worst, a most unseemly triumph of political interest over loyalty and duty to the King' (Douglas-Home, n 67 above, p 18). Cross's view seems the more objective.

[72] Jenkins, n 2 above, p 183.

[73] Recorded in the King's Diary and quoted in H Nicolson, *King George V: His Life and Reign* (London, Constable & Co, 1952), at p 138. As if to confirm the significance of Knollys's misleading advice, George V added that this was 'the only alternative to the Cabinet resigning, which at this moment would be disastrous.'

[74] Blewett, n 9 above, p 200.

[75] Jenkins, n 2 above, pp 191–92.

[76] *Ibid*, p 187.

voters throughout the United Kingdom voted, and this dropped only slightly to 81.4 per cent in December.[77] Such a turnout today is unimaginable. If the voters were apathetic in 1910, they are far more so at the beginning of the twenty-first century. In fact, as Blewett writes, what is clear from the 1910 elections is 'the remarkable interest of the electorate, as measured by the only meaningful criterion that can be used, the proportion of the electorate which could and did cast its vote.'[78]

The new Parliament opened on 6 February 1911, and the government immediately reintroduced its Parliament Bill into the House of Commons. Meanwhile, in the House of Lords, Lord Lansdowne announced his intention to introduce a House of Lords Reform Bill.[79] Rosebery's earlier argument of 'reform or be destroyed' was still providing some impetus for self-reform in the second chamber but, unfortunately, the Unionists were not united on any single plan for reform.[80] What they were united by was a desire to strengthen the House of Lords by increasing its legitimacy and thus defeating the government's attempts to curb its powers. This was vital for the Unionists, who were in reality Conservatives whose very reincarnation as the Unionist party clearly portrayed their primary goal of preserving the Union. Blewett recognises that, amongst many Unionists, 'concern for the Lords was already overshadowed by anxiety about the Union … Some were already preparing to sacrifice the Lords in order to save the Union, as the year before they had given way on the Budget to save the Lords.'[81] The government's Parliament Bill scheme was widely perceived as a mere prelude to a Home Rule Bill in the following session, which could only be stopped by a veto from the House of Lords. Lansdowne's plan was for composition reform along the lines of: one third elected by all hereditary peers; one third indirectly elected; and one third appointed by government.[82] It would have heralded a very different second chamber for the twentieth century if successful, but it soon foundered when the government declared that the Parliament Bill scheme would still be pursued and that even a reformed House of Lords would have its veto power removed. There was no genuine desire for composition reform amongst the majority of the Lords, and therefore efforts were concentrated upon the House of Lords' approach to the Parliament Bill itself, which finally reached the Upper House in May (having passed successfully through the House of Commons).

The Unionists passed the Bill at the second reading stage in the House of Lords but then proposed sweeping amendments during the committee stage which took the form of 'a six-day massacre of the government's proposals.'[83] The opposition amendments included a proposal to substitute a joint committee for the Speaker in the vital task of classification of Bills as money Bills, and a

---

[77] Blewett, n 9 above, p 377.
[78] *Ibid*, p 380.
[79] Jenkins, n 2 above, p 197.
[80] *Ibid*, p 198.
[81] Blewett, n 9 above, p 206.
[82] Jenkins, n 2 above, p 202.
[83] *Ibid*, p 210.

proposal to introduce a referendum on legislation of national importance which had been twice rejected by the House of Lords.[84] By the time that the Bill returned to the House of Commons, it had been amended out of all recognition. On 14 July, the Cabinet sent a minute to the King in which they explained that the Lords' amendments would be rejected en bloc by the House of Commons and that a deadlock between the two Houses would then emerge. They explained that, in such circumstances, 'it will be the duty of Ministers to advise the Crown to exercise its Prerogative so as to get rid of the deadlock and secure the passing of the Bill' and ominously warned that 'Ministers cannot entertain any doubt that the Sovereign would feel it to be his constitutional duty to accept their advice.'[85] The King agreed and it was only at this stage that the earlier November guarantee was made public. On 20 July, Asquith wrote to both Balfour and Lansdowne confirming that the government would, if necessary, ask the King to use his prerogative to secure the Bill's passage and that he had agreed to act on that advice.[86]

d) Divided Opposition

This revelation caused chaos within the Unionist party. The Shadow Cabinet meeting of 21 July, as well as a meeting of Unionist peers on that day, revealed a serious split in the party. On the one side, Balfour and Lansdowne both now argued that, in light of the government's threat to create peers, the Parliament Bill should be allowed to pass. Those who supported this argument were soon to be named the 'hedgers'. On the other side of the argument were the so-called 'ditchers' who would fight to the last ditch to oppose the Parliament Bill.[87] Lansdowne attempted to illustrate the futility of this position in a crucial debate in the House of Lords on 9 August 1911:

> the House is no longer in a position to offer effectual resistance to the policy of His Majesty's Government, and in these circumstances some of us, myself amongst the number, are convinced that further insistence on our Amendments would be not only unprofitable but detrimental to the public interest.[88]

[84] *Ibid*, pp 210–11.
[85] Cabinet minute, 14 July 1911, quoted in *ibid*, pp 213–14.
[86] Jenkins, n 2 above, p 219. Asquith himself was unhappy with the prospect of a mass creation of Liberal peers. In the words of Grigg, 'it appalled him scarcely less than it appalled Balfour or Lansdowne' (Grigg, n 15 above, p 277). While the political world was divided on the issue of whether the government was entitled to use the threat of creating peers, one minister, Churchill, 'was almost alone in wanting to carry out the threat' (Jenkins, n 29 above, p 223).
[87] Jenkins, n 2 above. p 220.
[88] *Hansard*, HL Deb, 5th Series, Vol 9, col 887. Without a trace of irony, Lansdowne also expressed concern that a mass creation of Liberal peers may create difficulties for a future Unionist government: 'I think it would be a serious misfortune to us if we found ourselves confronted by an obstinate and, perhaps, obstructive Radical majority in this House' (col 891). That any non-Unionist

In reply, the Earl of Halsbury, a 'ditcher', defended his position: 'It seems to me that upon a question of principle, if I believed a thing to be wrong, I ought to do my best to prevent it.'[89] Tempers were running high and on 24 July 1911 Asquith was shouted down in unprecedented scenes in the House of Commons as he tried to outline the government's intentions: 'For half an hour the Prime Minister stood at the box, unable to make any full sentence heard to the House, and unable to fill more than a staccato half-column of Hansard.'[90]

In an attempt to unify the party, Unionist leaders tabled votes of censure in each House in which they accused the government of 'a gross violation of constitutional liberty,'[91] and in which they particularly drew attention to the issue at the core of their party: 'under the coercion of the Government, the Prerogative is to be used ... in order that home rule may be forced through the two Houses of Parliament without the people of this country being consulted.'[92] In response Asquith defended his relationship with the King by saying, 'I have consistently striven to uphold the dignity and just privileges of the Crown,' but also argued with great force that 'I hold my office not only by favour of the Crown but by the confidence of the people, and I should be guilty indeed of treason if in this supreme moment of a great struggle I were to betray their trust.'[93] So once more both sides of the constitutional conflict were claiming to be fighting to give effect to the will of the people. It was an argument with less force from the hereditary peers, given their past record of listening to the people,[94] but was not particularly convincing from either side of what was essentially a political dispute, albeit one with great constitutional implications.

Before using his prerogative to create peers, the King insisted that the Parliament Bill be returned to the House of Lords to give the Lords a last chance to pass the Bill without the need for new Liberal peers. The government agreed and thus on 9 August 1911 the House of Lords faced the final battle to determine the nature of the second chamber. The two-day debate in the House of Lords was 'almost unique amongst major parliamentary occasions of the past eighty years in that the result was not known beforehand.'[95] When a division was called on 10 August, the result was 131 for the government and 114 against.

government would inevitably face such obstruction from the currently constituted House of Lords seems to go unnoticed.

---

[89] *Ibid*, col 899.

[90] Jenkins, n 2 above, p 230. When Balfour replied, he was heard in silence but when FE Smith, one of the leaders of the disruption, rose to speak, the government backbenchers were in uproar and proceedings were suspended (pp 231–32).

[91] *Hansard*, HC Deb, 5th Series, Vol 29, col 795; HL Deb, 5th Series, Vol 9, col 815 (7 and 8 August 1911, respectively).

[92] Balfour, HC Deb, 5th Series, Vol 29, col 797.

[93] *Ibid*, col 817. This is an interesting acknowledgement of the dual power base of the prime ministerial position through history, and is discussed in more detail in ch 3. By the beginning of the twentieth century, there was no doubt that the electorate had overtaken the Crown as the primary creator of Prime Ministers.

[94] As, for example, during the protracted passage of the Great Reform Act, discussed in ch 4.

[95] Jenkins, n 2 above, pp 251–52.

The 'hedgers', guided by the Unionist leadership of Balfour and Lansdowne, abstained, while the 'ditchers' voted against the Bill. But, crucially, Earl Curzon rallied 37 Unionist peers to vote with the government and for the Bill in order to cancel out the activities of the 'ditchers'. The split in the Unionist party was to have long-term implications and Balfour's leadership did not long survive. Ultimately, amongst this political intrigue, the Parliament Bill, which removed the legislative veto of the House of Lords, was passed by the Lords under the threat of a mass creation of Liberal peers. In the words of Cross, 'the oldest legislative assembly in the world, had abdicated.'[96]

III. The House of Lords under the Constitution

a) The Powers of the House of Lords, the Doctrine of the Mandate, and Popular Sovereignty

The protracted passage of the Parliament Act 1911 highlighted the fundamental debate which arises every time reform of the UK's second chamber is proposed. If the House of Lords needs to be reformed, is it preferable to change its composition or to limit its powers? The key principle which guides this debate is that of legitimacy. During the period of Liberal government between 1906 and 1911, the Lords' use of its absolute veto was criticised as being illegitimate because it frustrated the wishes of the elected government. Reforming the membership of the House by removing the hereditary peers would have been one solution. Indeed, Unionist peers made some efforts to initiate such reform in the hope that if the House's composition was seen as more representative of the people, it would be justified in opposing the government's radical plans. This solution would obviously have posed some danger for the government. It would be a rare government indeed that voluntarily permitted a second chamber to increase the legitimacy of its powers to oppose government policy. So it was not surprising that Asquith's government chose to curb the powers of the second chamber while retaining its largely discredited composition. The retention of hereditary peers also had a further advantage for the government at this time in constitutional history because, as George V had demonstrated in 1910–11, a monarch could, if the conditions were right, be persuaded to swamp the Upper House with pro-government peers. Such a solution would be very controversial, but in extreme circumstances it was a useful threat on which to be able to rely.

The problem with the 1911 solution was that, while the Lords' powers were limited, they were not removed entirely, and yet the Upper House remained permanently dominated by only one political party. Thus Lloyd George warned

---

[96] Cross, n 12 above, p 129.

in December 1910 that, even with the government's proposed reforms, 'there will still be inequality. The Veto Resolutions will stop Liberal legislation for two years … They will not stop Tory legislation at all. That is inequality. We must proceed to reform the constitution in such a way as to extend equal treatment to both sides.'[97] The Liberal government never pursued this promised further reform, and subsequent governments failed to rectify the political imbalance until very recent years. Lloyd George was certainly correct to foresee that political inequality in the House of Lords would endure post-1911. Grigg argues that for this reason the Parliament Act was 'a singularly misconceived piece of legislation' because it invited the Lords' obstruction of non-financial Bills and:

> unless and until the second chamber was reformed, this meant in effect … that a two-year veto could operate against many Liberal measures. Without the Parliament Act to define and legitimize their delaying power, the Lords might have been a little chary of risking further conflicts with the people's elect. But with the sanction of a new law they could do so cheerfully.[98]

It was an ominous situation for the Liberal government and shows that legitimising the (reduced) powers of the House of Lords was ultimately dangerous without tackling the far more difficult issue of composition. It is a lesson subsequent governments have also been slow to learn.

There is an argument, however, that there was no need for reform of either powers or composition in 1911. Not all commentators at the time regarded the Unionist-dominated House of Lords' policy of opposition to the Liberal government as illegitimate. Dicey explains that 'the point at which the Lords must yield or the Crown intervene to create peers is properly determined by anything which conclusively shows that the House of Commons represents on the matter in dispute the deliberate decision of the nation.'[99] The essence of the Lords' justification for their refusal to yield in 1909–10 was that the government did not have the 'deliberate decision of the nation' supporting it. Indeed, there is some support for this argument, in that the House of Lords finally yielded on the 1909 Budget once the people had given their explicit approval to it at the polls. Such an approach is termed the 'doctrine of the mandate' and first emerged over 40 years before the 1909 Budget when the Lords claimed a constitutional duty to veto major issues unless they had been put to the country in the winning election manifesto.[100] Dicey has recognised the existence of the doctrine of the mandate: 'No one till 1910 and 1911 seriously disputed the doctrine that the House of Lords in modern times had the right to demand an appeal to the people whenever on any great subject of legislation the will of the electorate was uncertain or

[97] Speech at East Ham, 15 December 1910, quoted in Grigg, n 15 above, at p 284.
[98] Grigg, n 15 above, p 289.
[99] AV Dicey, *Introduction to the Study of the Law of the Constitution*, 8th edn (London, Macmillan, 1915), p 427.
[100] See I Loveland, *Constitutional Law, Administrative Law and Human Rights: A Critical Introduction*, 3rd edn (London, LexisNexis Butterworths, 2003), pp 157–58.

unknown.'[101] As a corollary to this, a convention emerged that the House of Lords would not block any Bills which had proven popular support. The development of this doctrine may be traceable to the transformation in the legitimacy of the House of Commons post-1832. Prior to this date, as explained in the chapter 4, members of the House of Lords were able to influence General Elections and thus indirectly control the House of Commons. Once this power was lost, the House of Lords' veto power became more significant. Simultaneously, however, it became more threatened, as it had now to be justified in democratic, rather than aristocratic, terms.[102] Dicey's approval of the self-denying doctrine of the mandate was rather pragmatic. In private correspondence, Dicey wrote that 'what for example the King or the House of Lords or the House of Commons can effectively do, is what each has a right to do … If you ask what I mean by "can effectively do" I answer I mean that which the electors will support …'[103] In the context of the 1909 Budget dispute, Dicey, perhaps influenced by his strong pro-Unionist sympathies, argued that 'from a constitutional point of view, I consider amendment or rejection equally lawful, equally unusual, and in the circumstances equally legitimate.'[104]

The reliance of the House of Lords upon the doctrine of the mandate has led to an interesting argument that, between 1832 and 1911, the British constitution operated under popular, rather than parliamentary, sovereignty. Weill has recently argued that, during this period, the British Parliament repeatedly admitted its lack of authority to enact constitutional changes without the explicit approval of the people.[105] This policy ceased after 1911 when the House of Lords lost its ability to force the referral of constitutional issues to the electorate.[106] Under Weill's theory, not only the 1832 Reform Act and the 1911 Parliament Act, but also the second and third Reform Acts of 1867 and 1884 and the Irish Church Act 1869, were constitutional changes owing their existence to the primacy of popular sovereignty. It is an interesting theory but ultimately an unconvincing one for a variety of reasons.

First, some of the 'constitutional moments' identified by Weill were not characterised by elections but by popular agitation. Thus, the people's involvement in the decision was not through a formal deliberative procedure but through extra-parliamentary activity. While there is no doubt that such popular agitation is influential,[107] it is no different in essence from the usual political limitations upon Parliament's actions. As Dicey famously noted, Parliament

---

[101] AV Dicey, *A Leap in the Dark on Our New Constitution* (London, John Murray, 1893), pp 177–79.

[102] See R Weill, 'We the British People' [2004] *PL* 380, at 384. In the words of Loveland, 'the more "democratic" basis of the post-Reform Act Commons had significant implications for the power that a non-elected Lords could realistically expect to wield' (Loveland, n 100 above, p 157).

[103] 'Strachey Papers', Dicey to Strachey, 22 July 1909, quoted in Blewett, n 9 above, p 95.

[104] *Ibid*, 16 September 1909, quoted in Blewett, n 9 above, at p 96.

[105] See Weill, n 102 above, at 381.

[106] *Ibid*, at 383.

[107] See, for example, the significance of the political unions' campaign for parliamentary reform in 1831–32, as noted in ch 4.

(even if regarded as legally unlimited) is always subject to political limits of both an internal and external nature.[108] The latter is often identified by popular protest. There was nothing unusual in terms of public involvement in political issues of the day in the period 1832–1911, which Weill argues is a unique period of popular sovereignty in our constitutional history.

Second, Weill notes, but does not seem to appreciate the significance of, the fact that the House of Lords 'were practising their veto against regular and not just constitutional measures.'[109] This undermines Weill's theory, because the House of Lords was not merely referring issues to the electorate based upon their constitutional significance but rather on the basis of political self-interest for the Unionist party. This is evident from the January 1910 election, which focused upon Lloyd George's Budget, rather than any broader constitutional issue. This very fact, and Weill's misunderstanding of it, forms a third reason for doubting the popular sovereignty theory as a whole. Weill claims that 'in 1910, the electorate endorsed the Parliament Bill twice in two separate elections, almost a year apart, and in both elections the Bill reached the top of the electoral agenda.'[110] This is simply not true. Although the Lords/Commons conflict was an underlying issue in the January election, it was never a major issue before the electorate at that stage, and indeed Weill admits this later in the article by stating that the January election 'focussed on the budget and only indirectly touched upon the Lords' power.'[111] Given that only a page earlier, it had been claimed that the 'electorate endorsed the Parliament Bill twice,' there is an inconsistency underlying the article which undermines a crucial aspect of Weill's theory.

Furthermore, a fourth problem emerges when Weill mentions the House of Lords' failure to pass the Home Rule Bill in 1892. According to Weill's popular sovereignty theory, as the people had been consulted on this huge constitutional change and had signified approval, the House of Lords should have passed the Bill. Weill, however, seeks to distinguish this situation because there was only a small House of Commons and electoral majority, the election was not solely on home rule, and the details of the Bill were not referred to the people. The latter two excuses would equally apply to the January 1910 election and yet were ignored in reference to that election, and thus the attempt to distinguish the Home Rule Bill's rejection seems unconvincing.

It can be argued, therefore, that, despite the people being invited to express their opinion on a number of crucial constitutional changes during the nineteenth century and early twentieth century, Weill's theory of the emergence of popular sovereignty in this period is inadequately evidenced. Ultimately, 'the people' were consulted out of necessity when the normal political brokering failed, not, as Weill claims, because Parliament admitted its lack of authority to

---

[108] AV Dicey, *Introduction to the Study of the Law of the Constitution*, 10th edn (London, Macmillan, 1959), pp 76–82.

[109] Weill, n 102 above, at 399.

[110] *Ibid*.

[111] *Ibid*, at 400.

enact constitutional law.[112] Indeed, the House of Lords' amendment of the Parliament Bill after the December 1910 election proves that, in the words of Jenkins, the Lords 'had declined to accept the verdict of the second 1910 general election.'[113] The people, even those who had obtained the vote, were not in possession of sovereign powers over the evolution of the constitution during 1832–1911, even if they did, then as now, have a degree of political influence over the policy of the elected government.

b) The Parliament Act in Practice

During the protracted and disputed passage of the Parliament Act, the Unionists regarded it as a means to an undesirable end: a necessary prelude to Irish home rule. To some extent this concern was justified because home rule was a desired policy of Asquith's Liberal government, and the government wasted no time in introducing a Bill to achieve this controversial goal. In the very next session of Parliament following the passage of the Parliament Act, the Government of Ireland Bill (introducing home rule) was placed before Parliament, together with a Welsh Church Bill (disestablishing the Welsh Church). Both were rejected by the Unionist-dominated House of Lords and provided the government with two early opportunities to exercise the Parliament Act procedure.[114] The enduring inequality of which Lloyd George had warned in 1910 became apparent immediately as the government's policies on Ireland and Wales were subjected to a two-year delay of its own imposition. Grigg even goes so far as to argue that until 1914 'the Parliament Act served as a most effective check, not upon the power of the Lords, but upon the power of the Liberal Government.'[115] The delay imposed on home rule certainly had serious implications as, with the intervention of the First World War and civil war in Ireland, it was a policy which never came into force. The failure to resolve the Irish question at this opportunity has left a tragic legacy.

For the next 30 years there was no reliance upon the Parliament Act, as the Lords did not resort to the use of their final remaining power of a two-year suspensory veto. It may be significant that for most of this period either the Conservatives or a coalition government were in power. The post-war election of 1945 created a new stage for conflict between the two Houses of Parliament,

---

[112] *Ibid*,at 381.

[113] Jenkins, n 2 above, p 212.

[114]   The two early uses of the Parliament Act procedure have led to a perception that only major constitutional changes would be passed without the consent of the House of Lords and that more mundane party political matters might not be appropriate for this procedure. However, Asquith's government also seriously considered using the Parliament Act procedure to ensure the passage of the Temperance (Scotland) Bill and the Plural Voting Bill, but a compromise was reached with the House of Lords on the former Bill, and war intervened in respect of the latter, thus negating the need for further use of the Parliament Act by Asquith's government (Jenkins, n 2 above, p 273).

[115] Grigg, n 15 above, p 290.

however, as a strong Labour government was elected with a mandate for extensive social, economic and political change. The Conservative leader in the House of Lords, Lord Salisbury, established a convention that the House of Lords would not even delay any government Bills implementing the government's manifesto commitments. Nevertheless, Attlee's Labour government was unwilling to risk the imposition of a two-year delay on its radical measures[116] and introduced a second Parliament Bill in 1947 which reduced the House of Lords' delaying power to one year. Following the breakdown of a Conference of Party Leaders in 1948, the Bill became law in 1949 through the use of the 1911 Parliament Act procedure – that is, without the consent of the House of Lords.

Thus the third use of the Parliament Act procedure to pass an Act of Parliament without the House of Lords' assent was by far the most controversial. The Parliament Act 1949 reduces the period by which the Lords can delay the passage into law of a Bill it has rejected. The 1949 Act procedure was never relied upon by the Attlee government, and for over 40 years it remained untested. Then in 1991 the War Crimes Act became law after only a one-year delay imposed by the House of Lords' rejection of the Bill. Ironically, given the background to the abolition of the House of Lords' absolute veto, the government in power in 1991 was a Conservative one. Blair's New Labour government has more recently resorted to the Parliament Act procedure to ensure the passage of the European Parliamentary Elections Act 1999 and the Sexual Offences (Amendment) Act 2000, after the House of Lords objected respectively to the introduction of a party list system for European elections and the lowering of the age of consent for homosexual intercourse. Most recently, the Hunting Act 2004 – Labour's belated attempt to ban hunting with hounds – was also passed in this manner, and the controversial nature of this Act has inspired a legal challenge to the use of the Parliament Act procedure.[117]

There is a reasonable argument that these uses of the 1949 Parliament Act procedure are invalid. This argument is based upon the fact that the 1949 Act was itself passed under the earlier 1911 Parliament Act procedure – that is, by the House of Commons and monarch acting without the House of Lords. The influential constitutional commentator, HWR Wade, has argued that the 1911 Act created a new form of delegated legislation: 'The sovereign legislature has always been regarded as having three component parts, and an Act to which the Lords does not assent is not an Act of the sovereign Parliament at all.'[118] Thus, under

---

[116] The government was particularly concerned about its plans to nationalise the iron and steel industries, which had not been specified in its 1945 manifesto and thus were not protected under the Salisbury convention from rejection by the House of Lords. (See O Hood Phillips and P Jackson, *Constitutional and Administrative Law*, 8th edn (by P Jackson and P Leopold) (London, Sweet & Maxwell, 2001), p 169.)

[117] *Jackson v Attorney-General* [2005] 3 WLR 733.

[118] HWR Wade, 'The Basis of Legal Sovereignty' [1955] *CLJ* 177, at 193. Dicey fudges this issue further in his 1915 Introduction to the 8th edition of his textbook: 'sovereignty still resides in Parliament, ie in the King and two Houses acting together, but ... the Parliament Act has greatly increased the share of sovereignty possessed by the House of Commons and has greatly diminished the share thereof belonging to the House of Lords' (Dicey, n 99 above, p xxiv).

this argument, the Government of Ireland Act 1914, the Welsh Church Disestablishment Act 1914 and, significantly, the Parliament Act 1949 are not Acts of Parliament but, rather, a species of delegated legislation. If this argument is accepted, the first two of these pieces of legislation are legally valid, although reliant upon the Parliament Act 1911 for legal authority. A complicating factor arises, however, with the 1949 Act because in this piece of 'delegated legislation' the delegate (that is, a body comprising only the House of Commons and the monarch) sought to increase the scope of its delegated authority. In the words of Jackson and Leopold, this:

> offended against the general principle of logic and law that delegates (the Queen and Commons) cannot enlarge the authority delegated to them. We are not, of course, arguing – as it is impossible in English law to argue – that an Act of Parliament is invalid: what we are questioning is whether the measure called 'the Parliament Act 1949' bears the character of an Act of Parliament.[119]

If those commentators are correct, and the Parliament Act 1949 does not bear the character of an Act of Parliament, then the subsequent reliance upon it to pass the 1991, 1999, 2000 and 2004 Acts is ineffective and these 'Acts' are lacking in legal authority.[120] Such an outcome seems unrealistic, and Bradley and Ewing were inclined to regard it as a mere academic argument: 'with the passage of time and more frequent use of the Parliament Act procedure, it is one which may be more appropriate for the classroom than the courtroom.'[121] While this may have appeared true in 2003, the events of 2004 have proved that the status of the 1949 Parliament Act is far from a merely academic issue: the House of Lords recently faced exactly this issue in *Jackson v Attorney-General* in the context of a challenge to the Hunting Act 2004.[122]

The House of Lords held that the Parliament Act 1949 is a valid Act of Parliament because the 1911 Act cannot be construed so as to prohibit such a use of its terms. The Lords rejected the argument that the 1911 Act delegated legislative power and confirmed that Acts passed under the Parliament Act procedure are primary legislation, albeit enacted in a different manner to the norm, rather than a species of sub-primary parliamentary legislation. To some Lords, the 1911 Act redefined Parliament for certain purposes,[123] but to other Lords, this was not a

---

[119] Hood Phillips and Jackson, n 116 above, p 80.

[120] This even raises the possibility that convictions under the War Crimes Act 1991, non-convictions under the Sexual Offences Act 2000, and the results of the 2004 European Union elections are ultra vires.

[121] AW Bradley and KD Ewing, *Constitutional and Administrative Law*, 13th edn (Harlow, Longman, 2003), p 198.

[122] It should be noted, however, that some of the Law Lords, particularly Lord Hope, seemed to be influenced by the 'political fact' that the restrictions on the exercise of power by the House of Lords that the 1949 Act purported to make have been so widely recognised and relied upon that it is no longer open to the courts to say that the Act was not authorised by the 1911 Act. (n. 117 above, para. 128.)

[123] *Jackson*, n. 117 above, para. 86 (per Lord Steyn).

helpful view.[124] All of the Law Lords agreed, however, that the 1949 Act, and subsequent Acts passed under it, were valid Acts of Parliament.[125]

When the Court of Appeal passed judgment on this case, despite accepting the validity of the 1949 Parliament Act, the court claimed, obiter, that it did not necessarily follow 'that the 1911 Act can be used or amended, so as to produce results that will constitute a different constitutional settlement.'[126] The Court of Appeal gave examples such as an extension to the life of Parliament or the abolition of the House of Lords and held that these, unlike a reduction in the delaying power by one year, would be changes 'so fundamental, that they could only be enacted or expressly made possible by what is traditionally the sovereign Parliament. That is to say by the triumvirate of the Monarch, the Lords and the Commons.'[127] This is a significant limitation upon the efficacy of the 1911 Act, and the distinction drawn by the Court of Appeal, between Acts which are valid under the 1911 procedure (such as the 1949 Act) and purported Acts introducing constitutional changes which would not be valid, is tenuous. The Attorney-General was particularly keen for this part of the Court of Appeal judgment to be overruled[128] and the House of Lords obliged. The Court of Appeal's distinction between fundamental constitutional changes and other uses of the Parliament Act procedure was held to be untenable for a number of reasons, including the fact that one of the original objects of the Parliament Act was to secure home rule; undoubtedly a fundamental constitutional change in itself.[129]

Lord Steyn's view of a redefinition of Parliament in 1911 has support from Jennings who, unlike Wade, regards the Parliament Acts as Acts which changed the law as to the manner and form of the exercise of the sovereign legal power.[130] Thus, in Jennings' view, the legal sovereign is, for certain purposes, no longer the Crown, Lords and Commons, but merely Crown and Commons. There is, as Wade keenly points out, little judicial evidence that the British sovereign

---

[124] Ibid, para. 113 (per Lord Hope).

[125] Of broader significance, at least two senior Law Lords expressed reservations about the continued application of Dicey's theory of parliamentary sovereignty. Lord Steyn regarded Dicey's view as 'out of place in the modern United Kingdom' and suggested that parliamentary sovereignty is a 'construct of common law' which could be changed if necessary. (para. 102.) Lord Hope agreed and held that, although the British constitution is dominated by the sovereignty of Parliament, 'parliamentary sovereignty is no longer, if it ever was, absolute.' (para. 104.) Such comments would have been heresy only a few decades ago. The increasing judicial recognition of the need for an evolution of the constitutional principle of parliamentary sovereignty in response to the modern realities of the constitution is long overdue.

[126] [2005] QB 579, para 46.

[127] *Ibid*, para 48.

[128] Lord Goldsmith, the Attorney-General, has been quoted as saying that the Court of Appeal's conclusion that the 1911 Act procedure has limits was 'unwarranted and unworkable' and would bring 'chaos to the government's legislative programme' by which he seems to have in mind further reform of the composition of the House of Lords (C Dyer, 'Goldsmith urges Law Lords not to risk "chaos"' *The Guardian*, 15 July 2005).

[129] *Jackson*, n. 117 above, para. 31 (per Lord Bingham).

[130] I Jennings, *The Law and the Constitution*, 5th edn (London, University of London Press, 1959), p 161.

legislature is subject to such redefinition.[131] Wade also notes that such a theory of legislative sovereignty would leave the sovereignty of future Parliaments 'qualified and precarious'.[132] For example, if the House of Lords can be removed from the legislative equation, could not the monarch likewise be removed? One important restraint upon this course of action is that the threefold Queen-in-Parliament would need to consent to such a redefinition. The House of Lords, albeit subject to some government threats as to its future composition, voluntarily relinquished its absolute veto over legislation. Were the monarch to do the same, there is no reason why, under Jennings' theory, the sovereign legislature could not be so redefined. Indeed, it could be argued that Parliament has periodically been redefined through the successive Representation of the People Acts from 1832 onwards which have radically transformed the composition of the House of Commons. The line of succession to the throne has also frequently been changed during British constitutional history (including, in the twentieth century, by the Abdication Act 1936). Therefore, the body which claims sovereignty today is not a direct descendent of, for example, the 1689 Parliament established as part of the constitutional settlement of that year. Perhaps of particular significance for this chapter, today's Upper House is a radically different body from that which voluntarily relinquished its powers in 1911. The later twentieth-century redefining of the House of Lords removed (most of) the hereditary peers which had been so central to the 1910–11 conflict, and further reform to legitimise the composition may yet lead to a revival of the House of Lords' power to veto legislation. Such redefinition of the legislative branch of government is inevitable over the course of the centuries and, provided that the full legal sovereign of the day assents to the redefining, the newly defined body must carry with it full legal authority to legislate.

Is further reform of the second chamber likely to occur? House of Lords reform has been a thorn in the side of many governments since 1911. The Blair government, first elected in 1997, has made the most progress on reforming and seeking to legitimise the House of Lords by the removal of the hereditary peers in the House of Lords Act 1999. However, the government has since faltered on further reform, and the Upper House is now in an intermediary state of ambiguous composition.[133] Although few would doubt the desirability of limiting the hereditary right to legislate, the current House still lacks real legitimacy. As was discussed above, the composition of the House of Lords will govern the perceived legitimacy of its power. Indeed, as Russell and Cornes note, the composition of the House 'will govern its ability to effectively use its powers.'[134] It is this fact

---

[131] Wade, n 118 above, p 185.

[132] *Ibid.*

[133] The Report of the Royal Commission on the Reform of the House of Lords (Cm 4534) (2000) has yet to be implemented. For recent discussion of options for reform, see G Philipson, 'The Greatest Quango of them all, a Rival Chamber or a Hybrid Nonsense? Solving the Second Chamber Paradox' [2004] *PL* 352.

[134] M Russell and R Cornes, 'The Royal Commission on Reform of the House of Lords' (2001) 64 *MLR* 82, at 83.

which explains the relatively few instances of reliance upon the Parliament Act(s) procedure since 1911. Russell and Cornes argue that the weakness of the House of Lords in opposing the House of Commons during the twentieth century was 'not because of the chamber's powers ... but because its anachronistic membership made it difficult to justify challenging the elected lower house.'[135]

It is certainly evident that the removal of most of the hereditary peers has re-invigorated the Upper House. Since their removal in 1999, the House of Lords appears to have felt authorised to exercise its powers, as demonstrated by the Lords' rejection of the European Parliamentary Elections Bill in 1999, the Sexual Offences (Amendment) Bill in 2000 and the Hunting Bill in 2004. The government's use of the Parliament Act procedure in response to the Lords' exercise of their delaying power raises an argument that the Parliament Acts are being used inappropriately. If the Parliament Act procedure, under which one third of the sovereign legislature is bypassed, is regarded as a major interference with the UK's democratic constitutional tradition, it could be argued that this exceptional procedure should not be used for trivial measures. If the usual constitutional procedure is to be bypassed, this should only be done when a major constitutional measure is at stake, such as a refusal of supply by the Upper House or a measure to redesign the unitary state. The use of the Parliament Act for purely party political matters could, under this argument, be regarded as demeaning the entire democratic process.

Ultimately this is not a convincing argument, however, because the justification for the Parliament Acts is that the unelected should not be able to frustrate the wishes of the elected government, as happened in 1906–11. While an Upper House with greater legitimacy may feel justified in frustrating the wishes of the elected government to a much larger extent than previously, this cannot detract from the pre-eminent role which the House of Commons has under the UK constitution, as evidenced inter alia by the Parliament Acts, and will continue to have unless further and more radical composition reform is initiated. It is only through composition reform that the Upper House can reclaim a core role in legislating for the United Kingdom. This is a clear lesson from constitutional history which successive governments have failed, or for their own self-interest refused, to learn. The perceived illegitimacy of the House of Lords throughout the twentieth century was a far more effective restraint upon its powers than the Parliament Act had ever sought to be.

c) Implications for the Monarchy from House of Lords Reform

The hereditary nature of the House of Lords when it actively opposed the elected government in 1906–11 was a significant factor in the push for a curb on its

---

[135] *Ibid*, at 97.

powers. The other important hereditary element in the British constitution – the King – was aware of the precarious position in which an attack on the hereditary principle would place him. Edward VII had a conviction that any assault on the hereditary privileges of the House of Lords was equally an assault on the hereditary privileges of the monarchy.[136] Curiously, he was wrong. The House of Commons' dispute with the House of Lords was never developed into a conflict with the Crown's role in law-making, and yet, as Heffer notes, 'the King had a point.'[137] Why has the monarchy escaped attack from government and public attention, while the House of Lords is continually the subject of attempts at reform?

When Edward VII, and later George V, were dragged into the conflict between the two Houses, they were asked by Asquith's government to exercise their residual prerogative powers to load the dice in the Liberal party's favour by swamping the House of Lords with Liberal peers. It required Crown involvement in what was not only a constitutional conflict, but also a party political power struggle. For this reason (as well as others), both Kings were reluctant to become involved. The truth was, however, that political involvement could not be avoided, as a refusal to accede to ministerial requests for Liberal peers would in itself have been a blatantly controversial decision with political repercussions. There has been much debate on the question of whether George V made the correct constitutional choice in guaranteeing the passage of the Parliament Act by agreeing to exercise his prerogative if necessary. However, Grigg has argued that the Asquith government was wrong to grant the King this crucial discretion: 'It seems very curious, in retrospect, that his freedom to act or not to act upon Ministerial advice in what was, after all, a strictly political matter, was never questioned by the Government.'[138] In Grigg's view, the government should have emphasised to the King that he was obliged to follow ministerial advice. This seems unrealistic, however, given that both sides of the political divide were claiming that the other side was acting both unconstitutionally and contrary to the will of the people. The question of whether to initiate a mass creation of Liberal peers to swamp the Upper House, in order to force through a limitation on that House's legislative powers, was far from a 'strictly political matter'. It is in such circumstances that the monarch's residual powers have some enduring value. Controversial though this may be, it suggests that Douglas-Home is correct to describe the monarch as a 'referee of the constitution.'[139] As Douglas-Home argues, 'when its other constituent parts ceased to work properly together, only the Monarch held the key to unblocking the impasse and creating a new settlement. It put the monarchy in a very important position, but a very dangerous

---

[136] S Heffer, *Power and Place: The Political Consequences of King Edward VII* (London, Weidenfeld & Nicolson, 1998), p 226.
[137] *Ibid.*
[138] Grigg, n 15 above, p 278.
[139] Douglas-Home, n 67 above, p 21.

one.'[140] The fact that only the monarch is positioned to act as referee is explained by Brazier:

> The United Kingdom has no supreme court which could ensure that in the last resort the political actors behave in conformity with the norms of the constitution; Parliament is dominated by the government; voters cannot precipitate a general election; the only insurance of constitutional propriety in a dire emergency is the sovereign.[141]

It remains inappropriate that an individual chosen solely by accident of birth should wield such influence over the constitution. Even though convention has limited the practical influence of the Crown, it retains its key position as one third (or, under the Parliament Act, one half) of the sovereign legislature of the United Kingdom. While it does so, the Crown will continue to be a key player in major constitutional conflicts when normal power relations break down. The United Kingdom needs a 'referee of the constitution.' As a purportedly democratic and modern state, it needs one that does not rely upon the hereditary principle for its authority. If 1911 teaches us nothing else, it shows conclusively that a hereditary body lacks legitimacy for exercising its powers against elected politicians and will either have its powers curbed or its legitimacy increased. This is a lesson with implications for the future of both the monarchy and the British constitution.

IV. Conclusion

The legacy of the 1911 Parliament Act is an emasculated and illegitimate Upper House. The House of Lords lost its co-equal role in the sovereign legislature and retained a composition of questionable legitimacy in the all-important eyes of the public. This unsatisfactory state of affairs has barely been addressed since 1911. Although some important changes have been introduced since then – particularly by means of the Life Peerages Act 1958 and the House of Lords Act 1999, as well as the Parliament Act 1949 – the Upper House's membership has always remained on the political agenda for reform. A common theme whenever House of Lords reform is considered is the fear of creating an Upper House which could challenge the supremacy of the House of Commons. This is a red herring, however, for two reasons. First, there is a well-established convention

---

[140] *Ibid.*

[141] R Brazier, 'The Monarchy' in V Bogdanor, *The British Constitution in the Twentieth Century* (Oxford, Oxford University Press, 2003), p 83. Brazier proceeds, however, by recognising that the monarch's intervention is a last resort only: 'Representative parliamentary government has, however, ensured that governments are fully subject, in time, to the electorate: they know that they risk dismissal by an informed electorate if they were to do grave constitutional wrong. Because of that, the use of the sovereign's reserve powers has ceased to be a weapon of first resort against politicians who might be tempted to depart form the constitutional straight and narrow.'

that the government must command a majority in the House of Commons. Thus, it will remain this chamber which makes and breaks governments. Indeed, a common characteristic of second chambers worldwide is their lack of powers over the formation of governments.[142] It was the fact that the House of Lords challenged this reality, and sought to bring down a government by refusing supply, that led to the inevitable confrontation between the two Houses in 1909. Second, while the Parliament Acts remain in force, the powers of the Upper House are severely restricted. It cannot challenge the supremacy of the House of Commons and thus there is no excuse for a failure to legitimise the membership of the House of Lords.[143] The only consequence of a perceived democratic illegitimacy in the composition of the Upper House is a reluctance by the House of Lords to implement its suspensory veto. No doubt the moves towards a more democratic House of Lords in recent years have encouraged the Lords to reject Bills which they oppose and explains the recent uses of the suspensory veto.

1911 was a turning point in relations between the two Houses of Parliament. A conflict had been brewing since the House of Commons began on the road to democratic representation in 1832 (and simultaneously moved beyond the control of members of the House of Lords). There is no doubt that the House of Commons won the 1909–11 conflict, as the House of Lords has never since felt in a position to challenge directly the House of Commons in any prolonged manner.[144] The events described in this chapter, when combined with those of 1721–42 and 1832, discussed in the previous two chapters, laid the framework for a modern Parliament and executive for the twentieth century. All were guided by an increased democratisation of the British constitution, although the meaning of this concept was evolving slowly. By 1911 in British constitutional history, it was clear that the real source of power in the constitution was the executive-dominated House of Commons. This was to pose its own dangers: as one threat to the people was neutralised, another was just emerging.

---

[142] Russell and Cornes, n 132 above, p 83. Italy is a notable exception.

[143] See Lord Bingham of Cornhill, 'The Evolving Constitution' [2002] *EHRLR* 1, at 11: it is not 'necessary to deny democratic legitimacy to the Lords to preserve the constitutional dominance of the Commons.'

[144] It is significant that, on the same day as the House of Lords finally passed the Parliament Act, the government introduced a clause into the Appropriation Bill which authorised the payment of a salary to MPs. As Cross explains, 'between them the two events marked a decisive step in the evolution of the old oligarchical British Parliament into an institution fitted to the liberal fashion of political democracy' (Cross, n 12 above, p 132).

6

1953 – The European Convention on Human Rights: an External Influence Within the Constitution

This chapter deals with the first major international influence on the UK constitution. The negotiations, signature, ratification and coming into force of the European Convention for the Protection of Human Rights and Fundamental Freedoms (ECHR) occurred during the period 1948–53 and, as will be seen below, was a direct response to the horrors of the Second World War and to the continuing totalitarian threat in Europe. From the perspective of both international law and the UK constitution, the ECHR signalled a new world: the involvement of international treaties and institutions in what had previously been regarded as matters of domestic jurisdiction. The consequences for the UK constitution were profound. This chapter will begin by analysing the first moves towards international protection of human rights on a global scale and will then proceed to consider the negotiation process for the ECHR, and the UK government's role in this. The consequences of the coming into force of the Convention will then be highlighted before the chapter concludes with an evaluation of two subsequent developments which have enhanced the ECHR's influence within the UK constitution. The events of this chapter should be seen within the context of a constitution which, by the middle of the twentieth century, had evolved into an ostensibly democratic constitution but one in which Parliament was becoming increasingly overwhelmed by the strength of the executive within the House of Commons. Legal protection of individual rights was long overdue.

I. The International Protection of Human Rights

At the commencement of the Second World War, international protection of human rights was an unknown phenomenon. It is true that the idea of human rights had emerged in the seventeenth and eighteenth centuries and had led to domestic declarations of rights such as the US Bill of Rights and the French Declaration of the Rights of Man.[1] It is also true that international law had dabbled in related issues in the form of humanitarian laws of war, laws on piracy and slavery, and treaties for the protection of minorities, but in 1939 there was no universal international law on human rights. The minority treaties established under the League of Nations were the closest ancestors to human rights treaties but, crucially, these were far from universal. They imposed international obligations upon certain governments to protect the rights of minorities within their state, but this legal burden only weighed upon a limited number of states.[2]

During the course of the Second World War the idea of universal individual rights (and thus universal state obligations) began to be mooted, both by individual citizens[3] and by influential statesmen. On 6 January 1941, during a State of the Union address to Congress, President Roosevelt set out the 'Four Freedoms': freedom of expression and religion and freedom from want and fear. This speech has been described as combining the ideas expressed in the US Bill of Rights with the philosophy of Roosevelt's new deal.[4] It is certainly evident from the four freedoms proposed that Roosevelt wanted to include more than the traditional civil liberties. Indeed, freedom from want has been described as a 'synopsis of social and economic human rights.'[5] At the time of Roosevelt's speech there was no mention of the need for international protection of these freedoms, but the speech was 'to acquire, retrospectively, a practical and not merely rhetorical significance. It came to be read as implying that denial of the four freedoms, since this threatened security, was a matter of international and not merely domestic concern.'[6] As Simpson goes on to argue, 'the whole conception of the war as a justifiable crusade against atrocious behaviour carried with it this implication.'[7]

---

[1] Burgers describes two 'waves' of the idea of human rights: one in the seventeenth and eighteenth centuries, and then another in the twentieth century (JH Burgers, 'The Road to San Francisco: The Revival of the Human Rights Idea in the Twentieth Century' (1992) 14 *Human Rights Quarterly* 447, at 447).

[2] As Verzijl has described, 'This had as its consequence that, on the one hand, minorities in states not so legally burdened did not enjoy international protection and that, on the other, states that were so burdened felt the obligations imposed upon them as being unjustly one-sided, or even humiliating' (JHW Verzijl, *International Law in Historical Perspective (Vol V)* (Leiden, AW Sijthoff, 1972), p 201).

[3] For example, HG Wells was particularly influential as the drafter of the 'Sankey Declaration' published in the *Daily Herald* in February 1940.

[4] AWB Simpson, *Human Rights and the End of Empire: Britain and the Genesis of the European Convention* (Oxford, Oxford University Press, 2001), p 173.

[5] Burgers, n 1 above, p 469. Johnson also argues that Roosevelt 'articulated a concept which began to incorporate some understanding of economic and social rights' (MG Johnson, 'The Contributions of Eleanor and Franklin Roosevelt to the Development of International Protection for Human Rights' (1987) 9 *Human Rights Quarterly* 19, at 20).

[6] Simpson, n 4 above, p 175.

[7] *Ibid.*

This idea was soon formalised when first the Atlantic Charter and then the United Nations Declaration hinted at human rights as an Allied war aim.[8] It is evident that the 'contempt in which the human being was held'[9] in fascist states was an important impetus in uniting the allied states, but it must be noted that the allied governments themselves showed no great commitment in practice to human rights during the war. As Lauren has eloquently described,

> the Allied governments displayed great reluctance to take any serious action that might actually dissolve their colonial empires, assist those Jews caught in Hitler's Holocaust, modify their exclusive immigration restrictions, release those interned for the war solely because of their race, or change their domestic policies of segregation.[10]

Now, as later, human rights were for export rather than import.[11] Nevertheless, the inclusion of human rights as a war aim by the Allied powers created 'a troublesome mirror that reflected their own abuses.'[12] By 1944, a human rights movement had emerged, and the Allied governments' rhetorical reliance upon human rights to justify the war against fascism was 'coming home to roost.'[13]

Between August and October 1944, the four major Allied powers, including the United Kingdom, negotiated the structure and purposes of a post-war international organisation at the Dumbarton Oaks Conference. The United States proposed the inclusion of the principle of respect for human rights as one of the guiding principles of the new organisation, but the United Kingdom and the USSR both opposed this. The UK government was concerned that such an inclusion could threaten the continuance of the colonial empire.[14] The policy of the Foreign Office at this time was to support a new world organisation but one which would only be able to intervene in a domestic dispute if it threatened international peace and security.[15] Thus, the final document to emerge from the Dumbarton Oaks Conference failed to meet the expectations of the newly formed human rights movement.[16] Human rights were mentioned but not as one of the basic purposes of the proposed 'United Nations'. Also, controversially, the structure of this proposed organisation would favour the four main Allied powers (the United States, the USSR, China, and the United Kingdom), who would all be entitled to permanent membership of the Security Council. The

---

[8] The so-called Atlantic Charter was a declaration agreed by Roosevelt and Churchill in August 1941; the United Nations Declaration dates from January 1942, shortly after the United States had entered the war.

[9] I Szabo, 'Historical Foundations of Human Rights and Subsequent Developments' in K Vasak (ed), *The International Dimensions of Human Rights (Vol 1)* (English edition by P Alston) (Westport, Greenwood Press, 1982), p 21.

[10] PG Lauren, *The Evolution of Human Rights: Visions Seen* (Philadelphia, University of Pennsylvania Press, 1998), p 161.

[11] Simpson, n 4 above, pp 347–48. See further below.

[12] Lauren, n 10 above, p 160.

[13] Simpson, n 4 above, p 220.

[14] Johnson, n 5 above, p 24.

[15] See Simpson, n 4 above, p 245.

[16] Burgers, n 1 above, p 474.

more democratic General Assembly was to have only very limited powers of debate. The proposals caused an outcry both amongst the human rights movement and amongst other state governments, who resented their exclusion from the design process of a new world order.[17] When the San Francisco Conference opened on 25 April 1945, these two dissatisfied groups were influential in increasing the emphasis on human rights in the new world organisation.

The Charter of the United Nations which was agreed and signed at San Francisco on 26 June 1945 closely resembled the earlier Dumbarton Oaks proposals (and the great powers retained their self-appointed dominant roles in the Security Council), but human rights became more prominent in two major ways. First, respect for human rights was elevated to a basic purpose of the new organisation.[18] Second, the establishment of a Human Rights Commission was mandated under the Economic and Social Council. In achieving these two advances, two groups were particularly influential. The Latin American states were united in pressuring for greater focus upon human rights in the Charter following the Chapultepac Conference in February–March 1945 in which human rights took centre stage,[19] and 'consultants' from US non-governmental organisations 'prodded' the US government towards greater human rights obligations.[20] The increased emphasis on human rights in the Charter must, however, be seen in context. The Charter's terms were inevitably a compromise, and Article 2(7) made clear that states intended to ensure that their national sovereignty was preserved intact: 'Nothing contained in the present Charter shall authorise the United Nations to intervene in matters which are essentially within the domestic jurisdiction of any State ...' As Lauren writes, when one reads this Article, 'it is easy to conclude that the delegates who drafted and signed the Charter of the United Nations engaged in nothing less than deliberate duplicity. That is, they cynically and capriciously took away with one hand what they had given with the

---

[17] Lauren claims that the Dumbarton Oaks proposals 'opened up a vociferous public debate and launched a steam of protest that extended around the world. In the minds of those who advocated a new kind of universal peace with human rights, the meeting exposed the crass self-interests and the old politics of the Great Powers alone. The prominence of the Security Council, the diminution of the General Assembly, the emphasis on states rather than individuals, the absence of any provisions at all concerning colonial empires, and the sole mention of human rights practically buried in the text ... provoked shock, resentment and anger' (Lauren, n 10 above, p 173).

[18] Human rights are referred to in the Preamble ('to reaffirm faith in fundamental human rights, in the dignity and worth of the human person, in the equal rights of men and women and of nations large and small ...') and twice in Art 1: 'To develop friendly relations among nations based on respect for the principle of equal rights and self-determination of peoples' (Art 1(2)); 'To achieve international co-operation in ... promoting and encouraging respect for human rights and for fundamental freedoms for all without distinction as to race, sex, language or religion ...' (Art 1(3)).

[19] Indeed it was from the Organisation of American States that the very first international human rights treaty would emerge in 1948 in the form of the American Declaration of Rights and Duties of Man.

[20] Johnson, n 5 above, p 25. The US government was determined to avoid a repetition of Wilson's failure to obtain Senate approval to the Covenant of the League of Nations after the First World War and therefore invited 42 NGOs to send representatives to San Francisco to act as consultants to the US delegation (Burgers, n 1 above, p 476). Many of these consultants urged amendments to strengthen the position of human rights in the Charter.

other.'[21] Lauren regards this as an insufficient explanation of the terms of the Charter, but there is no doubt that Article 2(7) signifies a continued commitment to non-intervention in domestic matters. Simpson has argued that there is some justification for such a view, in that the inter-war years demonstrated the threat to peace and security which could arise from external interference in a state's domestic jurisdiction:

> Pre-war experience over the Minorities Treaties and over Hitler's policy of incorporating German populations in greater Germany, suggested that if peace was to be maintained states should not be in any way encouraged to champion the rights of citizens of other countries. That was indeed just what Hitler had done. So protecting domestic jurisdiction was thought to contribute towards keeping the peace, the primary task.[22]

The difficulty with this view is that the horror stories then emerging from the concentration camps vividly indicated the extent of suffering which could be caused if a state were free to treat its citizens in any manner of its choosing.

In December 1946, UK government officials took a decision which was to prove crucially important for the UK's future involvement in the international protection of human rights.[23] Human rights were now to be handled by the Foreign Office. For the Foreign Office, human rights were 'a weapon to be deployed against other governments.'[24] Other government departments took a very different view of human rights, regarding their international protection as 'a rod which might fall upon their own backs.'[25] As Simpson notes, the conflict in views is about the nature of the operation itself: 'Was foreign policy or domestic policy involved? Was it a question of exporting human rights or importing them?'[26] The 'export theory' of human rights may explain the inclusion of Article 1(3) and Article 2(7) of the UN Charter in close proximity with each other: human rights violations were seen as something that had to be prevented in other states but that either did not occur, or were justified, within a state's own territory.

The UN Charter was the starting point for international protection of human rights but the Human Rights Commission which it established was keen to move quickly on to a second and more detailed stage. The Commission, chaired by Eleanor Roosevelt, decided to draft an international bill of rights. Unable to agree upon the means of implementation of a legally enforceable covenant, the Commission agreed to a compromise under which a non-binding declaration would be drafted first, followed by a legally enforceable covenant. The latter stage did not materialise, however, for another 20 years. The first stage became the

---

[21] Lauren, n 10 above, p 199.
[22] Simpson, n 4 above, p 245.
[23] *Ibid*, p 337.
[24] *Ibid*, p 338.
[25] *Ibid*.
[26] *Ibid*, p 500.

Universal Declaration of Human Rights (UDHR), which was adopted by the General Assembly of the new United Nations on 10 December 1948. Forty-eight states agreed to this list of human rights, and there were eight abstentions.[27] Views on the significance of the Declaration differ drastically. Simpson says it 'represented little more than an exhalation of pious hot air,'[28] while Lauren claims that it 'enormously accelerated the evolution of international human rights.'[29] Lauren also recognises, however, that at the time of the adoption of the UDHR, 'no state – not one – regardless of location, level of development, or culture, could meet its standards of achievement. Champions and opponents of human rights alike thus wondered what would happen and what it all would mean.'[30]

The UDHR broke new ground in obtaining widespread international agreement on the existence and identity of fundamental human rights and freedoms. The governments of 48 states, including the United Kingdom, were willing to agree to abide by these rights, and yet in practice were violating a number of them on a daily basis. The challenge of turning the worthwhile theory into a practical reality proved to be too much for the UN at this stage in its history, but a new European regional document was soon to emerge that would seek, in the words of its Preamble, to 'take the first steps for the collective enforcement of certain of the Rights stated in the Universal Declaration.'[31]

II. Drafting the ECHR

In the General Election of 1945, a Labour government led by Clement Attlee was elected to power. It faced uniquely challenging times. The Attlee administration had to attempt to rejuvenate the United Kingdom after the war, while being committed to widespread domestic reforms (including a programme of nationalisation and the creation of the National Health Service) and dealing with an unstable international situation.[32] As Roberts notes, at the end of the war, the United Kingdom:

---

[27] The eight abstaining states were the USSR, Byelorussia, Czechoslovakia, Poland, Saudi Arabia, Ukraine, South Africa and Yugoslavia.

[28] Simpson, n 4 above, p 11.

[29] Lauren, n 10 above, p 239.

[30] *Ibid*, p 240. Verzijl also argues that the adoption of the Declaration 'brims with international hypocrisy' (Verzijl, n 2 above, p 205).

[31] Preamble of the ECHR.

[32] In addition to a devastated Europe and the beginnings of the Cold War between the USSR and United States, the United Kingdom was also involved in Indian independence, withdrawal from Palestine and unrest in the colonies in Africa and Malaya. (See D Childs, *Britain since 1945 – A Political History*, 5th edn (London, Routledge, 2001), ch 3.) Clement Attlee, the Prime Minister, has admitted that, 'The disturbed international situation was a constant anxiety during the whole of our period of office' (CR Attlee, *As It Happened* (London, William Heinemann Ltd, 1954), p 169).

had the status and the responsibility of one of the three victorious powers, with enormous prestige but none of the resources of the United States or even, taking a longer view, of the Soviet Union … Britain was infinitely weaker than the other two and yet had to play its full part in resisting Soviet pressures and in restoring Europe, while also undertaking the formidable task of converting an Empire into a Commonwealth.[33]

By 1950, the Attlee administration was also struggling for its own political survival with a majority of only six following the election of February 1950.[34] The government was therefore distracted by other concerns during the period 1945–51, and yet the ratification of the ECHR has proved to be an important legacy of this government and, indeed, very much a product of its time. As Simpson notes, it would have been 'quite inconceivable for any such treaty to have been negotiated in pre-war Europe,'[35] but it was also unlikely at a later stage, as indicated by the UN Covenants of 1966, which are 'pale creatures in comparison, with weak mechanisms for enforcement.'[36] Thus, the late 1940s and early 1950s represented a brief window of opportunity for a document such as the ECHR, largely due to the perceived communist threat to western democracies at that time. This is in accordance with Moravcsik's theory that governments turn to international enforcement of human rights only when an international commitment enforces the policy preferences of the government at that point in time.[37] Thus, in Moravcsik's view, it was mainly the 'new' democracies in Europe[38] which sought international enforcement of human rights (as their nature of government was under threat from communism), but an established democracy may also support an international human rights regime if 'democratisation is expected to pacify a potentially threatening neighbour or solidify opposition to a common non-democratic enemy.'[39] This was exactly the position in which the United Kingdom found itself in the post-war years.

The division of Germany in 1948 transformed the identity of Europe and, in the view of the British government, necessitated the formation of a western bloc

---

[33] FR Roberts, 'Ernest Bevin as Foreign Secretary' in R Ovendale (ed), *The Foreign Policy of British Labour Governments, 1945–1951* (Leicester, Leicester University Press, 1984), p 27.

[34] Howarth claims that there was 'an assumption that a single figure majority was unworkable and must soon lead to another dissolution' (TEB Howarth, *Prospect and Reality – Great Britain 1945–1955* (London, Collins, 1985), p 155). In fact the government, with a majority of six, survived from February 1950 to October 1951, at which time it lost the election despite gaining more votes than any political party before or since.

[35] See the previous section for explanation of this assertion.

[36] Simpson, n 4 above, p 8. Of course, the fact that the Covenants were negotiated on an international, rather than regional, level may also provide a partial explanation for the discrepancy.

[37] A Moravcsik, 'The Origins of Human Rights Regimes: Democratic Delegation in Postwar Europe' (2000) 54 *Int Org* 217, at 220.

[38] Moravcsik regards Austria, France, Italy, Iceland, Ireland and Germany as falling into this category.

[39] Moravcsik, n 37 above, at 229. Moravcsik continues by explaining that in such cases 'established democracies can be expected to support rhetorical declarations, in favour of human rights and regimes with optional enforcement that bind newly established democracies but exempt themselves.' As will be seen below, this mirrors exactly the approach of the United Kingdom during the drafting of the ECHR.

in opposition to Soviet communism.[40] The Foreign Secretary, Ernest Bevin, made clear that the factor which would most clearly distinguish west from east was respect for human rights.[41] The first step towards a western European political organisation was launched in March 1948 when the United Kingdom, together with France, Netherlands, Belgium and Luxembourg, signed the Brussels Treaty. The Preamble of this Treaty included a commitment to human rights, but this was not enforceable and the Treaty was primarily a military defence pact in direct response to the communist coup in Czechoslovakia in February 1948. At the same time, however, a non-governmental pan-European movement was becoming influential in shaping the future direction of western Europe. The 'United Europe Movement' was established in January 1947 (with Winston Churchill playing a key role). The Movement sought a federal Europe. In May 1948, a Congress of Europe was held in The Hague with over 600 delegates from 16 countries.[42] In Britain it became a party political issue: the British Labour party boycotted the Congress, while Churchill chaired it.[43] Two important proposals emerged from the Hague Congress: the establishment of a European Parliamentary Assembly and the drafting of a European charter of human rights (to include, crucially, the establishment of a court and individual petition).[44] The UK government had a rather different vision of co-operation in Europe and, in October 1948, Bevin proposed a 'Council of Ministers of Western Europe'.[45] This would have amounted to a Council of Europe solely comprised of government delegates. Other states, especially France, were not keen on this proposal.[46] In January 1949, a compromise was reached which would include both the Hague Congress and Bevin's proposals. A 'Council of Europe' would be established which would include both a committee of ministers and an assembly (albeit one with no legislative powers).[47] In May 1949, the Statute of the Council of Europe was signed in London by the Brussels six, plus Italy, Ireland, Sweden, Denmark and Norway. The Statute included an emphasis upon human rights, largely at the request of the UK government, who were concerned that the proposed assembly might become a platform for communists.[48] The priority for the UK government was to obtain a clear and narrow definition of rights and only then to consider what methods might be most appropriate for implementing these rights.

---

[40] See Simpson, n 4 above, p 555.

[41] *Ibid*, p 570. Simpson goes so far as to regard the submission of papers to Cabinet on this issue in 1947–48 as 'in retrospect, … the first step in the process which was to generate the ECHR.'

[42] *Ibid*, p 603.

[43] Churchill's role in the European Movement is very interesting. In the late 1940s, he appeared to be a strong advocate for a federal Europe of which the United Kingdom would be a member (Simpson, n 4 above, pp 560–61) but, by the time he returned to power in 1951, his interest had faded.

[44] Simpson, n 4 above, p 607.

[45] *Ibid*, p 626.

[46] *Ibid*, p 830.

[47] See Simpson, n 4 above, pp 636–37.

[48] *Ibid*, p 639.

The first session of the consultative assembly in Strasbourg on 10 August 1949 included a debate on human rights (despite the committee of ministers' attempt to exclude human rights from the agenda[49]). Two key points emerged from the debate, which was based on a motion proposed by Teitgen and Maxwell-Fyfe. First, the function of the document to be drafted would be solely to preserve existing rights. Teitgen has subsequently written that, 'As we were concerned at the time only with rights or freedoms inherent in any democratic form of government, they were by definition already present in the internal law of each of the states in question; all we had to do was to identify them.'[50] Second, the need to draft a convention which provided a collective guarantee was emphasised. This was to be the distinctive feature of the Convention. It would not be innovative in terms of the rights protected but in 'the fact that its aim is to organise their protection, within the framework of the Council of Europe, through commitments entered into and common action undertaken by all member states of that organisation.'[51] Crucially for the United Kingdom, Teitgen's plan included a European court as central to the scheme. When the matter was referred to a committee on legal and administrative questions, a dispute arose as to whether the 'collective enforcement' which was so vital to the Convention should be via legal or political mechanisms. The UK representatives, Layton and Ungoed-Thomas, followed the government's wishes in opposing legal enforcement through a regional court, but they were in a minority. The report which emerged from the committee therefore met with a negative UK response. For example, Le Quesne of the Foreign Office believed that 'the proposals seem to be as unrealistic and unacceptable as they could be.' [52] However, as Simpson notes, a wholly unco-operative attitude was not viable: 'The Council of Europe was, after all, an institution, monstrous or not, which Bevin was largely responsible for creating in the first place. And it was Bevin and his officials who had positively encouraged it to become concerned with human rights.'[53] Bevin himself also took the view that a human rights convention might be less of a danger, from a loss of sovereignty perspective, than political or economic union, and so should be supported.[54] Therefore, the Foreign Office proposed the establishment of a body of national representatives who were experts in the field and could determine the rights to be included in a convention.[55]

The first meeting of experts was held in February 1950 and immediately a divergence was evident between the civil and common law approaches. The United Kingdom favoured a more narrowly defined series of rights. Many states

---

[49] *Ibid*, p 667.

[50] P-H Teitgen, 'Introduction to the European Convention on Human Rights' in RStJ Macdonald, F Matscher and H Petzold (eds), *The European System for the Protection of Human Rights* (Dordrecht, Martinus Nijhoff, 1993), p 3.

[51] *Ibid*.

[52] FO 371/78937 (Le Quesne, Foreign Office).

[53] Simpson, n 4 above, p 683.

[54] *Ibid*, p 684.

[55] *Ibid*, p 686.

with a civil law tradition, such as France, Italy and Belgium, preferred the evolution of a jurisprudence of rights by a court. A preliminary draft convention was formed which adopted the latter approach but, by including no precise definition of the rights listed, a general limitations clause and the establishment of a court, it was unacceptable to the United Kingdom.[56] The second meeting of experts in March 1950 sought a compromise but was unsuccessful, and thus two alternative texts were produced. Alternative A enumerated the rights, and alternative B defined the rights. Because of the complexity of state views on the nature of the proposed convention, both alternatives A and B included one version with the establishment of a court and one without. The committee of ministers agreed to compose a conference of senior officials to choose between these variants. The conference met in June 1950 and was able to produce a single draft convention with majority support. The United Kingdom was successful in obtaining alternative B – that is, a convention with clearly defined rights. For example, alternative A merely mentioned that 'Everyone has the right to life …' whereas the final draft to emerge from the conference of senior officials declares a number of tightly defined limitations which can now be seen in Article 2 of the ECHR. The only substantial difference between alternative B and the compromise draft was the addition of Article 8's protection for the right to respect for family and private life, home and correspondence.[57]

However, the United Kingdom remained in a minority on the key question of enforcement, and the compromise draft achieved by the conference of senior officials included the right of individual petition (with jurisdiction of a European court optional). This was the vital innovation of the European regional system, as was explained by Teitgen early in the drafting process:

> That the international machinery should be at the disposal of the victims is … the only means we have of persuading the men and women of Europe that something new has been done and that an advance has been achieved. We must say to them that even if the states take no further interest in them, and even if no one takes any action on their behalf, they may, by virtue of their dignity as men, avail themselves on their own behalf of an international organ of protection.[58]

The UK government did not share this vision. As Marston explains, 'notwithstanding the Attlee administration's willingness to subscribe to statements of

---

[56] The United Kingdom was joined in its opposition to the establishment of a court by Luxembourg, Norway, Denmark, Turkey, and Greece.

[57] This was a controversial right for Sir Stafford Cripps, the Chancellor of the Exchequer, who claimed that 'a Government committed to the policy of a planned economy could not ratify it' (CAB 128/18, Minutes of Cabinet Meeting, 1 August 1950). The objection was not convincing, however, and, as Bevin noted, Art 8 'appears to have nothing to do with economic planning,' adding 'I should only look foolish if I tried to oppose it on those terms' (FO 371/88754, telegram to Prime Minister, 3 August 1950). See E Wicks, 'The UK Government's Perceptions of the European Convention on Human Rights at the Time of Entry' [2000] *PL* 438, at 444–45.

[58] G Robertson, *Collected Edition of the Travaux Préparatoires* (The Hague, Martinus Nijhoff, 1977), Vol 2, p 178.

human rights and even to take the lead in their formulation, it set its face against their implementation by a system of individual petition and a court of compulsory jurisdiction.'[59] The government's objections to individual petition were twofold.[60] First, there was a widespread concern among members of the government that an individual petition would be used for political purposes by members of the Communist party. In other words, that it would be 'just as much at the service of democracy's enemies as at its friends.'[61] Le Quesne, one of the UK's representatives to the Council of Europe, described the concern as follows: 'It seemed likely that in the present circumstances of the cold war the right of an individual to submit such complaints was liable to abuse and could become more a weapon of political warfare than a means of ventilating genuine grievances.'[62] Thus, while the Communist threat was a spur for the creation of a western European organisation and a human rights convention, in the minds of members of the UK government it also cautioned against introducing a right of individual petition. A second important concern for the UK government at this time was its colonial empire. The Colonial Secretary, Jim Griffiths, strongly opposed individual petition on the following basis:

> The bulk of the people in most Colonies are still politically immature and the essence of good government among such people is respect for one single undivided authority which they are taught to recognise as responsible for their affairs. The right of individual petition to an international body would obscure this principle.[63]

Thus, when the draft Convention went before the Cabinet for the first time on 1 August 1950, the Cabinet 'expressed a violent if ill-informed dislike' of it.[64] The Cabinet criticised the Foreign Office for allowing the draft Convention to reach such an advanced state of preparation before being brought before ministers and requested that the draft be remitted to the member state governments for further consideration.[65] Bevin refused to make this request but instead succeeded in convincing the committee of ministers to agree to make individual petition an optional provision.[66] Thus satisfied, the Cabinet agreed to approve the Convention on 24 October 1950. The reason for doing so was clear: politically the government felt that it had no choice. For example, a Foreign Office paper prepared by Bevin for the Cabinet meeting described the position as follows:

---

[59] G Marston, 'The United Kingdom's Part in the Preparation of the European Convention on Human Rights, 1950' (1993) 42 *ICLQ* 796, at 825.

[60] For more detail on this point, see Wicks, n 57 above, at 447–50.

[61] *Travaux Préparatoires*, n 58 above, Vol 2, p 256 (Mr Nally).

[62] FO 371/88754, Memorandum by Le Quesne, 20 July 1950.

[63] CAB 129/41, Memorandum by Griffiths, 28 July 1950.

[64] FO 371/88755, Minute by Le Quesne, 11 September 1950.

[65] See Simpson, n 4 above, p 729.

[66] See *ibid*, pp 731–32, and Wicks, n 57 above, p 451.

> We must sign the convention on human rights, which is the only positive achievement of the Council of Europe to date. The compromise reached on this within the committee of ministers was agreed in order to attain our adherence, and a retreat on our part at this stage would put us in a most embarrassing position.[67]

Even Lord Jowitt, the Lord Chancellor, and the most vociferous opponent of the Convention,[68] regarded it as 'inevitable that for political reasons we must – in some form or other – accept this draft convention,' even though 'from the point of view of administration of law', Jowitt regarded this necessity as 'an unqualified misfortune'.[69]

The draft of the Convention agreed to by the committee of ministers faced one final challenge from the consultative assembly when this body proposed a number of amendments which would have transformed the Convention once more. However, the committee of ministers rejected these amendments (with the exception of the proposed additional rights of property and education which it was agreed would be further considered for inclusion in a protocol). The Convention, in a form acceptable to the UK government, was finally signed on 4 November 1950.[70] In accordance with the Ponsonby Rule, the Convention was laid before Parliament for 21 days prior to its ratification.[71] No objections to ratification were raised.[72] The Convention was ratified by the United Kingdom on 8 March 1951. The government entered no reservations to its provisions, but did not accept the two optional provisions relating to individual petition, and jurisdiction of the European Court of Human Rights.[73] Perhaps most significantly, no changes were made to domestic law. As Marston has noted,

[67] CAB 129/42, Memorandum for Cabinet by Bevin, 19 October 1950.

[68] Lord Jowitt said that the Convention was 'so vague and woolly that it may mean almost anything' (CAB 130/64, Memorandum by Lord Chancellor for discussion at ministerial meeting on 18 October 1950).

[69] *Ibid.*

[70] An additional protocol containing three further rights was signed on 20 March 1952. The United Kingdom entered its only reservation to Art 2 of this protocol. On this issue, see Simpson, n 4 above, ch 15 for more details.

[71] The 'Ponsonby Rule' describes the practice under which the text of treaties signed by the United Kingdom will be laid before Parliament in the form of a Command Paper for a period of 21 days, after which the executive will proceed to ratification. Ponsonby himself (the Under-Secretary of State for Foreign Affairs, who outlined this 'intention' of government during a second reading of the Treaty of Peace (Turkey) Bill in the House of Commons on 1 April 1 1924) claimed the practice would: 'give Parliament, not arbitrarily in this or that case, but completely in all cases, an opportunity for the examination, consideration, and if need be the discussion of all treaties before they reach the final stage of ratification' (HC Deb, Vol 171, col 2002, 1 April 1924). This worthwhile goal is overly optimistic. Whilst the practice of laying signed treaties before Parliament does ensure the legislature is informed of the actions of the executive on the international plane (and is to that extent preferable to the situation previously), it does little more. Furthermore, it should be noted that the 'Ponsonby Rule' is in fact a misnomer. It is not a 'rule', because it is not binding upon the government. It is merely a statement by a junior minister as to the intentions of the 1924 government. Nevertheless, over 70 years later, the 'rule' is still being practised, suggesting that Ponsonby was prescient when he spoke of the 'paradox that under the British Constitution, it is rules that depend solely on practice and usage which are the most immutable' (*ibid*, col 2003).

[72] A Lester, 'Fundamental Rights: The United Kingdom Isolated?' [1984] *PL* 46, at 54.

[73] Arts 25 and 46, respectively, in the ECHR as drafted.

for political reasons the Attlee administration preferred to have the Convention regarded as a statement of general principles rather than – what it really was – as an internationally binding instrument: the absence both of reservations and of implementing legislation would serve to emphasise such an impression.[74]

However, a rubicon had been crossed. The UK government was committed, at international law, to protecting (certain of) the rights of its citizens. As Merrills has noted, the proper relations between the citizen and the state were now 'a legal as well as a political issue.'[75] The implications for the British constitution from this new approach were to prove enormous.

III. The ECHR and the British Constitution

a) The Treaty in Force

The ECHR came into force on 3 September 1953.[76] For some time to come, however, the practical importance of the entry into force of the Convention was minimal. As Simpson correctly notes, this was not unexpected because the raison d'etre of the convention was 'to preserve the liberty which was already enjoyed in Western Europe.'[77] A convention which sought to preserve the democratic nature of western European states would, it might be expected, be superfluous until a threat to democracy arose. This was indeed the view of the UK government when negotiating the terms of the ECHR: 'What was desired was to set up an effective organisation which could take action immediately if, as a result of political changes in any country, the observance of those rights was threatened.'[78] In the absence of such 'political changes' – presumably a communist takeover – the UK government could feel safe from interference. However, this was a mistaken assumption. As early as 1956 (only three years after the Convention came into force), the United Kingdom was challenged by Greece on the basis of human rights abuses in Cyprus.[79] It immediately became obvious that this convention was not only aimed at non-democratic governments but could also be used against ostensibly democratic regimes which nevertheless were violating the rights of their citizens. As Simpson graphically explains: 'An export trade in

---

[74] Marston, n 59 above, at 826.

[75] JG Merrills, *The Development of International Law by the European Court of Human Rights* (Manchester, Manchester University Press, 1988), p 2.

[76] This is the date on which Luxembourg became the tenth state to ratify the Convention.

[77] Simpson, n 4 above, p 809.

[78] Samuel Hoare, Deputy Under-Secretary in the Home Office, in *Travaux Preparatoires*, n 58 above, Vol IV, p 106..

[79] On this issue, see Simpson, n 4 above, ch 18.

human rights had suddenly taken on the appearance of an import trade and a most unwelcome one at that.'[80]

The Greek application of 1956 was only the beginning. By 1975 (and subsequent to the United Kingdom accepting individual petition and the jurisdiction of the Court[81]) the Strasbourg institutions had indicated their willingness to be pro-active in interpreting the Convention rights. For example, in *Golder v United Kingdom*,[82] which was the first case against the United Kingdom considered by the European Court of Human Rights and in which a violation was found, the Court implied into Article 6 a right of access to the courts. The Court was adamant that its judgment did not represent an 'extensive interpretation forcing new obligations on the contracting states,'[83] but held that the express protection of a right to a fair and public hearing within a reasonable time before an independent and impartial tribunal would be meaningless without a prior right of access to the courts: 'The fair, public and expeditious characteristics of judicial proceedings are of no value at all if there are no judicial proceedings.'[84] This is a logical argument. Nevertheless, the result of the *Golder* judgment is that a contracting state is bound by more than just the rights which appear on the face of the Convention. As the counsel for the United Kingdom argued before the Commission in this case, 'the United Kingdom had no intention of assuming, and did not know that it was expected to assume' an obligation to accord a right of access to the courts.[85] And yet, in international law it was held to be bound by such a right. The Court did accept that such an implied right would also necessitate implied limitations, but this only substantiates allegations of judicial legislating by the Court.

The UK judge, Sir Gerald Fitzmaurice, issued a strong dissenting judgment in *Golder* in which he argued that the ECHR had 'broken entirely new ground internationally, making heavy inroads on some of the most cherished preserves of governments in the sphere of their domestic jurisdiction'[86] and that such considerations must be said:

> not only to justify, but positively to demand, a cautious and conservative interpretation, particularly … where extensive constructions might have the effect of imposing upon the contracting states obligations they had not really meant to assume or would not have understood themselves to be assuming.[87]

---

[80] *Ibid*, p 923.
[81] On this matter, see below.
[82] (1975) Series A, No 18; 1 EHRR 524.
[83] *Ibid*, para 36.
[84] *Ibid*, para 35.
[85] See n 24 in Fitzmaurice's dissent, in which he quotes from the verbatim record of oral hearing on merits held in Strasbourg before the Commission on 16–17 December 1971.
[86] Fitzmaurice's dissent, para 38.
[87] *Ibid*, para 39.

The majority disagreed and Nicol has characterised this as a dispute between two competing philosophies:

> a minority of judges believed that the purpose of the ECHR should be solely to ward off fascism and communism, whereas the majority wanted the ECHR to have a more far-reaching character … In other words, the disagreement in the courtroom replicated the disagreement of the negotiating chambers.[88]

Thus, even though the United Kingdom was successful in ensuring that the Convention was narrowly defined, it now faced a further battle in respect of the interpretation of the Convention rights. By papering over the disagreement as to the ECHR's purpose, Nicol argues that 'the negotiators simply passed the baton to the judges to continue the disagreement.'[89]

A further example of such a philosophical disagreement can be seen in *Tyrer v United Kingdom* in 1978, when the majority declared that the ECHR 'is a living instrument which … must be interpreted in the light of present-day conditions.'[90] This principle has been of fundamental importance in the evolution of human rights law in Europe. It has enabled the Strasbourg institutions to update a 1950s document so as to continue to serve a relevant role in the twenty-first century.[91] But in the 1970s, when the principle was developed, it encapsulated the broader tension over the role of the Convention and its interpretive organs.[92] The United Kingdom was quickly learning that it may have taken on more than it had bargained for with this particular international treaty.

b) The Impact upon the UK Constitution

Ratification of the ECHR transformed the UK constitution in three discernible ways: by introducing an external legal influence; by entrenching the concept of a democratic society; and by transforming the nature of rights under the law. Each of these innovations will now be considered in turn.

The introduction of an external legal influence into the UK constitution is, perhaps, the most obvious change wrought by the ratification of the ECHR. Feldman has described this as follows: 'other states acquire an interest in the ways in which a state is treating people within its jurisdiction. That interest can be pursued not only through international diplomacy, but also through

---

[88] D Nicol, 'Original Intent and the European Convention on Human Rights' [2005] *PL* 152, at 167.

[89] *Ibid*, at 172.

[90] (1978) Series A, No 26; 2 EHRR 1, para 31.

[91] For example, the UK's failure to provide legal recognition of a transsexual's change of gender was finally declared to be a violation of Art 8's right to respect for private life in *Goodwin v United Kingdom* (2002) 35 EHRR 18 (after a series of cases in which a violation was not found) due to the changing perceptions of personal morality throughout Europe.

[92] Judge Fitzmaurice again issued a strongly worded dissent in *Tyrer*.

international law.'[93] This was a landmark change and, for the reasons explained above, was only accepted by the UK government because of the perception of a communist threat within Europe. Simpson makes an important point when he explains that the reason underlying the UK's willingness to accept the Convention 'must be sought not in the history of English constitutional thought, but in the general political history of the period.'[94] To agree to be bound by international obligations which had no direct reciprocal advantages for the United Kingdom was an unprecedented move. It sits especially uneasily with the dominant theory of parliamentary sovereignty under which Dicey had convinced most English lawyers that there was only one supreme lawmaker under the constitution and that it was unlimited in law. The involvement of international bodies and other states in the UK government's relations with its own citizens has no precedent in constitutional history (hence its categorisation as a 'key moment' in this book), and yet is entirely explainable in the context of international politics following the Second World War. The perceived political and military advantages in ensuring that other western European states did not violate the rights of their citizens was felt by the UK government to outweigh the dangers inherent in subjecting its own treatment of its citizens to external perusal. Of course, the export theory of human rights helped here: the UK government did not imagine that its own treatment of individuals would necessitate external intervention because of the evolution of a democratic constitution. Nevertheless, the UK's commitment in Article 1 ECHR to 'secure' the Convention rights to all within its jurisdiction, coupled with Article 32's acceptance of the decisions of the Committee of Ministers as binding, imposed legal limits upon the freedom of all branches of the UK government. As Merrills describes, 'when governments know that policies must be justified in an international forum an additional element enters their decision-making.'[95] The addition of a new international law element into the UK constitution transformed the nature of the constitution so that, from 1953, it can no longer be explained in purely domestic law terms. The ECHR (and subsequently other human rights treaties) influences the direction of the constitution and the actions of those who act under it.

The second major influence stemming from ratification of the ECHR is the entrenchment of the concept of a democratic society. The fact that the Convention is aimed at preserving democracy is evident from a number of sources. For example, the Preamble to the ECHR declares the contracting states'

> profound belief in those fundamental freedoms which are the foundation of justice and peace in the world and are best maintained on the one hand by an effective political democracy and on the other by a common understanding and observance of the human rights upon which they depend.

[93] DJ Feldman, *Civil Liberties and Human Rights in England and Wales*, 2nd edn (Oxford, Oxford University Press, 2002), p 35.
[94] Simpson, n 4 above, p 18.
[95] Merrills, n 75 above, p 1.

The terms of the ECHR also prioritise the preservation of democracy by identifying this goal as the only justification for a limitation of the rights to private and family life, freedom to manifest one's religion or belief, freedom of expression, and freedom of peaceful assembly and association with others.[96] In other words, the rights in the ECHR must be upheld by the contracting states except when to do so would threaten one of the core elements of democratic society itself.[97] In addition, it was clear during the negotiations of the ECHR that the UK government perceived the primary goal of the Convention to be the preservation of democracy in western Europe. For example, one of the UK's representatives to the Council of Europe, Lynn Ungoed-Thomas,[98] argued that 'what we are concerned with is not every case of injustice which happens in a particular country, but with the question whether a country is ceasing to be democratic.'[99] As I have argued elsewhere, Ungoed-Thomas's assumption that the Council of Europe should not be concerned with 'every case of injustice' is open to criticism in that such small injustices may gradually diminish the democracy of a state and, indeed, may be an early warning of such a diminution.[100] But it is clear that the United Kingdom committed to the ECHR largely because it foresaw the value of human rights in the task of preserving democracy, especially in other vulnerable European states.[101]

Previous chapters have highlighted the slow but steady development of democracy under, and becoming a core part of, the UK constitution. It was argued in chapter 4 that the 1832 Reform Act represented the opening of a door to democratic governance, and subsequent extensions of the franchise consolidated democracy as an important aspect of the constitution. Furthermore, the 1911 entrenchment of House of Commons' supremacy, discussed in the previous chapter, can also be regarded as a natural consequence of the evolution of a democratic constitution. Thus, by the early 1950s, democracy had acquired a fundamental position within the UK constitution. The acceptance of an international commitment to preserve that concept, both in constitutional theory but also, most crucially, in constitutional practice by means of laws and executive practices which uphold, rather than violate, a number of specified rights, can be regarded as the final confirmation that the UK constitution's democratic nature is inviolable.[102] That this should arise from a human rights treaty is rather ironic,

---

[96] Arts 8–11 all include the phrase 'necessary in a democratic society' as a core element of any permissible limitation or restriction upon the specified rights.

[97] Examples of such core elements to be found in Arts 8–11 include the protection of national security and public safety, the prevention of disorder or crime, and the protection of health and morals.

[98] Ungoed-Thomas was a Labour MP for 17 years and served as Solicitor-General in 1951, later becoming a High Court judge.

[99] *Travaux Preparatoires*, n 58 above, Vol II, p 166.

[100] See Wicks, n 57 above, p 442.

[101] See Moravcsik's theory on this: Moravcsik, n 37 above, especially at 233.

[102] Of course, as discussed in ch 4, further international co-operation and domestic diffusion of power has more recently threatened to overwhelm the traditional conception of democracy. (See ch 4, pp 80–81.)

however, as, although protection of rights is a core element of a democratic society, it may also conflict with the wishes of the majority. So, once more (as in chapter 4), the complexity of democracy as a concept becomes clear: it requires far more than merely majoritarian government. It is for this reason that the extension of the franchise in the late nineteenth and early twentieth centuries was not sufficient in itself to create, or ensure, a democratic form of government. With the legal entrenchment of human rights in the ECHR, the final important piece of the democracy jigsaw fell into place in 1953.

The third and final impact upon the constitution from the ratification of the ECHR is a transformation in the nature of individual freedoms. Prior to the ECHR, the UK constitution sought to protect a residual idea of liberty: 'Until recently, the general approach to protecting rights in the United Kingdom was to think in terms, not of liberties or freedoms, but liberty or freedom. The dominant idea has been that of an undifferentiated mass of liberty.'[103] This idea of, in Feldman's words, 'an undifferentiated mass of liberty' is a legacy of the Diceyian tradition under which an individual would be free to do anything not prohibited by the law. Under a constitution which encourages Parliament to believe itself to be free to make any laws, this was a very precarious freedom. Its residual nature ensured that no rights or freedoms were guaranteed to endure. The UK's traditional mistrust of codified lists of rights (and codified constitutional law in general) had only occasionally been overcome in constitutional history (as, for example, with the 1689 Bill of Rights, discussed in chapter 1). Commitment to a codified list of rights in the form of an international human rights treaty was, therefore, a significant step for the United Kingdom. Indeed, many members of the Attlee administration remained distrustful of such a commitment and unconvinced of the need for it. The Lord Chancellor, Lord Jowitt, contrasted unfavourably the 'half-baked scheme' of the Convention with the UK's 'whole system of law, which we have laboriously built up over the centuries.'[104] The commitment to abide by the specified rights was, therefore, an important change in direction for the protection of rights under the UK constitution. As such, it had a significant impact upon judicial reasoning within the UK courts. Long before the ECHR was incorporated into domestic law in the Human Rights Act 1998, English judges were using it to increase human rights protection in domestic law. Beloff and Mountfield, writing in 1996, helpfully identified 12 ways in which the ECHR was being given some domestic effect by the courts.[105] The three most influential of these are: its use as an aid to construction of ambiguous primary or delegated legislation;[106] its use to resolve uncertainty, or increase completeness, in the common law;[107] and its use to determine the way in which

---

[103] Feldman, n 93 above, p 70.

[104] LCO 2/6274, Note by Jowitt to Dalton, 3 August 1950.

[105] MJ Beloff and H Mountfield, 'Unconventional Behaviour? Judicial Uses of the European Convention in England and Wales' [1996] *EHRLR* 467, at 489–91.

[106] *R v Miah* [1974] 1 WLR 683 at 694, HL.

[107] *Derbyshire County Council v Times Newspapers* [1992] 1 QB 770 at 812 (Balcombe LJ) and 830 (Butler-Sloss LJ), CA.

judicial (but not administrative) discretion should be exercised.[108] Furthermore, the ECHR served a more general role in influencing the courts' judgments. This was recognised, for example, in *Airedale NHS Trust v Bland* when Lord Goff described the ECHR as 'a begetter, explicitly or implicitly, of an increased sensitivity to fundamental rights generally.'[109] It would be misleading to give the impression that all was well in the world of individual rights in the United Kingdom subsequent to 1953. The UK judges were limited in their freedom to refer to the ECHR as a guide due to the failure of successive governments to incorporate the Convention into domestic law. Nevertheless, the impact which the ECHR did undoubtedly have upon judicial reasoning, especially in terms of introducing the idea of codified, positive rights, as opposed to the residual idea of liberty, cannot be ignored. Furthermore, it was, perhaps, inevitable that, once the UK government had agreed to be bound at international law by the Convention rights, further steps towards effective enforcement of these obligations would follow.

IV. Subsequent Developments

a) 1966: Acceptance of Individual Petition

As discussed above, in 1950 the UK government refused to accept the optional provisions of individual petition and the jurisdiction of the European Court of Human Rights. The Attorney-General at the time, Sir Hartley Shawcross, regarded individual petition as 'wholly opposed to the theory of responsible Government.'[110] In stark contrast, by 1965 the Lord Chancellor, Lord Gardiner, was able to say with confidence that the acceptance of individual petition 'would cost us nothing.'[111] The most plausible reason for this change of heart by the government's legal officers is that in the years between 1953 and 1965 the ECHR was 'a sleeping beauty (or slumbering beast, depending upon one's viewpoint).'[112] The Commission had been 'building confidence in the system among governments,'[113] and the Court had only decided two cases.[114] In 1965, therefore, Lord Gardiner was able to say that 'we confidently anticipate there will be hardly

---

[108] *AG v Guardian Newspapers (No 2)* [1987] 3 All ER 306.
[109] [1993] AC 789 at 864, HL.
[110] LCO 2/5570, Letter by Shawcross, 4 October 1950.
[111] Quoted in Lord Lester of Herne Hill, 'UK Acceptance of the Strasbourg Jurisdiction: What really went on in Whitehall in 1965' [1998] *PL* 237, at 239.
[112] Lord Lester of Herne Hill and L Clapinska, 'Human Rights and the British Constitution' in J Jowell and D Oliver, *The Changing Constitution*, 5th edn (Oxford, Oxford University Press, 2004), p 68.
[113] *Ibid.*
[114] *Lawless v Ireland* (1961) Series A, No 3; 1 EHRR 15, and *De Becker v Belgium* (1962) Series A, No 4; 1 EHRR 43.

any petitions of merit, in which case, apart from a certain amount of wasteful effort in Whitehall, the existence of the right of individual petition will do us no harm at all.'[115] Once the Convention rights had been accepted as binding at international law, and once earlier UK fears of communist abuse and colonial instability had been displaced, it was clearly felt that the acceptance of the optional provisions would be of little significance to the United Kingdom.[116] This probably explains why there was no Cabinet discussion of the acceptance of the optional provisions, no legislation introduced into Parliament, and no public consultation.[117] It was simply not seen as a significant step. But very soon the true impact of the acceptance of individual petition and the jurisdiction of the Court would become obvious.

The first individual petition against the United Kingdom in which a violation was found to have been committed was the case of *Golder* in 1975.[118] From then on, the successful petitions snowballed. The reactions of successive UK governments were not favourable. For example, there was outcry at the 1995 *McCann v United Kingdom* judgment, in which the United Kingdom was found to be the first contracting party to have violated the right to life.[119] Crucially, however, even if the government has often fundamentally disagreed with the Court's decisions, it has always complied with them (albeit often after considerable delay). The international law obligation to abide by the judgments of the Court has always been taken seriously by successive UK governments.[120] This in turn has increased the public knowledge of the Strasbourg procedure and Convention.

[115] Lester, n 111 above, at 249. Lord Gardiner continued by arguing that 'Past experience shows how very few cases go to the Court …' This was soon to change.

[116] The one exception at Cabinet level was the Home Secretary, Sir Frank Soskice, who objected to the acceptance of the compulsory jurisdiction of the Court and favoured the retention of 'utmost flexibility in defending ourselves against individual petitions' by continuing with enforcement solely by the political body of the Committee of Ministers rather than by the legal body of the Court (FO 371/184368, Letter from Soskice, 2 August 1965). Lord Gardiner understandably responded by pointing out that 'critics would probably suggest that we were seeking to achieve by political means what we could not achieve before independent judges' (FO 371/184368, Letter from Lord Chancellor to Foreign Secretary, 9 August 1965).

[117] Lester and Clapinska, n 112 above, p 67.

[118] As discussed above, this judgment indicated that the Court was willing to adopt a broad interpretation of the Convention's obligations.

[119] (1995) 21 EHRR 97; Series A, No 324. For criticism of the decision of the majority in this case, see Nicholas Bonsor, Minister of State for Foreign and Commonwealth Affairs: 'The judgement of the majority, based on no new evidence and defying common sense, has done nothing for the standing of the court in the United Kingdom' (HC Deb, Vol 265, col 60, written answers). Also, see the Attorney-General praising the view of the minority, claiming it was one with which 'every sensible person should agree' (HC Deb, Vol 265, col 14).

[120] The only possible exception has been on matters relating to the prevention of terrorism, where derogations have been entered under Art 15 due to the core national interest which is regarded as being under threat. The latest derogation, following the terrorist attacks of 11 September 2001, and its use to attempt to justify detention without trial of foreign nationals suspected of being terrorists (Anti-Terrorism, Crime and Security Act 2001, s 23) is regrettable evidence that even a binding international law treaty can never compel complete obedience to the rights of individuals, especially where national security is perceived to be at issue. The House of Lords has issued a declaration of incompatibility in respect of this statutory provision notwithstanding the derogation order (*A v Secretary of State for Home Department* (2005) 2 WLR 87).

The key distinguishing feature of the ECHR when it was drafted – the involvement of individuals in ensuring effective implementation of the rights protected – was finally made relevant for UK citizens. The gradual increased involvement of individuals on the international plane, an arena traditionally reserved for states, added a new dimension to the idea of democratic society and, after 13 years of being excluded from this opportunity, in 1966 UK citizens finally had the chance to complain to an external body about any mistreatment by their government. The relationship between the UK government and its citizens, which faced its first major upheaval in 1953 when the relationship became a matter of law as well as politics, was fundamentally changed for ever by the introduction of individual petition. As welcome as this was, the possibility of petition to the Strasbourg institutions also cast light upon the absurdity of a European Court seeking to enforce Convention rights in the United Kingdom while domestic courts were prevented from doing so. The increased use, and publicity, of the right of individual petition to Strasbourg placed pressure on political parties in the United Kingdom to consider introducing the Convention rights into domestic law so that the long and expensive journey to Strasbourg could be reserved as a last resort rather than being the only option available. The extensive impact of the ratification of the ECHR (discussed in the previous section) had ensured an external influence in the constitution but had left an increasingly obvious gap: where was the protection for individual rights and freedoms under the domestic law? When the presence of this gap coincided with a Labour government obsessed with a need to modernise Britain and its constitution, it was perceived as time to bring rights home.

b) 1998 – The Human Rights Act

Until 1993 both major political parties were opposed to the incorporation of the ECHR into domestic law. In that year, following a major policy review (headed, incidentally, by Tony Blair), the Labour party changed its policy. The reasons for the change in policy can be discerned in the following quote from Mandelson and Liddle: '[W]ith a Bill of Rights enforced by a reformed independent judiciary, the modern age of citizenship will have begun and no one will ever be able to accuse Labour of being prepared to sacrifice individual rights on the altar of collectivist ideology.'[121] Ewing has accurately described this statement as 'simultaneously hyperbolic and defensive.'[122] When Labour was elected to government in 1997, its manifesto promised wide-ranging reform of the UK constitution, from

[121] P Mandelson and R Liddle, *The Blair Revolution – Can New Labour Deliver?* (London, Faber & Faber, 1996), p 196.
[122] KD Ewing, 'The Human Rights Act and Parliamentary Democracy' (1999) 62 *MLR* 79, at 81. Indeed, these two emotions could even be regarded as representing the two key aims of New Labour in respect of the entirety of its programme of constitutional reform: to take radical (but populist) action and to live up to its name of New Labour by avoiding all accusations of worshipping at 'the alter of collectivist ideology.'

devolution for Scotland, Wales and Northern Ireland,[123] to parliamentary reform in terms of both reform of the House of Lords and electoral reform (the latter, regrettably, never materialising). This 'flood' of constitutional legislation, as Lord Bingham has referred to it,[124] included, in the first parliamentary session of the new government, incorporation of the ECHR in the Human Rights Act 1998 (HRA).

This Act is in essence a compromise. It seeks to increase effective protection for human rights by, in the terms of the Bill's populist tagline, 'bringing rights home' from Strasbourg to the domestic constitutional arena, but it seeks to do so within the confines of the existing constitutional structure. The Home Secretary at the time, Jack Straw, explained that, 'Having decided that we should incorporate the convention, the most fundamental question that we faced was how to do that in a manner that strengthened and did not undermine, the sovereignty of Parliament.'[125] The government, therefore, drafted and enacted the HRA with the preservation of its orthodox view of parliamentary sovereignty[126] as an essential pre-requisite. The reason why this consideration was regarded as so important has also been explained by the Home Secretary: '[it] is no part of the project to call into question constitutional arrangements that have evolved in this country to make us one of the world's most stable democracies.'[127] This statement of intent is disappointing because, contrary to the Home Secretary's assertion, to 'call into question' traditional orthodoxies, albeit with due respect, would seem both entirely appropriate for a majority government with a mandate for widespread constitutional reform and also entirely possible under an evolving constitution.

Nevertheless, the government's intent was clear, and thus the HRA had to bring rights home within the confines of the existing UK constitution. This was achieved by the adoption of what Straw has acknowledged is a peculiarly British approach,[128] with an emphasis on statutory interpretation, parliamentary scrutiny and an innovative means of avoiding judicial review of Acts of Parliament, entitled declarations of incompatibility. Section 3 of the HRA imposes an obligation upon domestic courts to interpret legislation in a way which is compatible with the Convention rights 'so far as it is possible to do so.' While this 'goes far beyond' the previous rule in the view of the Lord Chancellor of the time, Lord Irvine of Lairg,[129] it is not a radical change in approach but extends the

---

[123] This important reform will be discussed in detail in ch 8.

[124] Lord Bingham of Cornhill, 'The Evolving Constitution' [2002] *EHRLR* 1, at 1.

[125] HC Deb, Vol 306, col 769, 16 February 1998.

[126] Straw's understanding of the requirements of parliamentary sovereignty is strictly orthodox: 'I mean that Parliament must be competent to make any law on any matter of its choosing' (*ibid*, col 770).

[127] *Ibid.*

[128] 'We came up with our own approach – it is a British answer to a British problem – fundamental to which is the sovereignty of Parliament' (HC Deb, Vol 313, col 420, 3 June 1998).

[129] Lord Irvine of Lairg, 'The Development of Human Rights in Britain under an Incorporated Convention on Human Rights' [1998] *PL* 221 at 228.

judiciary's pre-existing and important interpretive role. Section 4 introduces a new judicial power in the form of a declaratory power. If the court is unable to interpret primary legislation in a manner compatible with the Convention rights, it may issue a declaration of incompatibility. This 'does not affect the validity, continuing operation or enforcement of the provision in respect of which it is given.'[130] This provision – a direct response to the perceived inability of the courts to strike down primary legislation under the UK constitution – ensures that it is Parliament which retains the ability to determine whether to comply with the Convention rights or not. This responsibility is supplemented by section 19, under which a minister must make a statement of compatibility when introducing a new Bill or, if he cannot do so, explain that he wishes the Bill to proceed notwithstanding its incompatibility. While this ensures that Parliament can still make any law, even one violating the ECHR, it may make it politically more difficult to do so by drawing parliamentary, media, and public attention to the intended violation. Thus, sections 3, 4, and 19 work together to ensure that Parliament is ultimately free to violate rights, provided that it circumvents some obstacles first. None of this detracts from the fact that the United Kingdom remains bound at international law to comply with the ECHR and with the judgments of the Strasbourg Court. The fact that Parliament is now discouraged, but not prevented, from legislating contrary to the ECHR is a welcome addition to the arsenal of rights protection, but it is only a very small piece of a much larger picture.

The preservation of parliamentary sovereignty under the constitution means that Parliament can chose to ignore a declaration of incompatibility or, if the courts take an expansive approach under section 3, Parliament could chose to legislate again to reinstate its intended violation. There is no guarantee, therefore, that an individual's rights will receive effective protection from Parliament under the HRA.[131] Furthermore, not all of the rights protected in the ECHR have been incorporated into domestic law. The exclusion of the additional protocols to which the United Kingdom has not agreed to be bound at international law is understandable. Similarly, it is perhaps understandable that Article 1 of the ECHR, the general obligation to 'secure' the rights to all within the contracting state's jurisdiction, is not an appropriate clause for incorporation as it is directed at the states in international law. However, Article 13, the right to an effective remedy, is also omitted from the Convention rights in the HRA. This means that, if a violation of one of the other Convention rights is found by a domestic court and if that court is unable or unwilling to provide an effective remedy, there is no recourse within domestic law. The United Kingdom remains bound by Article 13 at international law, and so an individual's recourse in such a situation would be

---

[130] Section 4(6)(a) of the HRA.

[131] The government reaction to *A v Secretary of State for Home Department* (2005) 2 WLR 87 revealed the potential ineffectiveness of a declaration of incompatibility. However, rights will be protected against violation from a public body under s 6 of the HRA. It is perhaps on this aspect of domestic law that the HRA makes the most significant contribution to the protection of rights.

to Strasbourg. Both the failure to incorporate Article 13 and the retention of Parliament's ability to violate the Convention rights mean that rights have not been brought home at all. An individual will often need to proceed to Strasbourg in order to obtain justice, and the HRA represents little more than an additional domestic remedy which needs to be exhausted before proceeding to that European Court.

This brings into question the relationship between the Strasbourg Court and the domestic courts implementing the HRA. Section 2(1) declares that domestic courts 'must take into account' the jurisprudence of the Strasbourg institutions. This is a fascinating provision, because it tells us two important facts while omitting to answer a crucial third question. First, it tells us that the Strasbourg jurisprudence is not binding upon domestic courts. This means that the domestic courts could legitimately choose to interpret the Convention rights in a manner different from that pursued at Strasbourg so that two distinct lines of reasoning on particular rights might emerge. Second, section 2(1) makes clear that the obligation to 'take into account' the jurisprudence of Strasbourg is mandatory by the use of the word 'must'. Thus, a domestic court which ignored or failed to cite a relevant Strasbourg judgment would have acted unlawfully under the HRA. However, section 2(1) leaves unanswered the question of what 'take into account' actually means. Presumably, it does not require following a Strasbourg judgment for that would amount to being bound by it, which was deliberately avoided in the wording of the HRA.[132] Section 2(1) is a significant provision because it opens the door to the development of a domestic law of human rights. The Convention rights can be used as a mere launching pad from which the courts can proceed to develop rights in a way most suited to the British state and constitution. It is this possibility which represents the HRA's greatest potential, because if domestic courts merely follow wherever Strasbourg leads then the HRA is merely one more (not always effective) layer of protection for the ECHR. A genuine domestic law of human rights would be a much more worthwhile venture, subject, of course, to the ECHR's international supervision to ensure that the minimum requirements of the Convention are met. Whether such a domestic law will develop, however, is entirely in the hands of the British judges, and it may take some time. In the future, it may be that 1998 can be regarded as a key moment in British constitutional history because of the opportunity which the HRA offered for domestic protection of human rights under the constitution. But, for now, the HRA can only really be regarded as an offshoot of international protection of human rights, which was a landmark development which came into fruition for the UK constitution in 1953.

---

[132] See E Wicks, 'Taking Account of Strasbourg? The British Judiciary's Approach to Interpreting Convention Rights' (2005) 11 *European Public Law* 401.

V. Conclusion

Before 1953 the UK constitution was a self-contained entity. It regulated the relationship between the state and the individual, and between the different parts of government, on purely domestic terms. In 1953, however, the government of the time introduced an international element into the relationship between the state and the individual. The evolving nature of the constitution enabled this international element to be incorporated into the constitution and to transform the nature of rights and freedoms in the United Kingdom. No longer was there solely an idea of liberty but, rather, a specified list of positive rights and freedoms by which the government had agreed to abide. No longer was the relationship between the government and its citizens solely a matter of domestic jurisdiction but, rather, the concern of an international treaty and the regional bodies established under it. And underlying these radical changes was the idea of preserving democracy within Europe and, by default, within the United Kingdom itself. The moves towards a democratic form of government in the late nineteenth and early twentieth centuries were now supplemented by a belated recognition that the protection of human rights is essential if democracy is to survive and prosper. Thus, the international protection of human rights could serve to entrench a democratic form of government throughout western Europe. Even if in 1950 the UK government was oblivious to the need for active protection of rights within the United Kingdom, and of the precarious nature of democracy without such active protection even in a state where a form of democracy is long-established, by 1998 when the ECHR was finally incorporated into domestic law, the then Lord Chancellor felt able to acknowledge the complexity of the relationship between democracy and human rights:

> In a democracy it is right that the majority should govern. But that is precisely why it is also right that the human rights of individuals and minorities should be protected by law. I am convinced that incorporation of the European convention into our domestic law will deliver a modern reconciliation of the inevitable tension between the democratic right of the majority to exercise political power and the democratic need of individuals and minorities to have their human rights secured.[133]

Lord Irvine is entirely correct to recognise that, far from being unnecessary, rights protection is fundamental to the survival of democracy (even if his incorporation of the Convention rights was subject to the perceived need to preserve Parliament's freedom to violate rights). The evolving recognition of the need for human rights protection in order to secure British democracy is indicative of a wider trend. The impact of the ECHR on the United Kingdom has also evolved since 1951. Initial reluctance to permit individual petition, compulsory jurisdiction of the European Court of Human Rights, and domestic incorporation of the

---

[133] HL Deb, Vol 582, col 1234, 3 November 1997 (Lord Irvine of Lairg).

rights have all been overcome. The ECHR is now closely entwined with the UK's democratic constitution. The evolution is such that Simpson has argued that 'It is because of what it has become … rather than what it originally was, that the convention has achieved its contemporary importance.'[134] We should not forget, however, that it is what the Convention originally was when the United Kingdom signed and ratified it in 1951 which has been the basis for all subsequent developments. If it has contemporary importance, it is because the original document had understated and unforeseen potential.

[134] Simpson, n 4 above, p 3.

7

1972 – The European Communities Act: European Legal Supremacy under the UK Constitution

One of the most fundamental changes to the UK constitution occurred in 1972 with the passage of the European Communities Act. Although a politically divisive issue at the time, the constitutional implications of the Act went largely unnoticed, at least by the public. It has increasingly become obvious, however, that this Act of Parliament shattered many traditional constitutional assumptions. The core idea of the constitution, promoted by Dicey, that Parliament can make or unmake any law, no longer holds true in its pure form and only survives when accompanied by extensive explanation. European legal supremacy now holds a central place in the UK constitution. The changes wrought by the 1972 Act raise issues of state and parliamentary sovereignty, democratic legitimacy and the hierarchy of laws. This chapter will begin by explaining the UK's relationship with the European Community (EC) from its formation to UK entry in 1973. The subsequent 1975 referendum on membership will be analysed with a view to determining the extent of democratic legitimacy for the fundamental constitutional changes introduced in the 1972 Act. These constitutional implications will then be subjected to detailed analysis with emphasis upon both parliamentary and state sovereignty debates. The previous chapter saw the introduction of the first significant external influence into the UK constitution; this chapter sees an external body of law centrally, and superiorly, located within the constitution. One academic debate discussed in this chapter goes to the heart of this entire book: can such a fundamental change to the pre-existing constitution be regarded merely as another evolutionary step or is it more accurately portrayed as an overturning of the current legal order and thus a revolution?

I. 1957–72: The EC before UK Entry

As was seen in chapter 6, the immediate post-war era was characterised by efforts to unite Western Europe in order to prevent further wars commencing in Europe and to counter the growing influence of the communist Soviet Union. These dual goals were pursued both by European states and, significantly, by the United States which, through the Marshall Plan, was providing vital financial aid for Europe to rebuild. It was this scheme which necessitated the first European organisation in order to administer the financial aid. Thus, in 1948 the Organisation for European Economic Co-operation was established.[1] Further European co-operation followed with the Brussels Treaty in 1948, culminating in the establishment of the Council of Europe in 1949. However, as discussed in chapter 6, the Council of Europe was a mainly intergovernmental organisation (as opposed to a supranational one), largely due to the insistence of the United Kingdom. The French government was dissatisfied with this, and Robert Schuman, the French foreign minister, proposed an alternative organisation which would focus upon the task of pooling French and German coal and steel resources. This was seen as a way of ensuring that Germany could not re-arm without the knowledge of France and was therefore designed to ensure the retention of peace and co-operation in Western Europe. A plan for a European Coal and Steel Community (ECSC) was drafted by Jean Monnet and included the establishment of a 'High Authority' (an executive institution), an Assembly, a Council (with representatives of national governments) and a Court of Justice. In 1951, the Treaty of Paris, establishing the ECSC, was signed by France, Germany, Italy, Belgium, the Netherlands and Luxembourg ('the Six'). Unlike the Council of Europe, it was a purportedly supranational organisation. Craig and de Búrca argue that it was a significant development because of what it symbolised, namely that 'for its architects and proponents, this Community was not merely about coal and steel, but represented a first step in the direction of the integration of Europe.'[2] That the French government, at least, had grander plans than merely co-operation on coal and steel was obvious in 1950 when it proposed, first, a European Defence Community (EDC) in the Pleven Plan and then, subsequently, a European Political Community (EPC). The EDC Treaty was signed by the Six in 1952, but both projects failed in 1954 when this Treaty was rejected by the French National Assembly. Attention then turned to economic integration instead, and on this the Six were more successful in forging onwards. In 1957 they signed the Treaties of Rome establishing two further Communities: a European Atomic Energy Community (Eurotom) and a European Economic Community (EEC). These two organisations would share the ECSC's Court of Justice and Assembly but a new executive body was created (the Commission) as well as a new Council.[3] As with the ECSC, these new Communities were decidedly supranational in nature. A new era in Western Europe had begun.

---

[1] OEEC. This organisation was later renamed the Organisation for Economic Co-operation and Development (OECD) in 1960.

[2] P Craig and G de Búrca, *EU Law: Text, Cases and Materials*, 3rd edn (Oxford, Oxford University Press, 2003), p 9.

[3] The institutions were finally merged in 1965.

The United Kingdom had played a part in some of the early European co-operation including as a signatory for the Brussels Treaty and a founder member of the Council of Europe. However, the United Kingdom did not sign the Treaties in 1951 and 1957 which established the three Communities. As Ellis and Tridimas note, the UK's attitude at that time 'seems to have been a somewhat lofty one. Undefeated and unoccupied in wartime, she remained confident in herself and her greatness.'[4] Hibbert continues this theme by noting that, even in the 1960s, popular feeling in the United Kingdom:

> took it for granted that Britain was a world power, entitled to a seat at all the top tables. Europe was not then a top table. In so far as it might eventually be a candidate to become a top table, it would be natural for Britain to belong to it. But first it would have to qualify.[5]

The supranational nature of the EEC, with its proposed pooling of sovereignty, was a disincentive for the United Kingdom and, as an alternative, it proposed a European Free Trade Area (FTA), which would differ from the EEC by being purely economic (with no question of furthering political integration).[6] The Stockholm Convention, establishing the FTA, was signed in July 1959 by the United Kingdom, Austria, Switzerland, Portugal, Norway, Sweden and Denmark. This marked a defeat, rather than a victory, for the United Kingdom, however, as the Six proceeded with their more closely integrated community, unperturbed by the UK's proposals for a looser free trade area as an alternative.

Within only a few years, the economic success of the EEC became obvious to the United Kingdom. In 1961, Macmillan's Conservative government took the decision to open negotiations with the Six for entry to the Communities. The main reasons for this change in approach were twofold. First, there was the economic reason for entry: there was no doubt that the Six's economies were thriving while the United Kingdom was falling behind in economic terms. Second, there were broader political reasons for entry: to enhance the global influence of the United Kingdom. By 1961 these two factors suggested, as Lord has explained, that further postponement of entry would:

> represent the greater recklessness when it came to preserving the sovereignty of the British state. After all, if Britain was going to have to enter sooner or later to shore up

---

[4] E Ellis and T Tridimas, *Public Law of the European Community: Text, Materials and Commentary* (London, Sweet & Maxwell, 1995), p 9. Crucial to this confidence were the UK's links to the Commonwealth and the so-called special relationship with the United States. Indeed, it was when these links became more precarious that the United Kingdom eventually decided to bolster its position by applying to join the European Communities.

[5] R Hibbert, 'Britain in Search of a Role, 1957–1973; A Role in Europe, European Integration and Britain: A Witness Account' in B Brivati and H Jones (eds), *From Reconstruction to Integration: Britain and Europe since 1945* (Leicester, Leicester University Press, 1993), pp 114–15.

[6] D Gowland and A Turner, *Reluctant Europeans: Britain and European Integration 1945–1998* (Harlow, Pearson Education, 2000), p 112. The FTA would also differ from the EEC in that there would be no common external tariff, and foodstuffs would be excluded.

its diplomacy and its markets, it was essential that it should not remain aloof while the political forms of European collaboration were being decided, only to find that the community only became more supranational while Britain delayed.[7]

It is evident from this perspective that the 1961 decision to seek entry to the Communities was less of a positive choice and more of a concession of defeat. Gowland and Turner confirm this view: 'the decision to apply for entry was taken not in a fit of Euro-enthusiasm but out of a reluctant recognition that it represented the lesser of two evils.'[8] It is ironic, therefore, that the UK's negotiations for entry to the Communities in 1961–63 were ultimately unsuccessful. The lengthy and complex negotiations lasted from October 1961 until January 1963 and focused largely upon the two extremely difficult issues of the UK's commercial relations with the Commonwealth and domestic agriculture.[9] They came to an abrupt end in January 1963 when French President De Gaulle vetoed British membership. De Gaulle claimed that the United Kingdom was not a suitable candidate for membership, because of its distinct economic structure and commercial tradition and its links to distant Commonwealth countries and to the United States.[10] It could also be noted that UK entry was not in France's self-interest at this time; a factor which undoubtedly influenced De Gaulle's decision.

In 1963, when Macmillan's Conservative government sought entry, the Labour party was opposed to it. When Harold Wilson became Prime Minister in 1964 it seemed unlikely that his government would seek entry. However, the first of numerous Labour leadership U-turns on this issue soon occurred and Wilson began discussing the possibility of a second application to the Communities in 1966.[11] Both the Cabinet and the entire Labour movement was divided on the issue of Europe but, on 30 April 1967, the Cabinet voted by thirteen to eight to apply for entry.[12] The formal application was made in July 1967, and history repeated itself when, in November, De Gaulle issued a second veto on UK membership. It was now clear that the United Kingdom would not become a member of the Communities while De Gaulle remained in power.

Two years after the UK's second application, De Gaulle resigned from the French Presidency, thus transforming Anglo-French relations and the future direction of European integration. Ironically, De Gaulle had favoured the type of EC which the United Kingdom also favoured: one with the emphasis on

[7] C Lord, *British Entry to the European Community under the Heath Government of 1970–1974* (Aldershot, Dartmouth, 1993), p 14.

[8] Gowland and Turner, n 6 above, pp 115–16. Gowland and Turner continue by saying, 'perhaps it would be something of an exaggeration – though not much – to speak of desperation. But the mood of the government was entirely a sober one.'

[9] See Gowland and Turner, n 6 above, pp 126–31.

[10] *Ibid*, p 138.

[11] During Wilson's first period in office (October 1964–March 1966) his government had only a small majority, but the March 1966 Election gave Labour a strong majority of 97 and the door was opened for EC entry.

[12] Gowland and Turner, n 6 above, p 166.

intergovernmentalism and with only limited supranational power. With De Gaulle gone, the way was clear for the other states to transform the nature of the Community. At a summit of the Six held in The Hague in December 1969, three important decisions were taken: to enlarge the EC by opening negotiations with the United Kingdom, Ireland, Denmark and Norway; to move towards full economic and monetary union (EMU) by 1980; and to complete the first stage of economic integration.[13] The United Kingdom was now free to make a third application to join the EC, but it would do so at a time when the Communities were moving in a direction to which many in the United Kingdom remained opposed. Crucially for the United Kingdom, the new French President, Pompidou, made clear that he would not exercise a veto against UK membership. This change in French policy was probably largely due to French concerns about recent German growth.[14] But another reason, suggested by Young, for Pompidou's adoption of a new policy was a desire to spread the costs of the new (and controversial) Common Agriculture Policy (CAP).[15]

Harold Wilson and the Labour party lost the June 1970 election, and thus it was the new Conservative Prime Minister, Edward Heath, to whom it fell to initiate a third application for membership to the European Communities. He was ideally suited to the job as an avid pro-European. Indeed, for Heath, British membership of the EC was 'nothing less than a political crusade.'[16] In the words of Hugo Young, 'what he brought to the table, compared with every predecessor, was not merely a "European" policy but exceptional single-mindedness in pursuing it.'[17] Of course, the danger of such single-mindedness was that it would render Heath 'vulnerable to the accusation that he was willing to pay any price to fulfil a cherished political ambition.'[18]

II. UK Entry to the European Communities

In October 1970 negotiations for UK membership of the European Communites, including most significantly the EEC, began in Brussels. The major issues for discussion were the position of sterling, imports from the Commonwealth (especially New Zealand diary products and Caribbean sugar), the CAP (which would

---

[13] See *ibid*, p 172.

[14] *Ibid*, pp 170–71.

[15] JW Young, 'Britain and the European Economic Community, 1956–1973' in B Brivati and H Jones (eds), *From Reconstruction to Integration: Britain and Europe since 1945* (Leicester, Leicester University Press, 1993), p 112. Young also adds that Pompidou may have chosen this policy 'simply because he was not Charles de Gaulle.'

[16] Gowland and Turner, n 6 above, p 168.

[17] H Young, *This Blessed Plot: Britain and Europe from Churchill to Blair* (London, Macmillan, 1998), p 215.

[18] Gowland and Turner, n 6 above, p 169.

cause food prices to rise), and the UK's contributions to the EC budget.[19] But Lord has argued that these issues were no more than 'the terms of transition to a non-negotiable "acquis".[20] The core of the prospective relationship between the United Kingdom and the EC was not open for negotiation: if the United Kingdom wanted to join the EC it would have to sign up to the Community as already established, including to its supranational nature and the recently created judicial doctrines of direct effect and European legal supremacy.[21] As Lord explains:

> if the Governments had found a solution to all the questions on the agenda, it seemed to many that all the problems involved in entry must have been removed. It was easy to forget that the suitability of the 'acquis' itself to British interests had not even been up for discussion.[22]

Notwithstanding this important limitation upon the negotiations, the process was successfully completed in June 1971.[23] Some commentators, including Lord and JW Young, view the terms obtained by Heath as the best available at that time.[24] The terms were set out in a White Paper entitled 'The United Kingdom and the European Communities' issued on 7 July 1971. The first paragraph of the White Paper illustrates and explains the government's desire to enter the EC when it identifies the prime objective of any British government as being to 'safeguard the security and prosperity of the United Kingdom and its peoples' and proceeds to note that 'since 1961 successive British Governments have taken the view that these fundamental interests would be best served by British accession to the European Communities.'[25] If the negotiations with the Six had been slightly predictable due to the UK government's eagerness to join the EC, a real battle would now have to be fought before Heath's dream could become a reality. The European Communities Bill would have to pass through Parliament, and yet both main political parties were divided on the issue. With a majority of only 25, Heath's government had a real task ahead of it.

---

[19] See *ibid*, pp 177–78.

[20] Lord, n 7 above, p 67.

[21] See below.

[22] Lord, n 7 above, p 74. Hugo Young reiterates the point that the negotiations never dealt with the big issues: 'The deep, existential meaning for Britain, of getting into "Europe" was not considered. The way Britain would have to change had no place in the work of technocrats. The future of the nation-state wasn't on the agenda' (H Young, n 17 above, p 238).

[23] A crucial summit between Pompidou and Heath in May had created the foundations for agreement. See Hugo Young, n 17 above, pp 233–34.

[24] See, for example, Lord, n 7 above, p 93: 'independent contemporary assessments put them at the better end of expectations as to what had been thought attainable when the talks opened a year earlier.' See also JW Young, *Britain and European Unity 1945–1999*, 2nd edn (London, Macmillan, 2000), p. 105: 'Although Heath was accused by Labour of getting poor terms for Britain, at the time they seemed reasonable enough, especially given the fact that Britain was a supplicant with two failed applications behind it.'

[25] *The United Kingdom and the European Communities*, Cm 4715 (1971), para 1.

Since the 1967 application for entry, the Labour Party had moved away from such a pro-European stance, largely due to the rise of the Left of the party. Harold Wilson, now leader of the opposition, was in an extremely delicate position. He had led the government which had sought entry only five years previously. but now had to find a policy on entry to Europe which would avoid splitting a party in which the majority were now opposed to entry.[26] Wilson's solution was to claim that he was not opposed to entry in principle, but that he would not have accepted the terms obtained by Heath (even though the evidence suggests that he would have acted in the same way as Heath if he had won the 1970 Election).[27] This distinction enabled the Labour party to vote in opposition to the government on the issue, as the majority wished to do, but left the substantial number of pro-marketeers (as those in favour of entry to the EC were called) in the Labour party in a quandary. The focus of attention was a key vote on 28 October 1971 on the government motion '[t]hat this House approves Her Majesty's Government's decision of principle to join the European Communities on the basis of the arrangements which have been negotiated.' This vote on the principle of entry was merely a first step before the European Communities Bill was itself debated and voted upon. In an attempt to encourage the Labour pro-marketeers to vote for the government motion, Heath permitted a free vote for the Conservative party (even though this would enable a few Conservative anti-marketeers to vote against the government). Wilson did not reciprocate, however, and a three-line whip was imposed on the Labour party. Roy Jenkins was one of the pro-marketeer Labour MPs (and a leading member of the party) who faced a difficult personal choice as to how to vote: 'I was convinced that it was one of the decisive votes of the century, and had no intention of spending the rest of my life answering the question of what did I do in the great division by saying "I abstained".'[28] Jenkins, along with 68 other Labour MPs, defied the party's three-line whip to vote with the government on entry to the EC. Twenty further Labour MPs abstained, while 39 Conservatives voted against the government and two abstained. The motion on the principle of entry on Heath's terms was passed by 358 to 246: a majority of 112.

The actions of the Labour pro-marketeers in supporting the Conservative government on entry to Europe were extremely controversial at the time and remain so today. As Robins explains, many on the Left of the Labour Party felt

---

[26] Robins explains the change in approach to this issue within the Labour party by noting that between 1961 and 1971 the EC issue was 'domesticised'. Originally EC entry was regarded as a foreign policy issue, but by 1970–71 it was perceived (at least by the Left) as an aspect of the Conservative's domestic policy and thus was easier to oppose on the grounds of inflation, unemployment, industrial relations and, more generally, as being class-motivated (LJ Robins, *The Reluctant Party: Labour and the EEC 1961–1975* (Ormskurk, GW & A Hesketh, 1979), pp 82–84).

[27] Gowland and Turner, n 6 above, p 181.

[28] R Jenkins, *A Life at the Centre* (London, Macmillan, 1991), p 329. Jenkins continues by comparing this vote with other historical parliamentary occasions: 'I saw it in the context of the first Reform Bill, the repeal of the Corn Laws, Gladstone's Home Rule Bills, the Lloyd George Budget and the Parliament Bill, the Munich Agreement and the May 1940 votes and was consequently fortified by my amateur historical interest.'

that the 28 October vote was a missed opportunity: if all Labour MPs had opposed the motion, the government would have been defeated and would probably have called a General Election, which Labour may well have won.[29] This is a slightly unrealistic supposition, however, as it is unlikely that the 39 Conservatives who voted against the motion – on a free vote – would have done so if they had known that the future of their government was at stake. Heath regards winning the 28 October vote as his greatest success as Prime Minister: 'No Prime Minister in time of peace has ever asked the House to take such a positive and historic decision as I was asking it to do that night.'[30] Having voted in favour of the principle of entry, the Labour rebels now agreed to vote against the government on the European Communities Bill itself. The view was taken that it was for the government to ensure the passage of its own legislation. The Bill passed, albeit slowly, without a single clause being defeated. It is now well known that this miraculous feat was achieved by collusion between the government and the Labour pro-marketeers, who agreed to abstain or be absent when necessary to ensure that the government was not defeated on any clause.[31]

The Bill itself was astonishingly short, containing just 12 clauses. Cynicism has surrounded the government's choice to 'reduce nine Treaties and forty-three volumes of regulations to a Bill of just twelve clauses.'[32] There has also been criticism as to the lack of clarity on the real impact of Community law on the UK constitution.[33] There was no general clause stating clearly that Community law was henceforth to be supreme (although this is indirectly inferred by section 2(4)), and Hugo Young takes the view that this omission was part of a general policy amongst ministers to avoid telling the full truth.[34] Heath dismisses such criticisms:

> There was no question of the Bill, which consisted of twelve clauses and four schedules, having been deliberately drafted so as to mislead or to curtail debate. While a short, tight Bill naturally offers less scope for filibustering and wrecking amendments than a longer one, brevity is clarity. As the Bill was so concise, its purpose and implications were as clear as they could have been, and this had the virtue of concentrating parliamentary debate around the really important issues.[35]

The last point is easy to counter because, as will be discussed more fully below, the key issue (to modern eyes at least) of national sovereignty was not subjected to any detailed debate. Furthermore, the Bill was not concise in the sense of being succinct or to the point. For example, buried in the middle of the long paragraph

---

[29] Robins, n 26 above, p 106.
[30] E Heath, *The Course of my Life: My Autobiography* (London, Hodder & Stoughton, 1998), p 380.
[31] See Gowland and Turner, n 6 above, pp 182–83.
[32] Lord, n 7 above, pp 115–16.
[33] The issue of the implication of the European Communities Act 1972 for the constitution will be considered in detail below.
[34] H Young, n 17 above, p 247.
[35] Heath, n 30 above, p 383.

which is section 2(4) is the statement that 'any enactment passed or to be passed, other than one contained in this Part of this Act, shall be construed and have effect subject to the foregoing provisions of this section.' In effect, this says that EC law is to be supreme over domestic law, but it probably takes a lawyer to discern this. While such language from the parliamentary draftsman is not unusual, the European Communities Act 1972 (ECA 1972) is, at best, a missed opportunity to declare positively the fundamental nature of the constitutional change wrought by the Act. (At worst, it is an attempt to hide those constitutional implications.) At the time, the brevity of the Bill caused disquiet. As JW Young notes, anti-marketeers complained that the Bill 'made a mockery of the complex legal, financial and constitutional questions involved in entry.'[36] This had significant repercussions because, as Young also explains, 'The myth soon grew that Heath pushed membership through a reluctant House of Commons, without a popular mandate.'[37] This 'myth' provided a window of opportunity for Wilson when he returned to office in 1974 in charge of a bitterly divided party which remained unable to form a consensus on EC membership.

III. The 1975 Referendum: Providing Democratic Legitimacy?

The Labour government which took office in 1974 remained strongly divided on the question of Europe, as did the Labour movement as a whole. Indeed, it has been claimed that the division within Labour between 1970 and 1974 'came close to tearing the party asunder.'[38] In an attempt to avoid a massive split in the party, the February 1974 Labour manifesto promised that a Labour government would renegotiate the Heath government's entry terms and hold a popular vote on membership. These two promises were well chosen. The promise to renegotiate enabled Wilson's government to argue for continued membership of the EC whilst simultaneously attacking the Heath government which first achieved membership. The promise of a referendum was justified on the basis of the feeling that the public had not yet been consulted about the momentous and historical decision to enter the EC. In the 1970 General Election, all three party leaders supported entry so there was a valid argument that the electorate had thus far been deprived of the chance to say no to the EC.[39]

Having been subsequently elected to office on the basis of the 1974 manifesto

---

[36] Young, n 24 above, p 109.
[37] Young, n 15 above, pp 111–12.
[38] Gowland and Turner, n 6 above, p 199. The reasons for the depth of division on the issue of Europe were numerous: it was closely linked to the ongoing ideological battle in the party between left and right, as well as to the question of leadership, and the nature of the issue itself aroused strong passion amongst many MPs.
[39] *Ibid.*, p 202.

(and with a majority in a second election later in the year), the Wilson government identified four main issues for renegotiation with the EC: reform of the CAP; access to the EC for products of Commonwealth states; state aid to industry and regions; and the UK's contributions to the EC budget.[40] Crucially, however, it was decided that the renegotiations would take place within the terms of the existing EC Treaties.[41] This meant that from the outset there was no possibility of radical change to the principles of Community membership. This has led Jenkins to claim that 'the whole exercise had more of cosmetics than of reality about it.'[42] Beloff confirms, in relation to the renegotiations, that 'the intention to succeed robbed them of reality.'[43] Even if the Labour leadership did intend to succeed during the renegotiations, the Cabinet remained divided on the issue, with seven ministers voting against accepting the renegotiated terms.[44]

The idea of a referendum on the issue of EC membership had first arisen publicly in April 1972 when there was a parliamentary debate and vote upon the Conservative MP Neil Marten's referendum amendment.[45] The amendment was defeated by 286 votes to 237 but, significantly for the future, the Labour opposition voted in favour under a whipped vote. It was this decision which led Jenkins (a pro-marketeer) to resign from his position as deputy leader of the Labour party. By the time of the October 1974 election, the Labour manifesto pledged that 'within twelve months of this election we will give the British people the final say, which will be binding on the government – through the ballot box – on whether we accept the terms and stay in or reject the terms and come out.'[46] The wording here was intentionally vague, because it had not yet been finally decided whether the means of giving the people 'the final say' was to be through a referendum or another General Election. The reason for keeping these two options open can be found within the ideological conflict in the Labour party. The idea of a referendum was championed by anti-marketeers such as Tony Benn largely because it was assumed at this stage that the public would vote overwhelmingly against EC membership.[47] For the same reason, the pro-marketeers within the Labour party were opposed to the idea of a referendum. However, another election (following closely on the heels of two elections in 1974) was always going to prove impossible to achieve. This was partly because a third General Election would be damaging to both national

---

[40] *Ibid*, p. 191.

[41] *Ibid*, p. 190.

[42] Jenkins, n 28 above, p 387.

[43] Lord Beloff, *Britain and the European Union: Dialogue of the Deaf* (London, Macmillan, 1996), p 79.

[44] Gowland and Turner, n 6 above, p 203.

[45] HC Deb. 5th Series, Vol 835, cols 246–363, 18 April 1972.

[46] Quoted in P Goodhart, *Full-hearted Consent: The Story of the Referendum Campaign and the Campaign for the Referendum* (London, Davis-Poynter, 1976), p 80.

[47] See Gowland and Turner, n 6 above, pp 201–2: 'The conventional wisdom, backed up by opinion polls, was that a majority of the public was opposed to membership and would reject it if given the chance.'

stability and to the Labour party, but also because of the Labour party's division on the issue:

> How could the Labour Party possibly fight an election in support of a policy that a majority of its party activists rejected? And in any case who would they fight? For both the Conservatives and the Liberal parties were demonstrably more in favour of staying in the Common Market.[48]

It was no great surprise, therefore, when Wilson announced on 23 January 1975 that there would be a consultative referendum on EC membership by June.[49] Two months later he confirmed that the government's position would be to recommend staying in Europe.[50] However, as mentioned above, the Cabinet remained divided on the issue. Given this division, Wilson made a historic constitutional decision to allow ministers to campaign on different sides during the referendum campaign. Lord even claims that the idea of a referendum 'was partly a substitute for a decision by the party itself.'[51] The sight of Cabinet ministers campaigning against each other on this fundamental issue certainly supports this view. Such a suspension of the constitutional convention of collective responsibility was almost unprecedented[52] and illustrates the political difficulty facing the Wilson government on this issue. The long-term implications for the unity of the Labour party were significant. The pro-marketeers never really reintegrated into the party, and it is no coincidence that many were eventually to form the core of the new Social Democratic Party (SDP).

The referendum campaign was dominated by two issues: the potential loss of sovereignty and the economic consequences of membership.[53] There is no doubt that the latter was of more interest to the voters. While sovereignty is an issue inextricably linked to the debate on Europe today, the anti-marketeers were unable to summon public concern on this issue during the referendum campaign:

> The truth, incredible though it may seem twenty years later, is that the public were not interested. The potential loss of sovereignty did not bother them ... If the voters said Yes to Europe, it was because they did not care about the arguments pressed hardest on them to make them say No.[54]

Hugo Young continues by arguing that it was 'prices rather than independence, money rather than nation ... where the voters needed reassurance.'[55] And the

---

[48] Goodhart, n 46 above, p 84.

[49] HC Deb. 5th Series, Vol 884, cols 1745–50, 23 January 1975.

[50] HC Deb, 5th Series, Vol 888, col 1456, 18 March 1975.

[51] Lord, n 7 above, p 130.

[52] An 'Agreement to Differ' was revealed in McDonald's Cabinet in 1932 on the issue of import controls but, as a coalition National Government, the situation was less controversial.

[53] Gowland and Turner, n 6 above, p 211.

[54] H Young, n 17 above, pp 295–96.

[55] *Ibid*, p 296.

reassurance was forthcoming from the Yes campaign, which was staffed by senior and respected members of all three political parties.[56] Public opinion swung towards a yes vote, and the final outcome was 67.2 per cent in favour of continued EC membership with 32.8 per cent against. This was an impressive majority on a turnout of 65 per cent. Is this the democratic approval of the EC which would legitimise the UK's membership?

There are a number of arguments as to why democratic legitimacy for the EC's place in the UK constitution cannot be implied from the 1975 referendum result. First, the referendum was primarily a political device to prevent a split in the Labour party (and not an entirely successful one). Second, there was inequality between the two sides of the campaign in both monetary and political terms. For example, each household received three official leaflets during the campaign: one from the Yes campaign; one from the No campaign; and one from the government outlining its official recommendation, which also recommended a yes vote. Furthermore, respected, mainstream politicians from all sides of the political spectrum (including Wilson, Heath, Jenkins, and Thatcher, the new leader of the opposition) all campaigned, with varying degrees of enthusiasm, in favour of EC membership. On the No side they faced controversial extremists such as Tony Benn and Enoch Powell. Third, and this is the point which most undermines the legitimacy argument, the true nature of the EC was never put before the public. In part this is explainable by the different nature of the EC at that time. Closer political integration has evolved more recently, but in the 1970s the EC was primarily an economic organisation – a common market – and thus the public and political emphasis on the economic issue is perfectly understandable. The fact remains, however, that from its origins, the EC was, and was intended to be, a supranational body. By entering into the Community the United Kingdom was agreeing to (and entrenching in its constitution) the supremacy of Community law over domestic law.[57] Whether the British public has ever really assented to this remains open for debate. Whether they need to do so is a further relevant question, because there is no doubt that the people's elected representatives knew, or should have known, exactly to what they were assenting in 1972. In the UK's representative democratic system, that is usually regarded as sufficient legitimacy for a constitutional change. Indeed, this raises the fourth reason for doubting the achievement of democratic legitimacy through the 1975 referendum: the referendum is a device which inverts, rather than ensures, democratic legitimacy.[58] This argument was raised by a number of

---

[56] Goodhart argues that even if a referendum had been held in 1972 before entry, a majority would have voted in favour because the majority of politicians who commanded the most respect were in favour (Goodhart, n 46 above, p 191). In other words, it was personalities rather than policies which mattered most.

[57] On this issue, see below.

[58] It will be recalled from ch 5 that the Unionist opposition led by Balfour proposed a referendum scheme during the 1911 constitutional crisis. The proposal was that all parliamentary Bills of constitutional importance on which the two Houses could not agree would be referred to the people by means of a referendum. This was rejected by the Liberal government, mainly because of a dispute

politicians at the time. For example, Brian Walden, referring to the argument that EC membership violated parliamentary sovereignty, retorted that 'the referendum is the most brazen affront to parliamentary sovereignty in my lifetime.'[59] For all of these reasons, the 1975 referendum result cannot be regarded as providing democratic legitimacy for the role of the EC in today's constitution. It is now time to investigate that constitutional role in more detail.

IV. Establishing European Legal Supremacy

Long before the United Kingdom joined the EC, the European Court of Justice (ECJ) had orchestrated a 'transformation of the European legal system.'[60] This was achieved through the process of the preliminary ruling mechanism[61] and manifested itself in two fundamental legal principles: direct effect and European legal supremacy. Because these principles – which radically transformed the nature of the European legal system – were derived from judicial interpretation and not from the Treaty of Rome itself, they were unexpected and controversial although, by the time of UK entry, there was no doubt that they were also well established. Thus, the foundations for today's Europe are to be found in the European Communities as established before UK entry in 1972.

The first indication of judicial innovation on the issue of the nature of the Community legal order arose in the 1963 case of *Van Gend en Loos*.[62] This case was a preliminary reference from a Dutch trade tribunal on the issue of whether a provision of the Treaty of Rome was self-executing. This question was in some ways unique to the Netherlands because, under Dutch law, international agreements had precedence over national law if they were 'self-executing' in the national sphere. Thus, the Dutch reference was a question 'that probably no court in another country would have framed in the same way'[63] and provided the opportunity for the ECJ to introduce a doctrine of direct effect:

over home rule. By the 1970s the idea of consulting the people by means of a referendum remained a controversial constitutional mechanism, but the 1975 experience paved the way for future uses of the referendum, including on the constitutional issue of devolution for Scotland, Wales, and Northern Ireland. Today, a second referendum on the EC is possible, this time focusing upon the question of an EU Constitution. Unlike the first referendum, this one will concentrate public opinion upon the issue of the political and constitutional repercussions of European integration.

[59] HC Deb. 5th Series, Vol 889, col 1038, 8 April 1975.

[60] KJ Alter, *Establishing the Supremacy of European Law: The Making of an International Rule of Law in Europe* (Oxford, Oxford University Press, 2001), p 1.

[61] Originally Art 177 and now Art 234.

[62] *Algemene Transport – en Expeditie Onderneming van Gend en Loos v Nederlandse Administratie der Berlastingen* (Case 26/62) [1963] ECR 1, [1963] CMLR 105.

[63] Alter, n 60 above, p 17.

the Community constitutes a new legal order of international law for the benefit of which the states have limited their sovereign rights, albeit within limited fields, and the subjects of which comprise not only member states but also their nationals. Independently of the legislation of member states, Community law therefore not only imposes obligations on individuals but is also intended to confer upon them rights which become part of their legal heritage ...[64]

As is evident from this famous quote, the ECJ asserted that Community law creates rights for individuals which can then be relied upon directly before national courts. The ECJ's reasoning was based partly on reference to the text of the Treaty of Rome but mainly 'by reference to a vision of the kind of legal community that the treaties seemed designed to create.'[65] It was, therefore, largely a purposive or teleological approach, and indeed there is little indication in the words of the Treaty of Rome itself that its provisions would have direct effect in member states.[66]

This innovative approach to an international treaty was supplemented the following year in the case of *Costa v ENEL*.[67] This case concerned a challenge to the validity of the nationalisation of an Italian electricity company. An Italian small claims court sent references to both the ECJ and the Italian Constitutional Court on the question of whether the nationalisation was contrary to Community law and, if so, whether Community law was supreme over national law. The Constitutional Court ruled that Community law was not supreme but the ECJ held that it was:

The transfer by the states from their domestic legal system to the Community legal system of the rights and obligations arising under the Treaty carries with it a permanent limitation of their sovereign rights, against which a subsequent unilateral act incompatible with the concept of the Community cannot prevail.[68]

This was a hugely significant development: a 'subsequent unilateral act' within national law 'cannot prevail' if incompatible with Community law. The implications for national laws and national constitutions would be profound. However, the original six member states seemed surprisingly unperturbed by this judicial development. Alter explains[69] that both *Costa* and *Van Gend* were more significant to lawyers than to politicians because, while lawyers look for the doctrinal implications of a case, politicians tend to look only for the material and political impact of a decision. In both cases, although the doctrinal impact was huge, the material impact was minimal. In *Van Gend*, the money at stake was small, and in

---

[64] [1963] ECR 1 at 12.

[65] Craig and de Búrca, n 2 above, p 184.

[66] Regulations are, however, described in the Treaty of Rome as 'directly applicable in all member states,' and so it could be argued that there is some indication of the possibility of direct effect in the Treaty.

[67] *Costa v ENEL* (Case 6/64) [1964] ECR 585, [1964] CMLR 425.

[68] *Ibid*, p 593.

[69] Alter, n 60 above, pp 186–87.

Costa, the Italian government won the case (on the basis that the nationalisation was held not to be contrary to Community law by the ECJ). Thus, neither case was considered particularly significant by the governments at the time. In addition, the ECJ's view that Community law was supreme and created rights for individuals would be of limited utility if national courts chose not to follow this lead.[70] The response of national courts thus became crucial.

In *Costa*, the ECJ had suggested that national courts must apply the supremacy doctrine. and this instruction was made even more explicit in the 1978 decision of *Simmenthal*.[71] But, as Alter explains, there existed three conceivable ways in which national courts could respond: they could accept and follow the ECJ's view of a new legal order; they could reject this view and rely upon the implied repeal rule to give effect to a subsequent incompatible national law; or they could avoid such a stark choice by changing national doctrine so that it is no longer incompatible with Community law supremacy.[72] Alter claims that national courts elected to use this compromise, which enabled them to give supremacy to Community law while still rejecting the notion that the Treaty of Rome created a new type of legal obligation.[73] As will be seen below, this approach could indeed be regarded as reflecting the UK approach under which parliamentary sovereignty has often been redefined in order to incorporate the idea of Community law supremacy.

It is perhaps surprising that, while the supremacy of Community law is now widely accepted, member states have always declined to enshrine the principle within the Treaties.[74] De Witte poses the question of whether this could be because 'the governments and parliaments all agreed that such principles were too controversial to be written down and should be kept as secret passwords of courts, lawyers, and European law students so as not to awaken public opinion to their existence?'[75] This may change, because the recently drafted EU Constitution does include an explicit recognition of the supremacy doctrine.[76] This can, however, be regarded as confirming de Witte's underlying premise, that the public would be perturbed by such awareness, because the supremacy of Community law is a principle which has been dragged into the heated debate on the EU Constitution, often wrongly used as an example of the new proposed integrationist (or, worse, federalist) direction of the EU.[77] The outrage of many in

---

[70] *Ibid*, p 189.

[71] *Amministrazione delle Finanze dello Stato v Simmenthal SpA* (Case 106/77) [1978] ECR 629, [1978] 3 CMLR 263.

[72] Alter, n 60 above, p 37.

[73] *Ibid*, pp 37–38.

[74] *Ibid*, p 26.

[75] B De Witte, 'Direct Effect, Supremacy, and the Nature of the Legal Order' in P Craig and G de Búrca, *The Evolution of EU Law* (Oxford, Oxford University Press, 1999), p 194.

[76] Art 1(6): 'The Constitution and law adopted by the institutions of the Union in exercising competencies conferred on it shall have primacy over the law of member states.' The future of the Constitution is currently in doubt following its rejection by the French people in a 2005 referendum.

[77] See, for example, W Rees-Mogg, 'We the People Reject this Wretched Constitution', (2004) *The Times*, 21 June.

Britain stemming from this newly acquired knowledge of Community law supremacy suggests that successive UK governments have done a very effective job of failing to publicise this core principle, well established by the time of UK entry. This failure can be highlighted by a passage within the 1971 White Paper on entry:

> The English and Scottish legal systems will remain intact. Certain provisions of the treaties and instruments made under them, concerned with economic, commercial and closely related matters, will be included in our law. The common law will remain the basis of our legal system, and our courts will continue to operate as they do at present. In certain cases however they would need to refer point of Community law to the European Court of Justice. All the essential features of our law will remain ...[78]

This is extremely misleading information, not so much for what it says,[79] but for what it omits. There is no mention of the established principle that Community law will be supreme over national law. This may well have been regarded as a relevant piece of information for both the public and Members of Parliament at the time that Parliament voted to join the EC. Its omission from official documentation, such as the government White Paper, painted a very misleading picture of the nature of the EC. It was not, even in the early 1970s, an international organisation comparable to the Council of Europe, NATO or the United Nations. It was fundamentally different because of the recent evolution by the ECJ (and implicit acceptance by the original member state governments) of the principles of direct effect and Community law supremacy. It was, as the ECJ so clearly described it, 'a new legal order of international law for the benefit of which the states have limited their sovereign rights.'[80] For anyone in possession of the key facts, it would be immediately obvious that membership of such an organisation would involve considerable conflict with the existing constitution and would necessitate a radical evolution in the constitutional foundations of the United Kingdom.

Once the United Kingdom had joined the EC, the Community's evolution into a unique supranational body continued. It was perhaps ironic that the key advances in European legal doctrine discussed above occurred at a time when member states were actually scaling down the supranational aspirations of the Treaty of Rome.[81] During the period between the 1960s and 1986, the early supranational impetus gave way to greater intergovernmentalism, as evidenced by the Luxembourg compromise in 1966.[82] The implicit acceptance of the ECJ's

[78] White Paper, n 25 above, para 31.

[79] Although to assert that only 'certain provisions' of the Treaties will be 'included in our law' is clearly inaccurate.

[80] *Van Gend*, n 64 above.

[81] Alter, n 60 above, p 26.

[82] In 1965, the French government withdrew from the Council and declined to participate in the Council's legislative process in protest at increased use of majority voting. The crisis, known as 'the empty chair crisis', was resolved in 1966 by the Luxembourg Accords, agreed outside the terms of the Treaty (and inconsistent with its terms). The compromise agreed ensured that the Council would not invoke majority voting on any matter affecting a state's vital interests.

transformation of European legal doctrine notwithstanding, no significant steps were taken by member states towards closer integration. However, in 1986, the Single European Act 'heralded a revival of the Community momentum towards integration which has continued at a breathless pace since then.'[83] The Treaty on European Union, signed at Maastricht in 1992, the Treaty of Amsterdam in 1997, and the Treaty of Nice in 2000 all continued the theme of closer European integration, as does the EU Constitution currently under consideration in member states across a much enlarged Europe.

As the UK's participation in an increasingly integrated Europe continues and develops, an increasingly important question is: from where does European law derive its force? Does it rely upon national constitutions or does its primacy derive from its own authority? The approach of the national courts will again be crucial here. Do national courts find authority for Community law in the national legal order or in the jurisprudence of the Court of Justice?

> National courts see themselves as organs of their states and try to fit their Community mandate within the framework of the powers attributed to them by their national legal systems. For them (and, indeed, for most constitutional law scholars throughout Europe), the idea that EC law can claim its primacy within the national legal orders on the basis of its own authority seems … implausible … The national courts … see EC law as rooted in their constitutions, and seek a foundation for the primacy and direct effect of EC law in that constitution.[84]

This is not an easy task as most national constitutions fail to deal explicitly with the domestic effect of Community law. It is a very significant approach because if Community law gains its national legal force and supremacy from the national constitution, national courts will be unlikely to allow Community law to overrule core constitutional principles.[85] This is not the approach demanded by the ECJ, which ruled in *Internationale Handelsgesellschaft* that even a state's constitution is inferior to Community law:

> [T]he law stemming from the Treaty, an independent source of law, cannot because of its very nature be overridden by rules of national law, however formed, without being deprived of its character as Community law and without the legal basis of the Community itself being called into question. Therefore the validity of a Community measure or its effect within a member state cannot be affected by allegations that it runs counter to either fundamental rights as formulated by the constitution of that state or the principles of a national constitutional structure.[86]

---

[83] Craig and de Burca, n 2 above, p 19.

[84] De Witte, n 75 above, p 199.

[85] *Ibid*, pp 202–4. For example, the German Federal Constitutional Court has asserted its right to review Community provisions to ensure compliance with constitutional rights and principles, including most recently in *Brummer v The European Union Treaty* ('*Maastricht decision*') 2 BvR 2134/92, and 2 BvR 2159/92; [1994] CMLR 57.

[86] *Internationale Handelsgesellschaft GmbH v Einfuhr –und Vorratsstelle fur Getreide und Futtermittel* (Case 11/70) [1970] ECR 1125, [1972] CMLR 255, para 3.

This is unconvincing from a constitutional perspective. EC law is an external body of law given domestic force within the United Kingdom by the constitutional statute of the ECA 1972. As will be discussed in more detail below, there is no doubt that European legal supremacy is currently a core principle in the UK's evolving constitution. But, as such, there can likewise be no question of Community law being superior to the constitution itself. The only way in which such absolute supremacy could be established outside of member states' constitutions would be if the EU evolved into a state entity itself and thus, rather as in federal states, authority for Community law derived from the EU Constitution rather than national constitutions. This may indeed be the direction in which Europe is headed, but it will involve an immense change in the constitutional structure of European states, as well as public and political acceptance that the evolution of European states and their constitutions has reached its final destination. For now, at least, the UK constitution remains the source of all laws within the United Kingdom, including Community law. How, then, does the constitution, which prior to 1972 had evolved to prioritise Parliament's sovereignty, reconcile existing constitutional principles with the European legal doctrine of supremacy?

V. The Parliamentary Sovereignty Debate

The key question which has faced the national courts numerous times since 1973 is whether a European law should, and can, take precedence over a conflicting piece of UK legislation. The courts' initial response to this difficult constitutional dilemma was to deny that such a conflict existed. So, for example, in *Litster v Forth Dry Dock*[87] in 1989, the House of Lords adopted a purposive construction to UK law in order to interpret domestic law as conforming with Community law. The court regarded this as acceptable, even if it involves 'some departure from the strict and literal application of the words which the legislature has elected to use.'[88] Likewise in *Pickstone v Freemans*[89] the House of Lords adopted a purposive approach to interpretation of the relevant UK legislation. A relevant factor in both of these cases – and perhaps the decisive factor – was that the UK legislation was passed in order to give effect to the Community law. In *Litster*, the UK Regulations in question were passed to give effect to a Community Directive and, in *Pickstone*, the Equal Pay Act 1970 was amended by secondary legislation in order to comply with a ruling of the ECJ. It was no difficult task, therefore, for the House of Lords to argue that the UK Parliament had intended its legislation to be compatible with the Community law in question. When this assumption of compatibility could not withstand evidence to the contrary, the House of Lords

---

[87] [1990] 1 AC 546, [1989] 1 All ER 1134.
[88] Lord Oliver, *ibid*, at 559.
[89] [1989] AC 66.

took a very different approach, as can be seen in *Duke v GEC Reliance* in 1988.[90] In this case, the national legislation was passed prior to the relevant ECJ judgment and so could not be regarded as intended to comply with it. Thus, in *Duke*, the House of Lords refused to interpret national law in accordance with Community law. This case clearly portrays the limits to the construction approach in *Litster* and *Pickstone*. Nevertheless, those two judgments are constitutionally ground-breaking because they devastate the doctrine of implied repeal. Previously an aspect of the parliamentary sovereignty doctrine required that a later inconsistent piece of legislation would impliedly repeal an earlier one.[91] That rule was not applied in these cases, and thus a subsequent domestic piece of legislation was interpreted so as to comply with (rather than impliedly repeal) an earlier Community law. Furthermore, in neither case was the Community law in question one with direct effect. Such factors boded ominously for the future.

In 1991, the House of Lords faced a case with potential to be the landmark constitutional case of the century. The *Factortame* litigation was a complex and lengthy judicial process. It concerned the fishing rights of Spanish fishermen in the North Sea, which the UK government sought, through the Merchant Shipping Act 1988, to restrict in a way which potentially violated Community law. In *Factortame (No 1)*,[92] when the dispute first reached the House of Lords, the question for the court was whether to grant interim relief to the fishing companies pending the decision of the ECJ on the case's merits. The pressing problem facing the companies was that, as they were currently prohibited from fishing, they could become bankrupt before the ECJ's final decision was reached. The House of Lords refused to grant interim relief because it held that it had no power to grant an interim injunction against the Crown. However, the House of Lords also referred this point to the ECJ: whether the absence of administrative law remedies in this situation was itself a breach of Community law. The ECJ subsequently held that it was a violation of Community law and, based on the earlier judgment of *Simmenthal*,[93] affirmed that national courts must set aside any rule of national law which prevents them granting interim relief in a dispute on Community law.[94] It has been argued that this ECJ judgment is misleading in its reliance upon 'setting aside' terminology.[95] The UK courts would have to do far more than set aside a constitutional norm in order to comply with the ECJ judgment. In the words of de Witte, they would have to 'assume new jurisdictional powers and therefore create new law rather than simply choose between two applicable norms.'[96] The House of Lords agreed to do this and, accepting that as a matter of

---

[90] [1988] AC 618, [1988] 1 All ER 626.
[91] *Vauxhall Estates Ltd v Liverpool Corpn* [1932] 1 KB 733; *Ellen Street Estates Ltd v Minister of Health* [1934] 1 KB 590.
[92] *R v Secretary of State for Transport, ex parte Factortame* [1990] 2 AC 85.
[93] *Simmenthal*, n 71 above.
[94] *R v Secretary of State for Transport, ex parte Factortame (No 2)* (Case C-213/89) [1990] ECR I-2433.
[95] De Witte, n 75 above, p 191.
[96] *Ibid.*

Community law interim relief had to be available against the Crown, it suspended the application of the Merchant Shipping Act 1988.[97] The House of Lords emphasised that such relief would be rare, but held that on the facts (including the financial hardship suffered by the fishing companies and their likelihood of success in the final case), it should be available in this case.

There are various ways to interpret this judgment. On the one hand, for the first time since 1688 a court suspended the operation of an Act of Parliament. Contrary to Dicey's oft-quoted assertion, it appeared that there was now a body with power to set aside the legislation of Parliament, and that body was the House of Lords.[98] On the other hand, on the narrow issue in the case, the decision may be reconcilable with traditional parliamentary sovereignty. The rule preventing interim relief was the Crown Proceedings Act 1947. It could be argued that this was impliedly repealed by the later ECA 1972. However, few commentators feel able to close their eyes to the wider implications of the case, and even Lord Bridge felt compelled to tackle, albeit obiter, the constitutional impact of the ECA 1972 on parliamentary sovereignty:

> If the supremacy ... of Community law over the national law of member states was not always inherent in the EEC Treaty it was certainly well established in the jurisprudence of the Court of Justice long before the United Kingdom joined the Community. Thus, whatever limitation of its sovereignty Parliament accepted when it enacted the European Communities Act was entirely voluntary.[99]

Craig has described this reasoning as contractarian:

> [T]he United Kingdom knew when they joined the EEC that priority should be accorded to EEC law, and they must be taken to have contracted on those terms. If, therefore, 'blame' was to be cast for a loss of sovereignty then this should be laid at the feet of Parliament and not the courts.[100]

This does indeed appear to be the justification put forward by Lord Bridge but surely it is not a question of blame? What matters is the constitutional impact of the contract entered into, and the national courts are the vital factor in addressing this problem.

---

[97] *R v Secretary of State for Transport, ex parte Factortame (No 2)* [1991] 1 AC 603, [1991] 1 All ER 70.

[98] These broader implications of EC membership were at the fore again in the 1995 EOC case (*R v Secretary of State for Employment, ex parte Equal Opportunities Commission* [1995] 1 AC 1). In this case, concerning the compatibility of UK legislation on unfair dismissal and redundancy pay with Community law on discrimination, the House of Lords issued a declaration to the effect that national legislation violated Community law. As this case was not complicated by the additional factor of interim relief, the core point of European legal supremacy becomes even clearer.

[99] *Factortame (No 2)*, n 97 above, p 643.

[100] P Craig, 'Sovereignty of the United Kingdom Parliament after *Factortame*' (1991) 11 *Yearbook of European Law* 221, at 249.

A more recent judicial attempt to reconcile parliamentary sovereignty and European legal supremacy occurred in the case of *Thoburn v Sunderland City Council*.[101] In this case, Laws LJ, frequently an extra-judicial commentator upon constitutional principles, gave an immensely important, and controversial, judgment on the nature of parliamentary sovereignty. He held that the ECA 1972 is a 'constitutional statute' which is not subject to the doctrine of implied repeal. He also made clear that the supremacy of Community law derives from the UK constitution and not directly from Community law itself. As was discussed above, this is a vital distinction, because if Community law is supreme only because the constitution makes it so, it will not be able to override that constitution or other principles within it, such as the legislative supremacy of Parliament, as currently defined in the constitution. The relevant part of the judgment comprises three key propositions: the existence of constitutional rights; the existence of constitutional statutes; and the protection of the latter from implied repeal.[102] The first proposition draws some support from previous case-law,[103] but its implications for parliamentary sovereignty had not previously been acknowledged. Laws argues that, as a logical consequence of the existence of constitutional rights, there must also exist 'constitutional statutes'. He views this as part of a 'hierarchy of Acts of Parliament.'[104] This is a radical reinterpretation of the dominant theory of parliamentary sovereignty. Under Dicey's theory, such a hierarchy is impliedly prohibited because it is impossible to entrench any Act, even a constitutional one, from repeal. Laws' classification of the ECA 1972 as a 'constitutional statute' is not controversial in itself, but his belief that the statute is thereby immune from implied repeal is hard to reconcile with previous judicial approaches to parliamentary sovereignty.

The claim that this 'special status of constitutional statutes follows the special status of constitutional rights'[105] is, in fact, the least convincing aspect of Laws' *Thoburn* judgment. This is perhaps so because it is an unnecessary intellectual leap. If constitutional rights – that is, individual rights which are so fundamental to our democratic society that they are protected within the UK constitution – exist, they must be immune from infringement by all branches of government, including the legislature. The inclusion of such rights in particular statutes is irrelevant – it is not the statutes which are immune from repeal but, rather, the rights themselves. Hence a hierarchy of Acts is not necessary or desirable. Furthermore, the emphasis upon constitutional rights within Laws' judgment limits the application of his theory. If constitutional statutes follow from the existence of constitutional rights, only those statutes which contain provisions related to individual rights will be elevated to constitutional status. And yet, as

---

[101] [2002] 4 All ER 156.

[102] *Ibid*, at paras 62–63.

[103] See, for example, *R v Secretary of State for the Home Department, ex parte Simms* [2000] 2 AC 115 at 131 per Lord Hoffmann; *Pierson v Secretary of State for the Home Department* [1998] AC 539; *R v Lord Chancellor, ex parte Witham* [1998] QB 575.

[104] *Thoburn*, n 101 above, at para 62.

[105] *Ibid*.

Laws himself impliedly recognises, statutes may also have constitutional status by virtue of regulating the relationship between different organs of government.[106] The ECA 1972 does, as Laws claims, have 'profound effects on so many dimensions of our daily lives'[107] but it also, far more significantly for the UK constitution, creates a new layer of government superior to the central UK government. It is a constitutional statute, without doubt, but it is so for broader reasons than those outlined by Laws. The significance of this point is that, while Laws' linking of constitutional rights and statutes may be easily attacked, his underlying argument is far stronger. The ability of the constitution to impose constitutional limits upon the legislative branch of government is logical and hard to dismiss. The values in the UK constitution which are capable of imposing such limits include the issues of constitutional rights identified by Laws but also other broader values, such as democracy, natural justice, and the supremacy of EC law. Emphasis on this point is essential to encourage a wider acceptance of Laws' desire to uphold the constitution from attack by Parliament and was sadly lacking in the *Thoburn* judgment.

It is clear from *Thoburn* that the supremacy of Community law imposes judicially enforceable limits upon the UK legislature. But the significance of the judgment goes far wider. The UK Parliament remains 'sovereign' but (logically) subject to the constitution which made it sovereign. European legal supremacy is currently a constitutional principle and imposes some limits on Parliament's legislative freedom, but so do many other values. This proposition goes to the core of the evolving nature of the constitution. As this book has progressed, so it has been seen that various constitutional changes have resulted in new principles and values being incorporated into the evolving constitution. For example, in 1688 the constitution was transformed with the inclusion of parliamentary legislative supremacy; since 1707 the core principles of the Treaty of Union have been protected in the UK constitution; from 1832 onwards a fundamental principle of democracy has gradually evolved to transform the core nature of the UK constitution. Now, the constitutional significance of 1972 becomes clear: the idea of European legal supremacy – an idea arguably never given democratic legitimacy by the public – has been incorporated into the evolving constitution and joins with ideas such as democracy, union, and human rights in imposing limits on the legislative freedom of the Parliament established under the constitution.

Despite the apparent merits of the above theory, a number of commentators reject the idea of a sovereign Parliament subject to constitutional limits and argue instead that parliamentary sovereignty was destroyed in 1972 (or 1991). The distinguished constitutional commentator HWR Wade has expressed the view that the 1972 Parliament has bound its successors (at least for the duration of UK

---

[106] Laws lists the Acts of Union 1706 and the Scotland Act 1998 as constitutional statutes (*ibid*, at para 62). While these Acts do undoubtedly affect the citizens of Scotland, their wider significance is in respect of the organs of government.

[107] *Ibid*, at para 62.

membership of the EC), and that this amounts to a revolution.[108] Wade bases his argument on his interpretation of the *Factortame (No 2)* judgment. He acknowledges that the judges were faced with a novel situation in this case, but criticises them for their choice 'to depart from the familiar rules for the sake of political necessity.'[109] MacCormick succinctly describes Wade's argument as follows: 'A change ... was made in the fundamental rules of the constitution of a kind that the constitution as understood in 1972 could not have authorised.'[110] On Lord Bridge's dicta, quoted above, Wade comments that it is 'a statement which could hardly be clearer: Parliament can bind its successors. If that is not revolutionary, constitutional lawyers are Dutchmen.'[111]

However, Craig queries whether the reasoning of Lord Bridge is reconcilable with Wade's theory that the courts were making 'a political choice at the boundary of the legal system.'[112] Craig asserts that the courts do not wish to be seen as making political choices and 'prefer to express the matter as one in which the essential choice has been made by the legislature.'[113] This may explain the raising of the issue of blame, mentioned earlier. The courts have often sought to emphasise that any adaptation caused to the doctrine of parliamentary sovereignty was a voluntary act initiated by the Parliament of 1972. The courts have consistently pleaded not guilty to Wade's accusation of a judicial revolution and instead seem to recognise a constitutional evolution, traceable back to the Parliament which passed the ECA 1972. This is also the view of commentators such as Craig and Allan. Thus, Allan argues that in *Factortame* the House of Lords 'merely determined what the existing constitutional order required in novel circumstances.'[114] So, while Wade's constitution broke (resulting in a revolution), Allan's constitution merely bends (or evolves). The latter must be the better view in the light of the many constitutional changes identified in this book which have been incorporated into the existing constitution rather than causing its demolition. MacCormick supports this view:

> [There] are moments when, in response to changing circumstances, legislators or the people in a referendum make amendments, or judges engage in interpretative adjustment of principles and doctrines in a way that may produce great constitutional change but that does not thereby amount to radical or revolutionary discontinuity.[115]

Allan argues that the House of Lords judgment in *Factortame* represents 'a rational attempt to explore the boundaries of legislative sovereignty within the

---

[108] HWR Wade, 'Sovereignty: Revolution or Evolution?' (1996) 112 *LQR* 568.

[109] *Ibid*, p 574.

[110] N MacCormick, *Questioning Sovereignty: Law, State, and Nation in the European Commonwealth* (Oxford, Oxford University Press, 1999), p 79.

[111] Wade, n 108 above, at 573.

[112] Craig, n 100 above, at 252.

[113] *Ibid*.

[114] TRS Allan, 'Parliamentary Sovereignty: Law, Politics, and Revolution' (1997) 113 *LQR* 443, at 445.

[115] MacCormick, n 110 above, p 93. Many such examples have been discussed in this book.

contemporary constitution'[116] and concludes that, contra Wade, constitutional theory is now essential in order to determine the nature of the contemporary constitution. MacCormick regards the debate between Wade and Allan on this issue as a fundamentally important one: 'It poses sharply the issue of how it is possible to change a constitution in its fundamentals, while still acting in a constitutional and lawful manner and spirit.'[117] This dilemma goes to the heart of an evolutionary constitution. Both Craig and Allan argue convincingly that the answer lies in placing the doctrine of parliamentary sovereignty within broader constitutional justification. For example, Craig criticises much of the current literature for failing to pay attention to the reasons why Parliament should, or should not, be regarded as sovereign,[118] and Allan argues that the 'validity of traditional assertions of absolute sovereignty can only be determined by analysis of their normative grounding in political theory.'[119] Parliamentary sovereignty thus remains a core part of the constitution, but it is now sited within a constitution which has also incorporated the idea of European legal supremacy, and therefore new limits upon Parliament's competence have been asserted.

A problem arises, however, due to the questionable democratic legitimacy of the idea of European legal supremacy. As was discussed above, neither the 1970 Election nor the 1975 referendum can be regarded as providing public approval of this radical new introduction into the constitution. Given that democracy is a now well-established central tenet of the UK's constitution, the position of European legal supremacy within the UK constitution is precarious. If we are to follow Craig and Allan's advice, and seek the reasons underlying the assertion of a constitutional principle, we must accept that European legal supremacy appears vulnerable to claims that it is isolated from, and indeed may be contrary to, the core elements of the constitution within which it must reside if it is to be given any legal effect by domestic courts.

VI. National Sovereignty

As seen above, constitutional lawyers have been very preoccupied with the issue of parliamentary sovereignty and its reconciliation with membership of the EC. Popular debate, however, often focuses upon the question of national sovereignty and whether the United Kingdom remains a sovereign state while within the EC. The 1971 White Paper did address this issue (unlike the issue of parliamentary sovereignty) and stated categorically that '[t]here is no question of any erosion of essential national sovereignty; what is proposed is a sharing and an enlargement

---

[116] Allan, n. 114 above, at 448.
[117] MacCormick, n 110 above, p 81.
[118] Craig, n 100 above, at 221.
[119] Allan, n 114 above, at 449.

of individual national sovereignties in the general interest.'[120] As Hugo Young has pointed out, this was 'open, as intended, to many constructions.'[121] For example, what aspects of national sovereignty are to be regarded as essential? Does the word 'essential' add anything to the meaning of national sovereignty in this context? In his autobiography, Heath defends this passage in the White Paper and argues that the word 'essential' 'is very important' and insists that it 'is no mere sophistry'.[122] Heath defines essential national sovereignty as referring 'for example, to our powers of self-government, our right to safeguard national interests and to keep sole control of our armed forces.'[123] The difficulty with this definition is that reference to powers of self-government hardly seems to narrow the concept of national sovereignty to an essential component.

This crucial passage in the White Paper is also open to criticism in relation to its reference to a sharing and an enlargement of individual national sovereignties. In the words of Hugo Young, 'How individual national sovereignty could be shared, while at the same time being enlarged, without compromising its individuality, was a question to baffle any casuist.'[124] This question is addressed by Heath's distinctive theory of sovereignty, which he explained numerous times both inside and outside Parliament:

> There is a pooling of sovereignty … When we surrender some sovereignty, we shall have a share in the sovereignty of the Community as a whole, and of other members of it. It is not just, as is sometimes thought, an abandonment of sovereignty to other countries; it is a sharing of other people's sovereignty as well as a pooling of our own.[125]

This is a very pragmatic approach to the issue: national sovereignty can be exercised individually by a state or pooled with other states' sovereignties and used in conjunction with them. It is a pragmatic view shared by Heath's political opponent of the 1960s and 1970s, Harold Wilson,[126] and explains the reference to a sharing and enlargement of sovereignty in the White Paper. But it begs the question: what is this substance called national sovereignty which can be pooled? Sovereignty is often regarded as a form of independence or autonomy but, if this is so, how can independence be pooled without ceasing to be independent? If, instead, sovereignty refers to a form of power or influence on the international plane, then Heath's concept of pooling this entity becomes viable. Indeed, he may be correct to claim that the UK's power and influence is increased when

---

[120] White Paper, n 25 above, para. 29.

[121] H Young, n 17 above, p 246.

[122] Heath, n 30 above, p 716.

[123] *Ibid.*

[124] H Young, n 17 above, p 246.

[125] Quoted in Heath, n 30 above, p 357.

[126] 'The whole history of political progress is a history of gradual abandonment of national sovereignty … The question is not whether national sovereignty remains absolute or not, but in what way one is prepared to sacrifice sovereignty, and to whom and for what purpose' (HC Deb, 5th Series, Vol 645, cols 1666–67, 2 August 1961).

operating within the EC, because it merges with the international influence, power and reputation of other states. But is sovereignty merely another word for dominion? Regrettably, Heath does not investigate this issue in his public pronouncements on pooling sovereignty.

However, the idea of pooling sovereignty continues to attract heavyweight academic support. For example, MacCormick, in words which could have been spoken by Heath, argues that 'the sovereignty of the Community's member states has not been lost, but subjected to a process of division and combination internally and hence in a way enhanced externally.'[127] But MacCormick takes this argument to a place where Heath, and most modern-day politicians, would fear to go, when he argues that

> the process of division and combination has taken us 'beyond the sovereign state', indeed, well beyond it. Despite the rhetoric of politicians, it cannot be credibly argued that any member state of the European Union remains politically or legally a sovereign state in the strict or traditional sense of these terms.[128]

In many ways this is a far more logical conclusion than Heath's (and his successors') claim that sovereignty can be pooled and yet simultaneously retained. MacCormick convincingly argues that once national sovereignty is pooled in an external body, it is no longer available on an individual state level in the same way as it was previously. Thus, in MacCormick's view, no EC member states remain in possession of ultimate power over their own internal affairs.[129] This view is also open to criticism, however, because of its unqualified, dichotomous nature: a state either is sovereign or it is not. This seems to be an unrealistically stark view in today's globalised world. Every state is involved in relations on the international plane through trade agreements, international treaties, political alliances and international conflicts. The extent of international involvement seems ideally suited to explanation by a variable approach to sovereignty: a state can be more or less sovereign depending upon the extent of its residual freedom of action and decision.[130] Relevant factors in determining a state's degree of sovereignty may include its ability to influence other states and to be free of influence from others. No state in today's world retains absolute sovereignty, but there is a minimum beyond which sovereignty will be entirely lost. Once lost, however, the 'state' will no longer be a state at all, and it is likely that it will be governed by an external body or that there will be no effective government. Has the UK's sovereignty really fallen below this bare minimum? There seems little evidence of this, given that it continues to be governed by an internal body which, although often giving effect to Community laws, also frequently acts without EC prompting and even,

---

[127] MacCormick, n 110 above, p 133.
[128] *Ibid.*
[129] *Ibid,* p 132.
[130] See E Wicks, 'State Sovereignty: Towards a Refined Legal Conceptualisation' (2000) 29 *Anglo-Am LR* 282 for a more detailed investigation of this conception of state sovereignty.

sometimes, without EC approval. This internal government is subject to external influences beyond the EC – for example, from the US government – and is itself sometimes able to influence world affairs without doing so through the body of the EC. The United Kingdom remains free to withdraw from the EC, and the authority for its continued involvement in this organisation (and the organisation's superior legal status) derives, as was explained above, from the UK's constitution. There can be no doubt that the UK's sovereignty has been greatly diminished by entry into, and continued involvement in, the EC, but a sufficient degree of sovereignty remains in order for the United Kingdom to continue in existence as a sovereign state.

Whether this is a good thing or not is also open to question. MacCormick, for example, welcomes the loss of sovereignty that he perceives: 'Western Europe's successful transcendence of the sovereign state and of state sovereignty is greatly to be welcomed. It has been and will be a condition for the security of peace and prosperity among us.'[131] There is no doubt that the history of the twentieth century reveals the dangers inherent in national sovereignty. Much international conflict, as well as human rights abuses, has stemmed from the excessive use of national sovereignty. The forces of globalisation also indicate that many modern-day problems do not respect national borders.[132] But, while it is vital (if we are to learn the lessons of history) not to value national sovereignty as an inevitable good, we should also be clear that it is not always a threat. While much of Heath's pragmatic view of sovereignty is open to criticism, he makes a valuable point when he argues that 'sovereignty is not an absolute good in itself. Its value is defined by the use we make of it.'[133] National sovereignty is not intrinsically good or bad; it is an instrument whose value depends upon the purposes for which we use it. To celebrate the death of the sovereign state, as MacCormick and many other commentators do, is to conflate sovereignty's uses with its nature, and may fail to confront the forces which have from time to time corrupted the concept. These destructive forces, including nationalism, xenophobia and racism, are unlikely to be buried with the corpse of the sovereign state.

Whether the UK's national sovereignty is regarded as diminished (the view preferred here) or lost entirely, the possibility arises that the EU may merge all the pooled national sovereignties of member states and become a sovereign entity itself. Perhaps the EU could even become a sovereign state, much as the United States or Australia did when the individual states became united? Or, perhaps, the most fitting parallel would be the union of England and Scotland, and later Ireland, to become the United Kingdom? Democratic approval for such

---

[131] MacCormick, n 110 above, p 133.

[132] Heath recognised this and argued that 'it is only through international institutions, in which sovereignty is pooled, that we shall be able collectively to manage the many international problems which human progress brings in its wake: environmental change; trade liberalisation; economic and social dislocation; and criminal activity … In the modern world, so many of the problems and challenges that we face have no respect for national boundaries' (Heath, n 30 above, p 718).

[133] *Ibid.*

a step would be essential, however, and, unlike the incremental moves towards close European economic and political integration thus far, democratic approval would need to be explicit and informed. But is a gradual merging of sovereignties to form a new state possible? Can the degree of lost sovereignty from member states re-emerge at the supranational level? MacCormick usefully raises the question of whether sovereignty is like property 'which can be given up only when another person gains it' or whether we should think of it 'more like virginity, something that can be lost by one without another's gaining it.'[134] MacCormick chooses the analogy of virginity because he recognises that its loss 'in apt circumstances can even be a matter for celebration,'[135] but nonetheless this is a more fitting analogy than that of property. If, as has been argued in this section, national sovereignty is a matter of degree, and a state can be more or less sovereign depending upon its current international commitments, it is not something which can be passed on to another body. The only circumstance in which a state's sovereignty might be bequeathed to another body is if through a treaty (or, in the past, through conquest) a state ceased to exist in its entirety and title passed to another state.[136] In the normal course of events, with the UK's sovereignty ebbing and flowing on an almost daily basis, the EU cannot be the automatic beneficiary of every ounce of diminished UK sovereignty. This is not to say, of course, that the EU could not acquire a form of national sovereignty, but it will not do so by default as the supranational body responsible for diminishing aspects of the national sovereignty of its member states.

VII. Conclusion

The UK's entry to the EC in 1972 was the most significant constitutional event for centuries. It carried with it the potential to overwhelm not only the UK constitution but also the state itself. Even the most restrictive view of the implications of EC membership must acknowledge that a new principle of European legal supremacy has been incorporated into the UK constitution, necessitating a rethinking of parliamentary sovereignty and a diminution of national sovereignty. The constitution has survived, however, and is best seen as the source, rather than the victim, of European law. The sovereign state has also survived and is likely to continue to do so unless and until the people exercise their democratic right of self-determination to choose otherwise. The right to self-determination, an idea which will be encountered again in the following chapter, on devolution, has been defined by the International Court of Justice as 'the need to pay regard

---

[134] MacCormick, n 110 above, p 126.
[135] *Ibid.*
[136] As, for example, in respect of England and Scotland in 1707.

to the freely expressed will of the peoples.'[137] The absorption of the United Kingdom into a federal European state would require democratic approval under international law. Democratic legitimacy is also vital, of course, within domestic constitutional terms. Membership of the EC is an issue which continues to generate heated political and public debate, and often the important constitutional issues become clouded by euro-sceptic or europhile rhetoric. This is an issue, however, where public opinion is crucial. Many of the constitutional changes discussed in this book (those of 1832, 1911, 1998) have been given democratic approval, but many others (those of 1688, 1707, 1953) have not. It cannot be argued, therefore, that constitutional change necessitates an exercise of popular sovereignty in order to legitimise it. But the potential implications of closer European integration are so profound for the nature of the state that this may be one issue on which the ultimate decision will need to be taken by the public, especially given the central role which democracy retains within the UK constitution.

The impact of EC membership upon traditional doctrines such as parliamentary sovereignty has been illuminating in confirming the evolutionary nature of the UK constitution – a constitution which bends but does not break when confronted by a challenge to some of its most fundamental principles. Thus, as of 2005, the UK Parliament remains sovereign, albeit limited in its law-making powers in the European context (as in others) under the constitution; the United Kingdom remains a sovereign state, but one which has chosen for economic and political reasons to accept diminished freedom of action and decision; and the supremacy of European law over national law is the latest surprising addition to the UK constitution: not a revolutionary change but still an unprecedented evolutionary leap.

---

[137] *Western Sahara* [1975] *ICJ Reports* 12, at para 59.

8

1998 – Devolution to Scotland, Wales and Northern Ireland: Decentralising the Union State

In terms of constitutional reform, 1998 was a year unprecedented in its significance. Blair's New Labour government was elected to power with the potentially interesting combination of a huge parliamentary majority and manifesto commitments to a wide-ranging programme of constitutional reform, to include the incorporation of the European Convention for the Protection of Human Rights and Fundamental Freedoms, removal of the hereditary peers from the House of Lords, the enactment of a Freedom of Information Bill, a referendum on electoral reform for Westminster (the only significant reform never to materialise) and devolution for Scotland, Wales and Northern Ireland. It is the latter which forms the focus of this chapter and it is, notwithstanding the constitutional importance of the other reforms (many of which have been touched upon in previous chapters), the change with the greatest impact upon the UK's evolving constitution. The reason for this is clear: devolution calls into question the very nature of the United Kingdom, a state founded by unions between England and the now devolved territories and nations. Thus, not only for the constitution, but also for the state itself, the 1998 devolution Acts would be determinative of the direction of future evolution.

I. The Background to 1998 Devolution

a) A Union State

The United Kingdom of Great Britain and Northern Ireland is best described as a union state. It is the embodiment of various agreements between its component parts, on the basis of which the state continues to function. Throughout the history of the formation of this union, England has always been dominant. And yet it is difficult to pinpoint the origins of the English state, which evolved during the tenth century as Wessex expanded.[1]

The first 'union' – although here, as elsewhere, that is a euphemism – occurred during the thirteenth and fourteenth centuries, when Wales was conquered under the reign of Edward I and was then subsequently confirmed in two Acts of Parliament in the sixteenth century. The first of these, in 1536, entitled 'an Act for laws and justice to be ministered in Wales in like form as it is in this realm' declared that Wales had always been a part of England. The second Act, in 1543, was entitled 'an Act for certain ordinances in the King's dominions and principality of Wales', and together these two Acts can be regarded as the Acts of Union between England and Wales. Despite the one-sided nature of the initial union, it has evolved to be the most secure of the three unions which comprise the modern-day union state of the United Kingdom. As will be seen below, Welsh nationalism has developed in recent years but has been more concerned with the preservation of Welsh culture than with a desire to achieve political independence from England.

By contrast, Scotland was never conquered by England and instead negotiated the terms of a union with England and Wales in 1707, following a century of regal union. As discussed in chapter 2, there was never any doubt about who would be the senior partner in the union, but Scotland did obtain significant concessions to preserve Scottish identity within the union, in key areas such as church and law. Despite, or perhaps because of, this, Scottish nationalism (unlike that in Wales) has increasingly sought political independence and an end to the 1707 union.

The third 'union' which created the union state of the United Kingdom occurred in 1800 when Great Britain and Ireland united to form the United Kingdom of Great Britain and Ireland. This followed many years of subjugation of Ireland by England, culminating in the assumption of direct rule by Henry VIII in 1534. During the seventeenth century, many Scottish Protestants moved to Ulster in the north of Ireland, and in 1727 the Celtic, Catholic population was disfranchised. During the late eighteenth century, a Protestant Irish Parliament acquired significant powers but used these to negotiate and agree a union with Britain. The union did not provide the anticipated benefits for Ireland, however, and British indifference to Irish economic and social problems encouraged a growth in nationalist feeling. In 1921, after decades of political debate about Irish home rule, the Anglo-Irish Treaty enabled Ireland to become a self-governing dominion within the British Empire.[2] Six counties in the north chose not to join the newly formed Irish Free State and instead obtained home rule – or devolved – status within the United Kingdom under the Government of Ireland Act 1920.

---

[1] As Bogdanor explains, 'The English state never began. Rather, it evolved' (V Bogdanor, *Devolution in the United Kingdom* (Oxford, Oxford University Press, 1999), p 5).

[2] In 1949, the Irish Free State became the Republic of Ireland, severing all ties with the British Empire.

From these, often murky, origins the union state of the United Kingdom was founded. As each component part of the United Kingdom was incorporated, the terms of its incorporation were evident within the agreements. Thus, Walker has argued that the constitutional character of a union state such as the United Kingdom cannot be seen in isolation from the 'foundation parchments' of the union(s).[3] This view certainly resonates with the conclusions of chapter 2 in which fundamental aspects of the treaty of union between England and Scotland were argued to still reside within the modern UK constitution. Walker's argument logically continues with the recognition that the union state thus 'provides a key historical pathway towards a more general model of asymmetrical government, in which a heterogeneity of governance arrangements between regions becomes a normal and persistent feature.'[4] This convincing argument is illuminating for two reasons. First, it reveals that recent concerns about the development of an asymmetrical form of governance under the UK constitution are misplaced. As the composite of a number of unions between states and regions, asymmetry has always been a feature of the United Kingdom, and its current appearance within the context of the 1998 devolution arrangements and subsequent developments is, in the words of Walker, merely 'a new but essentially unremarkable chapter in a long and familiar constitutional narrative.'[5] Second, recognition of the United Kingdom as a union state provides a much more accurate, if complex, picture of the state than to focus solely upon its unitary nature. While it is true that the United Kingdom is a unitary (as opposed to federal) state, it is an entity with far more complexity than is indicated by the unitary label.

The United Kingdom has traditionally been a very centralised state. Indeed, Bogdanor claims that 'no other democracy seeks to manage the affairs of so large a population through a single parliament.'[6] The myth that this parliament is omnipotent only compounds the centralisation of governmental power in Westminster. Such a tradition sits uneasily, however, with the nature of the United Kingdom as a series of unions between states and/or regional entities. Keating has acknowledged the survival within Scotland, Ireland and, to a lesser extent, Wales of 'a concept of the UK as a political union rather than a unitary state.'[7] Perhaps only England – the dominant partner – would emphasise the unitary over the union. A recognition that Wales, Ireland, and Scotland united with England at various stages encourages the retention of distinct cultural, and in some cases political, national identities. That such identities would not remain compatible forever with the centralisation of power in London seems to present a foreseeable

---

[3] N Walker, 'Beyond the Unitary Conception of the United Kingdom Constitution?' [2000] *PL* 384, at 397.

[4] *Ibid*, at 397–98.

[5] *Ibid*, at 398.

[6] Bogdanor, n 1 above, p 1.

[7] M Keating, 'The United Kingdom as a Post-Sovereign Polity' in M O'Neill (ed), *Devolution and British Politics* (Harlow, Pearson Education, 2004), p 319.

danger to the unitary nature of the UK constitution. If change were sought to the constitutional arrangements, the extreme option would be secession: a dis-integration of the union state into its pre-existing components. Various factors mitigate against this extremity, however, including the political and frequently violent conflict in Northern Ireland; the fact that 'there was not and never has been, a clearly territorial Wales'[8]; and the long-established cultural, political and economic ties between all of the UK's component parts. This is not to say that there are not voices in favour of breaking up the union, particularly in Scotland. But increasingly secession and subsequent statehood are not seen as the only – or even the best – option for nationalists to pursue. As Tierney has identified, the models of institutional change now being advocated within sub-state nations such as Scotland, Quebec and Catalonia 'focus increasingly upon reconfiguring relations with their respective host states in preference to secession.'[9] These sub-state nations seek enhanced autonomy and recognition within a larger state, while also possibly seeking some measure of discrete international personality.[10] This is not an easier option, from a constitutional perspective. Secession is far less problematic in constitutional terms than an arrangement which seeks to recon-cile devolved powers with a unitary constitution.[11] A grant of independence to Scotland, for example, would involve little more in legal terms than the repeal of the Acts of Union 1707, whereas the solution achieved in 1998 of Scottish devolution requires far more complex legal and constitutional restructuring.

The term 'devolution' refers to 'a transfer of powers from a superior to an infe-rior political authority.'[12] As such it mitigates the centralisation of a unitary constitutional arrangement but falls short of a federalist arrangement under which supreme power would be divided between various regional or national parliaments. As Burrows notes, devolution takes place within a limited frame-work set out in legislation[13] and, as such, may be regarded as 'a paradise for lawyers' because, at least in relation to the United Kingdom, 'the written text is at the heart of the process [and] little will be left to chance.'[14] The details of the three distinct devolution schemes enacted in 1998 will be considered below. First, however, it may be illuminating to consider, briefly, the UK's earlier attempts to devolve power to Ireland, Scotland, and Wales, for it is these failures that created the conditions for the subsequent schemes and highlighted the pitfalls which the 1998 Labour government would need to avoid if its schemes were to be any more successful.

---

[8] KO Morgan, 'Welsh Devolution: The Past and the Future' in B Taylor and K Thomson (eds), *Scotland and Wales: Nations Again?* (Cardiff, University of Wales Press, 1999), p 201.

[9] S Tierney, 'Reframing Sovereignty? Sub-State National Societies and Contemporary Challenges to the Nation-State' (2005) 54 *ICLQ* 161 at 175.

[10] *Ibid*, at 162.

[11] *Ibid*, at 181.

[12] Bogdanor, n 1 above, p 2. The Report of the Royal Commission on the Constitution (the Kilbrandon Report) in 1973 defined devolution as 'the delegation of central government powers without the relinquishment of sovereignty' (Cmnd 5460, para 543).

[13] D Burrows, *Devolution* (London, Sweet & Maxwell, 2000), p 1.

[14] *Ibid*, p 2.

b) Ireland: The First Attempt at Devolution 1921–72

Home rule for Ireland emerged as the most convulsive issue in British politics between 1886 and 1914.[15] During this period, three Home Rule Bills were introduced into Parliament: the first, in 1886, was defeated in the House of Commons; the second, in 1893, was defeated in the House of Lords; and the third became law in 1914 after the first use of the Parliament Act procedure (as discussed in chapter 5). This third Home Rule Bill received the Royal Assent six weeks after the Second World War commenced and was therefore put on the statute book together with a Suspensory Act providing that it would not come into force until the end of the war. Significantly, Prime Minister Asquith also promised that it would not come into force without some special provision for Ulster, a province in the north of Ireland.[16] This concession acknowledged that a national and religious conflict existed in Ireland, which could lead to civil war unless special arrangements were made for the largely Protestant region of Ulster. The Government of Ireland Act 1920 subsequently revealed that the special arrangement would amount to a partition of Ireland. In an attempt to mitigate the partition, home rule would be available for both parts of Ireland, with separate parliaments in Dublin and Belfast. This proposed solution was far from satisfactory, however, because the North had not requested home rule, and the rest of Ireland wanted far more, namely secession from the union. In the words of Asquith, as quoted by Bogdanor, 'Northern Ireland was to be given a Parliament it did not want … while the rest of Ireland was to be given a Parliament it would not accept.'[17] The matter was superseded by the 1921 Anglo-Irish Treaty, which finally conceded the Irish demand for independence. The Treaty was embodied in domestic law in the Irish Free State (Agreement) Act 1922, which amends the Act of Union with Ireland of 1800 by excluding 26 counties from its ambit. The remaining six counties[18] retained their position under the 1800 Act of Union but subject to the terms of the 1920 Government of Ireland Act, which now came into force in the North only. Thus, the six counties of Northern Ireland were now left with a system of home rule which they had not desired: 'the relic of a failed attempt to resolve the Irish problem.'[19]

This period of home rule – the first experience of devolved government within the union state – lasted from 1921 until 1972. It is a unique precursor to later devolution across the United Kingdom, not least because uniquely it was accepted by the devolved region only in order to ensure that it remained within

---

[15] Bogdanor, n.1 above, p 19.

[16] *Ibid*, p 60.

[17] *Ibid*, p 66.

[18] The Ulster Unionists insisted upon a six-county exclusion, rather than one comprising all nine counties of Ulster, in order to be sure of retaining a Unionist majority and thus a veto on a united Ireland. As Bogdanor notes, the border created 'had little logic for it partitioned Ulster as well as Northern Ireland' (*ibid*, pp 64–65).

[19] *Ibid*, p 66.

the United Kingdom.[20] The Ulster Unionists came to recognise the advantages of home rule, however, particularly the role that the Northern Ireland Parliament could play as a veto on incorporation into a united Ireland. Home rule also had the unfortunate effect of enabling the Unionist majority to infringe the rights of the Catholic minority. The UK government remained indifferent to this until 1968 when Catholic dissent became violent. After decades of abdicating responsibility for the troubled region, in 1972 Westminster reasserted its authority by first proroguing[21] and then abolishing[22] the Northern Ireland Parliament. One further brief period of home rule between January and May 1974 failed and a prolonged period of direct rule began. As Bogdanor notes, this commonly used phrase of 'direct rule' is revealing, as it suggests a very different settlement than complete integration within the United Kingdom: 'No one claims, for example, that Scotland or Yorkshire is under direct rule.'[23] The failure of the home rule experiment had a number of democratic disadvantages beyond the failure of a peaceful settlement. Under direct rule, laws for Northern Ireland are made by Orders in Council without effective parliamentary scrutiny and by a Secretary of State for Northern Ireland who does not (and cannot, because of the existence of distinct political parties in the Northern Ireland polity) represent a Northern Ireland constituency. Furthermore, none of the Northern Ireland political parties have representation within the UK government, and thus voters in the province are unable to have any say in choosing the unitary government.[24] 'Direct rule' is not a viable long-term option within a purportedly democratic state. The lessons of the home rule failure make clear that any devolved alternative must involve both communities within Northern Ireland in order to be stable and enduring. Given the violent political conflict within Northern Ireland, this would not be an easy task, as the governments and parties discovered in 1998.

c) Scotland and Wales: The 1978 Devolution Acts

In the 1707 Union with England, Scotland had secured the independence of its legal system and Church – aspects of Scottish identity seen as critical at the time. However, by the twentieth century it was obvious that the institutions of government were becoming more important. During the late 1960s and early 1970s nationalist support in Scotland increased and the Scottish National Party (SNP) became a significant political force.[25] Welsh nationalism was also on the increase,

---

[20] *Ibid*, p 55.
[21] Northern Ireland (Temporary Provisions) Act 1972.
[22] Northern Ireland Constitution Act 1973.
[23] Bogdanor, n 1 above, p 100.
[24] *Ibid*, p 101.
[25] Bogdanor argues that one factor, among many, was that UK entry to the EC had ensured that England could no longer threaten the imposition of tariffs on Scottish goods if Scotland were to gain independence (*ibid*, p 127). Perhaps one economic union may be regarded as negating the need for an earlier one?

but was very different in nature. Plaid Cymru, established in 1925, was originally a movement to preserve the Welsh language. In a nation where 80 per cent of the population did not speak Welsh, this goal limited the party's electoral chances, but by the 1970s, despite diminishing public support, Plaid Cymru began to gain seats from Labour and thus a perception grew that nationalism was on the increase in Wales as well as in Scotland. In 1968, the Wilson government established a Royal Commission which reported in 1973. Its report (the Kilbrandon Report)[26] was not unanimous, and indeed there was very little agreement evident within it except that a federalist solution was rejected and a directly elected assembly for Scotland was proposed. Before this report was published, the idea of a Scottish assembly had obtained some support from Prime Minister Heath after it was recommended by the Scottish Constitutional Committee which he established. Heath included a Scottish assembly (to consider the second reading, committee and report stages of Scottish Bills) in the 1970 Conservative election manifesto, but it was a promise never implemented. Subsequently, the Conservative party retreated from its support for devolution, ironically just at the time that Labour warmed to the idea.

In September 1974, Wilson's Labour government published a White Paper entitled *Democracy and Devolution: Proposals for Scotland and Wales*[27] containing proposals for directly elected assemblies for Scotland and Wales, with legislative powers for Scotland but only executive powers for Wales. This was the first appearance of the asymmetrical legislative/executive distinction between Scotland and Wales, which was to form a core part of New Labour's reforms in the late 1990s and yet, as Bogdanor notes, it was never a decision of principle but rather a hasty response to a perceived electoral threat from the SNP.[28] In November 1975, the Labour government issued a second White Paper setting out the detailed proposals.[29] Then, in December 1976, the government, now led by Callaghan, introduced the Scotland and Wales Bill into Parliament. There was no clear majority in favour of devolution, and when the government lost a guillotine motion on 2 February 1977, the Bill was lost. However, the minority Labour government could only continue to govern with the support of the Liberals, and they insisted upon the introduction of a new devolution Bill. The second attempt was very similar to the first, although the government's rather transparent attempt to diffuse opposition to Welsh devolution by including it in the same Bill as Scottish devolution was discontinued and two separate Bills were introduced. The Bills were passed but would not come into force without the support of the Scottish and Welsh people. Referendums were held in Scotland and Wales on 1 May 1979. They proved disastrous for the government. In Scotland, there was a narrow majority in favour of devolution (51.6 per cent) but, on a low turnout, this failed to reach the 40 per cent of the registered electorate required by the Bill.

[26] Cmnd 5460 (1973).
[27] Cmnd 5732 (1974).
[28] Bogdanor, n 1 above, pp 178–79.
[29] *Our Changing Democracy: Devolution to Scotland and Wales* (Cmnd 6348).

In Wales, the situation was even more embarrassing for the government. Only 20.2 per cent voted in favour on a turnout of only 58.8 per cent. The government's devolution policy was in tatters. The Conservative opposition won a motion of no confidence (with the support of the Liberals and the SNP) on 28 March 1979, and the Callaghan government fell. Thus, in the midst of the severe economic problems and industrial unrest of the notorious winter of discontent, it was the government's failed policy on devolution which caused its collapse and heralded 18 years of Conservative rule.[30] Once in office the Conservative government wasted no time in repealing the devolution Acts, and devolution remained off the political agenda for nearly two decades. It should not be overlooked, however, that despite the fiasco of the 1979 referendums, a majority of Scottish voters in the referendum had voted in favour of devolution. And their causes of discontent were only to be intensified by 18 years of rule by a Westminster government with only minority (indeed minimal) support in Scotland.

II. 1998 Devolution

a) The Process

Given that the 1979 Labour government lost power due to its disastrous devolution referendums, it is astonishing that one of Labour's first acts once it finally regained power 18 years later, was voluntarily to hold further referendums on the same subject.[31] The long years in opposition had convinced many in the Labour party of the need to pursue devolution, especially for Scotland. In 1989, a Scottish Constitutional Convention was established, with participation by Labour and the Liberal Democrats as well as trade union and church groups (although neither the Conservatives nor the SNP participated). The establishment of the Convention was a direct response to an increasing sense of injustice in Scotland that it was governed by an English Conservative administration with little support in Scotland and even less concern for it. For example, in the 1987 Election the Conservatives had won only 10 out of the 70 Scottish seats. (By 1997 it would win none.) Two reports were issued by the Convention, and these broadly lay out the scheme for future devolution.[32] The 1990 Report is credited with changing the views of the then Labour leader, Neil Kinnock,[33] who in the 1970s had been one of the many Labour MPs strongly opposed to devolution on the basis that it would represent a loss of vital power of central government needed to remedy

---

[30] Bogdanor, n 1 above, p 191.
[31] B Taylor, J Curtice and K Thomson, 'Introduction and Conclusions' in B Taylor and K Thomson (eds), *Scotland and Wales: Nations Again?* (Cardiff, University of Wales Press, 1999), pp xxiii–xxiv.
[32] *Towards Scotland's Parliament* (1990), and *Scotland's Parliament, Scotland's Right* (1995).
[33] Bogdanor, n 1 above, p 198.

the very territorial inequalities which were causing discontent.[34] By the early 1990s, many in the Labour Party were prepared to rethink their traditionally centralist ideology.[35] Kinnock's successor as Labour leader, John Smith, was a far more committed believer in devolution and left a legacy which Tony Blair would not be permitted to ignore.[36] Blair himself, however, was less committed to devolution.[37]

Blair's reservations led him to insist upon referendums being held before the devolution legislation was introduced into Parliament and, ironically, this probably guaranteed the Acts' success by disarming parliamentary criticism. Other probable reasons for Labour's decision to hold new referendums in 1997 include an attempt to avoid division within the party (as the policy was decided in opposition before Labour's overwhelming parliamentary majority was foreseen) and a need to counter the damaging image of 'tax and spend' in the context of Conservative criticism of a so-called 'tartan tax'.[38] This last factor explains the inclusion of a specific supplementary question in the Scottish referendum on a potential tax-varying power for the proposed Scottish Parliament. The Scottish referendum was held on 11 September 1997. On a 60.2 per cent turnout, 74.3 per cent voted in favour of a Scottish Parliament and 63.5 per cent in favour of this Parliament having tax-varying powers. In Wales (where the referendum was held a week later in a rather blatant attempt to enable the vote to be swayed by a yes vote in Scotland) the outcome was less decisive. On a low turnout of 51 per cent, only 50.3 per cent voted in favour of a Welsh Assembly with 49.7 per cent voting against. Thus, only one in four of the Welsh electorate voted for devolution. It was hardly the positive endorsement for which the government hoped. Nevertheless, the government proceeded by introducing both the Scotland Bill and the Government of Wales Bill into Parliament. The government's huge majority in the House of Commons ensured an easy passage in the Lower House, and the House of Lords, constitutionally restricted by the Salisbury Doctrine, was obliged not to oppose this government manifesto commitment. Thus, the Government of Wales Act received the Royal Assent in July 1998 and the Scotland Act in November 1998.

---

[34] *Ibid*, p 140.

[35] As O'Neill explains, 'It was now more favourable to post-modern notions of community politics, cultural pluralism and democratic empowerment. "New Labour" broke with its own centralist past and embraced devolution for principled as well as for pragmatic reasons' (M O'Neill, 'Great Britain: From Dicey to Devolution' (2000) 53 *Parliamentary Affairs* 69, at 77).

[36] Blair himself has described constitutional reform, and especially Scottish devolution, as Smith's 'unfinished business which we must now finish' ('John Smith Lecture', 7 February 1996, reproduced in T Blair, *New Britain – My Vision of a Young Country* (London, Fourth Estate, 1996), p 310).

[37] Naughtie describes Blair's position on devolution as follows: 'Having launched himself as a constitutional reformer, Blair wanted the [devolution] legislation to pass quickly and with as little collateral damage to the party as possible. But no one believed that when Blair had gone anyone would find the word "devolution" engraved on his heart. In conversation he would raise his eyes heavenwards and hope it would soon be over' (J Naughtie, *The Rivals: The Intimate Story of a Political Marriage* (London, Fourth Estate, 2001), p 178).

[38] Taylor, Curtice and Thomson, n 31 above, p xxv.

The Scotland Act 1998 establishes a Scottish Parliament,[39] elected by means of the Additional Member System (AMS) form of proportional representation, with powers to legislate on all issues except certain 'reserved' matters.[40] The Parliament has a limited tax-varying power of three pence in the pound. There is also established a Scottish executive headed by a First Minister elected by the Scottish Parliament and appointed by the Queen. The Government of Wales Act 1998 establishes a National Assembly for Wales, elected by means of the AMS form of proportional representation, but devolves only executive powers (that is, those previously exercised by a minister) onto this Assembly.[41] The Assembly elects a First Secretary and Assembly Secretaries who form an executive committee.

The third devolution scheme of 1998 had a very different history. The IRA ceasefire of August 1994 opened the door for Sinn Fein to participate in multi-party talks. Under the chairmanship of Senator George Mitchell, the talks eventually culminated in the Belfast Agreement, or (more emotively) the Good Friday Agreement, of April 1998.[42] In fact, either name is a misnomer for there were two distinct agreements rather than one concluded at Stormont in April 1998. The multi-party agreement between the major Northern Ireland political parties was a hugely significant political breakthrough in the context of centuries of political mistrust and decades of violent conflict. But it was the British–Irish Agreement between the two governments which had legal significance as an international treaty.[43] As will be discussed in more detail below, the international nature of the Belfast Agreement, and subsequent settlement, positions the Northern Ireland experience beyond mere devolution of government within a unitary state. The terms of the Belfast Agreement(s) were given democratic legitimacy by overwhelming support in a referendum on 22 May 1998. On a turnout of 81.1 per cent (the stark contrast with low turnouts in Wales and Scotland no doubt reflecting the fact that the political conflict in Northern Ireland is unavoidably fundamental to the population's daily life), 71.1 per cent voted in favour of the Agreement. In a move that confirms the point made above about the international flavour of the Northern Ireland settlement, a referendum was also held in the Republic of Ireland in which 94 per cent voted in favour on a turnout of 56 per cent.[44] The Agreement's novel scheme of power-sharing, having been

---

[39] See s 1(1) of the Scotland Act 1998 for the stark statement that 'There shall be a Scottish Parliament.'

[40] Listed in Sch 5, including 'the Constitution', foreign affairs, defence, national security, fiscal, economic and monetary policy, and other, perhaps less obvious, matters where discrepancies across the United Kingdom were held to be unacceptable, such as immigration, telecommunications, broadcasting and abortion.

[41] The executive powers devolved are listed in Sch 2 of the Act and include agriculture and fisheries, economic development, education, environment, health, housing, social services and transport.

[42] For an interesting account of the multi-party talks, see GJ Mitchell, *Making Peace* (London, William Heinemann, 1999).

[43] A Morgan, *The Belfast Agreement: A Practical Legal Analysis* (London, Belfast Press, 2000), p 8.

[44] The Agreement necessitated an amendment to the Irish Constitution (relinquishing its territorial claim over the North), thus requiring a referendum within the Republic of Ireland.

approved by a convincing (cross-community) majority in Northern Ireland, was thus ready for implementation.

The Northern Ireland Act 1998 establishes a Northern Ireland Assembly, elected by the Single Transferable Vote (STV) form of proportional representation, with powers to legislate on all matters except for 'excepted' matters (similar to the reserved matters in the Scotland Act 1998) and 'reserved' matters (including policing and criminal justice which, given their controversial nature in Northern Ireland, require the consent of the Secretary of State). An executive is to be formed through a novel voting mechanism which ensures cross-community support and is headed by a cross-community partnership of a First Minister and Deputy First Minister. As Wilford notes, 'If the process of reaching the Agreement was itself tortuous, that of implementing it was to prove no less difficult.'[45] The political conflict in Northern Ireland, together with the international context of the Agreement, raised a number of difficulties unique to the Northern Ireland context. This will be considered below. First, however, the similarities between the three devolution schemes will be identified. Given the very different conditions, needs and demands of Scotland, Wales and Northern Ireland, it is perhaps the similarities, rather than the differences, between the three schemes which are most surprising and noteworthy.

b) The 1998 Devolution Acts: Common Principles

All three Acts have the same underlying premise: the sovereignty of the Westminster Parliament is not effected. Brazier has identified a 'triple lock' on the preservation of parliamentary sovereignty in the devolution Acts. First, existing constitutional principle ensures that powers conferred by Westminster could be reclaimed.[46] Under the Diceyian conception of parliamentary sovereignty, so dominant in English constitutional thought, no Act of Parliament could reduce Parliament's omnipotence in the future. As if to confirm this constitutional principle, the devolution Acts contain explicit protection of it. Section 28(7) of the Scotland Act 1998 states that: 'This section does not affect the power of the Parliament of the United Kingdom to make laws for Scotland.' In other words, even those matters not reserved to the Westminster Parliament in the Act remain subject to Westminster's overriding legislative competence.[47] While this clause may be regarded as the second lock on parliamentary sovereignty, it can also, as Loveland has pointed out, be regarded 'from a traditional constitutional

---

[45] R Wilford, 'Northern Ireland: Resolving an Ancient Quarrel?' in M O'Neill (ed), *Devolution and British Politics* (Harlow, Pearson Education, 2004), p 137.

[46] R Brazier, 'The Constitution of the United Kingdom' (1999) 58 *CLJ* 96 at 102.

[47] Brazier notes that this fundamental provision is hidden away in a subclause of s 28 of the Act and conjectures that 'it would not do to give too much prominence to the continuing and complete British legislative power in a measure designed to confer the maximum possible authority (short of independence) to the new Scottish institutions' (*ibid*, at 104).

standpoint, to be a wholly unnecessary provision.'[48] If Parliament is sovereign in the sense in which Dicey defined the term, it would be impossible for it to relinquish that sovereignty through any legislative measure. As Loveland notes, recent developments in the context of the EC (discussed in chapter 7) have caused a reassessment of such a stark approach, and perhaps section 28(7) is intended 'to deter the courts from allowing the *Factortame* principle to seep into non-EC related constitutional contexts.'[49] It is certainly a significant inclusion, raising thoughts perhaps of a Parliament that 'doth protest too much.' Rather than securing an extra lock on parliamentary sovereignty, section 28(7) suggests a vulnerability in the concept previously hidden from view. As Loveland argues, section 28(7) is significant because it suggests that 'the Blair government regarded entrenchment as politically undesirable, rather than legally unachievable.'[50] This would be a radical transformation in constitutional ideology.

Brazier's third lock for parliamentary sovereignty is also derived from the terms of the Acts: the express limitations on the powers of the devolved legislatures to legislate.[51] For example, the reserved matters within the Scotland Act include the constitution and the union between England and Scotland. Thus, neither parliamentary sovereignty nor the union state is susceptible to amendment by the Scottish Parliament under the terms of its constituent document. Whether this would constrain a nationalist-controlled Parliament and executive is, of course, another question. This raises the vital distinction between law and politics. Walker has argued that in the devolution Acts 'the British state has come closer than ever before to conceding that its retention of legislative omnipotence in the context of a devolution process is a matter of legal form rather than political substance.'[52] This distinction – if indeed it is one – will be discussed further below in relation to Scotland, for it is in this devolution settlement that parliamentary sovereignty is most challenged by constitutional realignments. However, it is worth noting here that the issue of 'legal form' in the devolution context is a matter for the judicial committee of the Privy Council.

This unusual judicial body was chosen by the Labour government to have competence for all devolution issues. That it was not the House of Lords which was chosen as the final court of appeal on these issues is perhaps understandable, given the political sensitivity of allowing Scottish criminal appeals to go to the House of Lords. The High Court of Justiciary has traditionally been the court of final instance for Scottish criminal appeals, and this is regarded as an important aspect of the independent Scottish legal system secured in the Act of Union. However, the Scotland Act 1998 does now permit appeals to the Privy Council, either by leave of the Scottish court or with special leave of the judicial

---

[48] I Loveland, *Constitutional Law, Administrative Law and Human Rights: A Critical Introduction*, 3rd edn (London, LexisNexis Butterworths, 2003), p 670.
[49] *Ibid.*
[50] *Ibid*, p 671.
[51] Brazier, n 46 above, at 106–7.
[52] Walker, n 3 above, p 397.

committee of the Privy Council, and this may be no less objectionable in Scottish eyes. Furthermore, arguments about the House of Lords being part of the Westminster Parliament (a sound criticism of the lack of separation of powers under the constitution) fail to pay adequate regard to, first, the Privy Council's nature as an ancient executive body and, second, the fact that many of the same judges will sit on the two judicial bodies. Although the Privy Council, as the final court of appeal for Commonwealth cases, may be the best option currently available, the complexity of the devolution schemes are best suited to a new, independent, Supreme Court.[53] This is one constitutional reform which has proven problematic to enact.

In the context of Labour's constitutional reform programme, promised in its 1997 Election manifesto, the use of proportional representation for elections to all three devolved institutions is significant. Despite the manifesto commitment to a referendum on the voting system for Westminster, no progress has been made in this regard, and the first-past-the-post system seems destined to endure for General Elections in the foreseeable future. In Scotland, Wales, and Northern Ireland, however, proportional representation is now a reality. The perceived need for a strong, majority, central government at Westminster does not apply to the devolved institutions and, in respect of Northern Ireland, proportional representation has a long history as an essential mechanism for ensuring cross-community representation. The introduction of proportional representation necessitates the exercise of coalition politics, although this has been more effective in some devolved areas than others. As O'Neill has recognised, coalition politics is better suited to a less polarised polity than Northern Ireland, but equally 'it is required here more than ever if reconciliation is to endure.'[54] After the first set of elections for each devolved region, no single party had a majority in any of them. In Wales, there was a minority (Labour) administration; in Scotland, a (Lib–Lab) coalition; and in Northern Ireland 'an artificially constructed cabinet in which all the political parties are represented.'[55] A new age of consensus politics has arrived throughout the United Kingdom, with only Westminster clinging to the old ideal of a two-party government and opposition dichotomy.

A further feature shared by all three devolution schemes is more problematic. Often referred to as the West Lothian question (after the MP for that constituency, Tam Dalyall, repeatedly raised it in the House of Commons), it is the constitutional imbalance of devolution to only three of the four component parts of the union state. This presents a dilemma because, in the absence of an English devolved parliament, Scottish, Welsh, and Northern Ireland MPs continue to speak and vote upon domestic English matters, while English MPs have no say on

---

[53] The Constitutional Reform Act 2005, Part 3 establishes a Supreme Court.
[54] M O'Neill, 'Reforming the British State: The 1998 Watershed' in M O'Neill (ed), *Devolution and British Politics* (Harlow, Pearson Education, 2004), p 202.
[55] Burrows, n 13 above, p 108.

matters devolved to those areas. While at present the West Lothian question may appear to be largely of academic concern, it would pose far more practical and politically contentious concerns if, for example, the Conservative party had a majority of English seats, but were outvoted on English matters by Scottish and Welsh Labour MPs. Blair's government's approach to the West Lothian question was to ignore it. As Hazell notes, 'Lord Irvine has famously said that the best way to answer the West Lothian question is to stop asking it: which led William Hague to retort that the best way to find an answer to the question might be to stop asking Lord Irvine.'[56] Indeed, given the Labour party's strength in Scotland and Wales, there seems little likelihood of a Labour party solution to the question. As Bogdanor has recognised, the logical solution is English devolution and a move towards a more symmetrical (perhaps federal) United Kingdom.[57] However, there is little demand for devolution in England, and the view is often taken that devolution should not be thrust upon those who do not want it. (Given that only one in four of the electorate in Wales voted for devolution, this is not an entirely convincing argument.) Keating has countered this argument by noting that it ignores the issue of England's motivation for rejecting the idea of devolution. If, as seems a reasonable summation, the people of England wish to retain a centralised system because of their own domination of it, their wishes may have to be overruled.[58] There are further objections to English devolution, however, particularly the argument that an English Parliament would be 'grotesquely overbalanced'[59] because of the disproportionate size, and economic power, of England within the United Kingdom. As Hazell notes, 'there is no successful federation in the world where one of the parts is greater than around one-third of the whole.'[60] When coupled with the fact that there is no public demand for it, and that there might still be a need for further dispersal of power to the English regions in order to ensure the democratic accountability and decentralisation which drove the 1998 devolution schemes, the English devolution option seems unrealistic.

The Labour government favoured regional devolution within England, and this may, inter alia, have provided a partial solution to the West Lothian question. Bogdanor goes so far as to prophesise that if regional devolution in England occurred, 'we would have embarked on a process of rolling devolution which could turn Britain into a quasi-federal state, still asymmetrical, but with a rough balance of power between Scotland, Wales and the English regions.'[61] The government chose an evolutionary approach, so suited to the British

---

[56] R Hazell, 'The English Question: Can Westminster be a Proxy for an English Parliament?' [2001] *PL* 268, at 275.

[57] Bogdanor, n 1 above, p 228.

[58] M Keating, 'What's Wrong with Asymmetrical Government?' in H Elcock and M Keating (eds), *Remaking the Union: Devolution and British Politics in the 1990s* (London, Frank Cass, 1998), p 207.

[59] Hazell, n 56 above, at 268.

[60] *Ibid.*

[61] Bogdanor, n 1 above, p 276.

constitution, and in a 1997 White Paper, *Building Partnerships for Prosperity*,[62] proposed the establishment of regional development agencies and indirectly elected regional chambers which could serve as first steps towards greater devolution.[63] The key would be public support and referendums on the establishment of elected regional assemblies in the three regions most favourable to the idea (the North East, the North West, and Yorkshire and the Humber) were arranged for Autumn 2004.

The concept of regional devolution had a number of shortcomings however. First, it would require reorganisation of local government, with a danger that if functions currently exercised on a county level were transferred to the regional level, devolution would amount to a centralisation, rather than a dispersal, of governmental power.[64] Secondly, Bogdanor's vision of a quasi-federal structure, with Scotland, Wales, and the English regions roughly balanced, ignores the crucial distinction between regions and nations. It is likely that Scotland would be dissatisfied with a similar degree of devolution to that accorded to English regions, and a snowball effect towards greater independence for the nations may commence. Finally, and the real stumbling block, there is little public demand for regional devolution. Thus, the first regional referendum in the North East on 4 November 2004 revealed a strong dislike of the government's plans for further regional devolution. The North East, the region considered most supportive of the regional idea, voted 78 per cent against the proposed elected regional assembly on a turnout of 48 per cent. Aware that if there was no support in the North East there would certainly be no support elsewhere, the Deputy Prime Minister, John Prescott, immediately announced that the other planned referendums would not take place. Regional devolution has therefore stalled, at least for now.

In the absence of any plans for devolution to England as a nation, the 1998 devolution schemes continue to present serious problems of asymmetry. Possible solutions, falling short of the establishment of an English Parliament, include a Secretary of State for England and an England Grand Committee to take the committee stage of English (and possibly Welsh) Bills.[65] Perhaps ultimately it is fitting to remember that an asymmetrical structure is at the core of the UK constitution and, while the 1998 devolution schemes have enhanced it, they did not create it and could not have remedied it short of tearing up the Acts of Union which first established the union state.

---

[62] Cmnd 3814 (1997).
[63] Bogdanor, n 1 above, p 272.
[64] *Ibid*, pp 270–71.
[65] D Oliver, *Constitutional Reform in the UK* (Oxford, Oxford University Press, 2003), p 291.

III. Constitutional Issues in the Three Devolution Schemes

Having identified the common features of the three devolution schemes, each will now be considered in turn with particular emphasis upon each scheme's distinctive impact upon the constitution of the United Kingdom.

a) Northern Ireland: New Approaches to Sovereignty and Self-determination

The first issue that must be discussed in this section on Northern Ireland is whether the 1998 political agreement in Northern Ireland can properly be termed devolution at all. Was it merely devolution of a region within a unitary state, or was it something far more complex and thus constitutionally challenging? Campbell, Aolain, and Harvey argue that seeing Northern Ireland through a 'devolution lens' is of limited utility and indeed may even be misleading.[66] These authors query pointedly whether 'the political parties that negotiated the Agreement, and the people who voted for it, really believe[d] they were signing up to devolution in a unitary state?'[67] The political conflict in Northern Ireland is such that its settlement cannot merely be an aspect of New Labour's domestic constitutional reform programme. Indeed, the Northern Ireland peace process which led to the Belfast Agreement pre-dated Labour's other constitutional reforms, including devolution to Scotland and Wales. As with so many issues in this troubled region, claims that it can be regarded as comparable to Scottish and Welsh devolution are politically motivated: the Agreement is much easier to sell to unionists if it is packaged as merely another example of devolution within the unitary state.[68] But the Agreement, by necessity, goes much further. A threefold network is created which goes beyond traditional constitutional paradigms. There is established a North–South Ministerial Council, with representatives from the Northern Ireland executive and Irish government, to discuss cross-border co-operation on devolved matters; a British–Irish Council, with representatives from the UK and Irish governments, devolved institutions, the Isle of Man and the Channel Islands (but not, significantly, England);[69] and a British–Irish Intergovernmental Conference, with representatives of British and Irish governments, to discuss only non-devolved matters. These networks derive from strands

---

[66] C Campbell, F Ni Aolain, and C Harvey, 'The Frontiers of Legal Analysis: Reframing the Transition in Northern Ireland' (2003) 66 *MLR* 317.

[67] *Ibid*, at 323.

[68] *Ibid*, at 321.

[69] Despite the potential of this body to create a new quasi-federal environment, it 'has not been an active or productive arrangement' (Oliver, n 65 above, p 267).

two and three of the Agreement in which the relationships between North and South and between the United Kingdom and Ireland are defined, while strand one deals with internal Northern Ireland relations. As Campbell, Aolain, and Harvey have noted, 'the intimacy and necessity of the tie between all three strands may be lost to the constitutional law analysis, with its natural bias to internal constitutional arrangements.'[70] Given that some aspects of strands two and three are of particular significance to one side of the conflict, the exclusion of such features from (traditional, constitutional law) analysis could jeopardise the subtle political balance of the Agreement.

A concrete example of the implications of adopting a constitutional law vision of the Belfast Agreement as internal devolution is provided by the suspension of devolution by the Secretary of State for Northern Ireland, which has occurred on four occasions, including most recently (and still continuing) in October 2002. Suspension of devolution is explainable in traditional British constitutional terms. All three devolution schemes ensure that parliamentary sovereignty remains dominant and that power given away can be retaken. But suspension of the devolved institutions in Northern Ireland was a huge departure from the terms of the Agreement.[71] Indeed, in order to suspend the Northern Ireland Assembly, the Secretary of State had to introduce new primary legislation outside the remit of the Agreement.[72] Negotiators of the Agreement could legitimately argue that they had not agreed to be bound by Diceyian concepts of the UK constitution when they signed the Agreement. The constitutional law paradigm of devolution is, therefore, an insufficient context in which to analyse the Belfast Agreement and subsequent events in Northern Ireland. Campbell, Aolain, and Harvey instead regard the Agreement as a hybrid between constitutional law and international law.[73]

In terms of an international law analysis, one of the Agreement's crucial features is its innovative approach to issues of territorial sovereignty and self-determination. In the Northern Ireland context, the right to self-determination of the people of the territory amounts to a decisive power to determine the future of the territory. This concept was prophesised in Judge Dillard's famous statement in the *Western Sahara* case that 'It is for the people to determine the destiny of the territory and not the territory the destiny of the people.'[74] However, the Northern Ireland concept goes much further than this International Court of Justice judgment was willing to concede. In *Western Sahara* the principle of self-determination became relevant only once it was concluded that

---

[70] Campbell, Aolain, and Harvey, n 66 above, at 323.

[71] *Ibid*, at 324.

[72] B O'Leary, 'The Character of the 1998 Agreement: Results and Prospects' in R Wilford (ed), *Aspects of the Belfast Agreement* (Oxford, Oxford University Press, 2001), p 52. O'Leary argues that this 'violated the will of the people of Ireland, North and South, expressed in two referendums: neither the Agreement, nor the people(s) had mandated the suspensory power' (p 66).

[73] Campbell, Aolain, and Harvey, n 66 above, at 333. These authors also regard a transitional justice approach as a third essential lens through which to view the Northern Ireland settlement.

[74] The *Western Sahara* case [1975] *ICJ Reports* 12 at 139.

Western Sahara did not belong to either Morocco or Mauritania.[75] Furthermore, the principle of self-determination played no role in the determination of Western Sahara's fate as the International Court of Justice authorised the division of the territory by Morocco, Mauritania, and Spain and ignored the claims of the Saharan independence movement.[76] The Belfast Agreement makes clear that the people of Northern Ireland may determine the future of their territory *regardless* of the sovereign rights of the United Kingdom (or Ireland). In Article 1 of the British–Irish Agreement, the two governments 'recognise the legitimacy of whatever choice is freely exercised by a majority of the people of Northern Ireland with regard to its status, whether they prefer to continue to support the Union with Great Britain or a sovereign united Ireland'[77] and affirm that if the people exercise their right of self-determination in order to bring about a united Ireland, 'it will be a binding obligation on both Governments to introduce and support in their respective Parliaments legislation to give effect to that wish.'[78]

Also of significance is the fact that it is the people of the whole of the island of Ireland who have the right to determine the future of Northern Ireland. This inclusion of population both internal and external to the jurisdiction in question represents 'a radical reconfiguration of both the theory and practice of state formation.'[79] Thus, analysis of the Belfast Agreement in terms of international law reveals an important development in state practice in respect of state sovereignty.[80] The UK's willingness (in order to ensure peace within its own borders) to subject its sovereign claim to Northern Ireland to the approval of the Irish people (those living in both the North and South) reveals a significant development. The Agreement stops just short of establishing a formal joint sovereignty over Northern Ireland with the Republic of Ireland, but there are undoubtedly co-sovereignty aspects within the Agreement.[81] Both states have agreed to abide by the wishes of the people of Northern Ireland and to play a part in cross-border institutions. The Agreement is built upon power sharing, both within Northern Ireland between political parties from both sides of the conflict but also, less well known but even more significant in international and constitutional terms, between the UK and Irish governments.

So what is the current constitutional significance of the 1998 moves towards 'devolution' in Northern Ireland stemming from the Belfast Agreement? In practical and political terms, the effect is clear: while the Northern Ireland Assembly

---

[75] See Campbell, Aolain, and Harvey, n 66 above, at 330.

[76] See E Wicks, 'State Sovereignty: Towards a Refined Legal Conceptualisation' (2000) 29 *Anglo-Am LR* 282, at 289–90.

[77] Art 1(i).

[78] Art 1(iv).

[79] Campbell, Aolain, and Harvey, n 66 above, at 330.

[80] 'The shift in state sovereignty marked by the Good Friday Agreement makes evident that it occupies a space in international legal discourse that is not simply expressive, but as an example of emerging state practice, is also constitutive' (*ibid*, at 332).

[81] O'Leary, n 72 above, p 68.

is suspended indefinitely and as such the devolution scheme has (for now, at least) failed, the Agreement nevertheless transformed the political landscape of Northern Ireland. The conflict has not ended but it now persists in a largely non-violent form,[82] and this disentanglement of politics and violence is a worthy achievement in its own right. Constitutionally, the Agreement was never concerned merely with devolution within a unitary state. The openness of the UK government to consideration of novel power-sharing schemes once more reveals the advantages of an evolving constitution. The Northern Ireland Act 1998 raises 'a statutory doubt about the continuance of the union between Great Britain and Northern Ireland.'[83] The 1800 Act of Union with Ireland (as subsequently amended) is expressly subject to the continuing consent of the people of Northern Ireland (and the Republic of Ireland). This condition has the force of international law behind it, as it forms part of an international treaty with Ireland. It is worth noting that such legal protection for the self-determination of the people is not mirrored in Scotland, where issues relating to the union between England and Scotland are expressly reserved to the Westminster Parliament.

When concluding on the Belfast Agreement it is impossible not to mourn the missed opportunity for a final resolution of the Northern Ireland conflict. The current state of affairs continues to depress and the revival of Northern Ireland devolution does not appear imminent. Nevertheless, the Agreement did leave a lasting constitutional (and international) legacy. The flexible view of sovereignty in Northern Ireland and the entrenched right of self-determination continue to find a place in the UK constitution, and the conflict remains political rather than violent. Finally, it is worth acknowledging that, as Wilford notes, 'the remarkable thing about the Agreement is that it was reached in the first place. That its implementation has proven to be fitful and difficult is no surprise.'[84]

b) Wales: Devolution as a Means of Democratisation

If Northern Ireland is unique due to the complexity of the political situation there, devolution in Wales has been equally distinctive (thus indicating that the three devolution schemes, although based on the same foundational principles, were each tailored to the particular needs of the territories concerned). The major distinguishing feature of Welsh devolution is that it confers only executive, and not legislative, powers onto the newly established National Assembly for Wales. This is an oversimplified description of the scheme, however, because the 'executive' functions devolved include the power, previously exercised by the Secretary of State for Wales, to make subordinate legislation on devolved

---

[82] Campbell, Aolain, and Harvey, n 66 above, p 344.
[83] Brazier, n 46 above, p 113.
[84] Wilford, n 45 above, p 151.

matters.[85] Given the legal uncertainty (discussed in the Scotland section below) as to the classification of Acts of the Scottish Parliament – as primary or secondary – the distinction between Scottish and Welsh devolved powers can be overstated. This is certainly the view of Jones and Williams, who reject the defeatist attitude that 'Welsh devolution exists only to be compared (unfavourably) with the Scottish (or Northern Ireland) model.'[86] Perhaps such comparison is inevitable, however, especially within Wales itself. O'Neill argues that 'it is in the very nature of such asymmetrical arrangements that they invite the less autonomous territorial polities in an uneven constitutional framework to "catch up" with the pacesetters, as circumstances change and aspirations burgeon.'[87] The legal/executive dichotomy is certainly suspect given that, as Jones and Williams note, there is no clear distinction between executive and legislative functions under the UK constitution,[88] so while it is true that devolution to Wales is primarily executive rather than legislative, the power to legislate should not be ignored. This is particularly true given that the Secretary of State for Wales had exercised significant legislative power and that 'there are no constitutional limits to the powers that can be exercised by means of subordinate legislation.'[89]

Perhaps in recognition of this potential, the Welsh Assembly has allowed itself to evolve significantly in nature. Under the Government of Wales Act 1998, the Assembly was a single, corporate body: there was no separate legislature and executive body as in Scotland and Northern Ireland. The Welsh Assembly soon rejected this structure, however, and, as Osmond explains, 'Insofar as it could within the framework of the Government of Wales Act 1998, the new institution immediately set about digging up its constitutional foundations.'[90] It did this by striving to separate its administrative and legislative roles. For example, steps were taken to ensure the independence of the Office of the Presiding Officer in October 2000; the name 'Welsh Assembly Government' was adopted in November 2001; and the 'Secretaries' were renamed 'Ministers' in June 2002.[91] Now legislative proposals are put forward by the Welsh Assembly Government, while the Assembly, acting as a legislative body, scrutinises, amends, and approves or rejects them.[92] The Assembly now comprises both an executive and legislative

---

[85] The devolved matters are listed in Sch 2 to the Government of Wales Act 1998. The Assembly acquires responsibilities either through a transfer order under s 22 (eg functions of the Secretary of State may be transferred) or through direct conferment of functions in an Act of Parliament (eg powers to reform health authorities and other public bodies, as in ss 27–28 of the Government of Wales Act 1998).

[86] TH Jones and JM Williams, 'Wales as a Jurisdiction' [2004] *PL* 78, at 79.

[87] O'Neill, n 54 above, p 177.

[88] Jones and Williams, n 86 above, at 80.

[89] *Ibid*, at 85.

[90] J Osmond, 'Nation Building and the Assembly: The Emergence of a Welsh Civic Consciousness' in A Trench (ed), *Has Devolution Made a Difference? The State of the Nations 2004* (Exeter, Imprint Academic, 2004), p 47.

[91] See Jones and Williams, n 86 above, at 86–87.

[92] *Ibid*.

body. This evolution may continue because the Richard Commission, which reported in 2004, proposed the complete separation of legislative and executive in Wales with the creation of a legislative assembly with primary legislative powers (and preferably tax-varying powers).[93] These recommendations seem unlikely to be adopted, however, given that Blair has no desire to revisit devolution.[94] But, as Hazell points out, the devolution settlement as it currently stands in Wales is unstable: 'It is a contingent settlement, excessively dependent on political goodwill between London and Cardiff to make it work. The moment that goodwill is removed, the settlement faces breakdown.'[95] Burrows also regards the Welsh Assembly as a work in progress given that in her view the Government of Wales Act 1998 established it as an Assembly without a purpose, and 'an Assembly without a purpose will inevitably seek one.'[96] This view, however, risks ignoring the vital purpose that the Assembly has always served: to increase democratic legitimacy of Welsh governance.

A lack of democratic legitimacy was perceived as a real problem pre-1998, and Wales was not alone in this concern, for in Scotland Conservative support was minimal, and in Northern Ireland the different party structure means that Northern Ireland voters never vote for, or are represented by, the government of the United Kingdom. The reason that the increase in democratic legitimacy is so vital to understanding Welsh devolution, however, is that in the other two devolved regions other, greater considerations dominate. So, in Scotland the re-establishment of a Scottish Parliament after nearly 300 years and its powers to legislate have a greater impact upon the UK constitution. Similarly, the Northern Ireland Assembly ensured a significant increase in democracy in Northern Ireland, but the political and public focus has always remained on its role in ending violence within a broader peace process. In Wales, due to the limited extent of devolution, the most important achievement of the 1998 scheme has been increased democratic legitimacy and accountability. Powers – both executive and legislative – previously exercised by a minister in London (and, under the Conservatives, a minister unlikely to even represent a Welsh constituency) are now exercised and scrutinised by Welsh politicians in Cardiff. This in itself is an important democratic development, although it is one with only limited impact upon the UK constitution. However, given the ambivalent public support for devolution in Wales, as evidenced by the 1997 referendum, a more momentous change to the governance of Wales was unnecessary and unjustified. In Scotland, the situation was rather different.

---

[93] See www.richardcommission.gov.uk for the 2004 Report.
[94] R Hazell, 'The Unfinished Business of Devolution' in A Trench (ed), *Has Devolution Made a Difference? The State of the Nations 2004* (Exeter, Imprint Academic, 2004), p 260.
[95] *Ibid*, p 272.
[96] Burrows, n 13 above, p 187.

c) Scotland: Reconvening the Scottish Parliament

In Scotland the concept of popular sovereignty survived the 300 years of union with England to re-emerge as an influential factor in securing devolution. The Claim of Right for Scotland (issued by a Constitutional Steering Committee of an all-party campaign for a Scottish Assembly in 1988) acknowledged 'the sovereign right of the Scottish people to determine the form of Government suited to their needs.'[97] This insistence that sovereignty in Scotland resides with the people, rather than the Westminster Parliament, receives some support from the 1997 (and 1979) Scottish referendum, which can be regarded as an act of self-determination by the Scottish people.[98] Furthermore, the famous words of the SNP's Winifred Ewing in 'reconvening' the Scottish Parliament suspended by the 1707 Act of Union with England, illustrated the survival of the view, at least among nationalists, that the Scottish Parliament established in 1998 is the 'legatee of an element of sovereignty that was never surrendered in the union of 1707.'[99] Such a view does garner some support from the 1953 case of *MacCormick v Lord Advocate* in which, as was discussed in chapter two, Lord President Cooper rejected the notion that parliamentary sovereignty had any place in Scottish constitutional law.[100] There is, therefore, some evidence that in Scotland the idea of popular sovereignty has endured the years of union and continues to assert influence over the development of the constitution as it effects Scotland. Nevertheless, the Scotland Act 1998 makes no such concession and, as we have seen, seeks expressly and impliedly to preserve the sovereignty of the Westminster Parliament. As O'Neill has explained, the legislation 'expressly maintained that sovereignty ultimately and irrevocably remained in the Union, albeit devolved in some degree, but in no way divested from central government or its institutions.'[101] Is this realistic, or even achievable, given that legislative powers have been devolved away from Westminster?

The key issue which must be considered in order to appreciate the constitutional implications of Scottish devolution and its effect on parliamentary sovereignty is whether Acts of the Scottish Parliament are a species of primary legislation or subordinate legislation. Burrows has effectively explained the significance of this apparently technical question:

> Underlying this seemingly simple legal question is a deeply political argument about the nature of devolution itself. To recognise that the devolved legislatures have the power to adopt primary legislation is to acknowledge that a transfer has taken place from one legislature to another, albeit in limited fields. To qualify such legislation as

---

[97] Bogdanor, n 1 above, p 290.
[98] For this view, see M Keating, 'The United Kingdom as a Post-Sovereign Polity' in M O'Neill (ed), *Devolution and British Politics* (Harlow, Pearson Education, 2004), pp 320–21.
[99] *Ibid.*
[100] 1953 SC 396 at 411.
[101] O'Neill, n 54 above, p 171.

subordinate ... [means that] Parliament has not transferred powers to but conferred powers on the devolved legislatures.'[102]

In the Human Rights Act 1998, Acts of the Scottish Parliament are treated as subordinate legislation,[103] but, as Burrows explains, this is not a decisive answer because the Scotland Act treats legislation which is contrary to Convention rights as outside the Scottish Parliament's legislative competence.[104] Thus, and notwithstanding the Human Rights Act, the Scottish Parliament could retain the power to create primary legislation within the fields specified in the legislation and subject to its legislative competence.[105] This approach enabled the Privy Council in *Anderson, Reid & Doherty v Scottish Ministers*[106] to avoid deciding whether an Act of the Scottish Parliament was primary or secondary legislation, and instead merely to ensure its compatibility with Convention rights. The Privy Council was helped in this regard by the provisions of the Scotland Act 1998. Section 29(1) states the general rule that an 'Act of the Scottish Parliament is not law so far as any provision of the Act is outside the legislative competence of the Parliament,' and section 29(2)(a)–(e) lists the provisions outwith the Parliament's competence, including incompatibility with Convention rights. But section 101 declares that a provision should be read as narrowly as is required in order for it to be regarded as within the Parliament's legislative competence, if such a reading is possible. There is thus a presumption that Scottish legislation is within the competence of the Scottish Parliament, which will help the courts in avoiding the question of whether it is primary or secondary (and the constitutional consequences of striking it down). Furthermore, there is some evidence to suggest that Acts of the Scottish Parliament are primary legislation. For example, under the Scotland Act, they require and are given the Royal Assent. The government seems to take the view that they do amount to primary legislation,[107] and the Scotland Act seems to distinguish between primary and secondary legislation.[108]

If we accept Burrows' argument, based on the above facts, that Acts of the Scottish Parliament are a form of primary legislation, the question arises as to how a conflict between two pieces of primary legislation (one from Edinburgh and one from London) can be resolved. As Burrows notes, if 'the site of authority for primary legislation is shared' – because Westminster retains the power to legislate for Scotland – then difficulties are sure to ensue. Burrows' conclusion is, perhaps surprisingly, that in the case of a conflict, the courts should uphold the legislation of the devolved legislature. The reason for this is that Westminster has transferred, rather than merely devolved, its primary legislative powers, in certain

---

[102] Burrows, n 13 above, p 57.

[103] Human Rights Act 1998, s 21.

[104] Burrows, n 13 above, pp 58–59.

[105] *Ibid*, p 59.

[106] [2003] 2 AC 602. See BK Winetrobe, 'Scottish Devolved Legislation and the Courts' [2002] *PL* 31.

[107] See Burrows, n 13 above, p 60.

[108] *Ibid*, pp 60–61.

areas, to the Scottish Parliament and, provided always that the Scottish Parliament operates within the limits of the Scotland Act 1998 (its constitutive document), the devolved legislation should be upheld by the courts: 'This does not give the courts a power to review the legality of United Kingdom legislation, merely to set it aside in case of conflict in order to ground the devolution settlement in objective principles based on the rule of law.'[109] Given the courts' continued, dogged adherence to the Diceyian conception of parliamentary sovereignty (subject to a willingness to pursue a flexibility absent from the original theory in the context of the EC), this is not a convincing argument. It seems extremely unlikely that the courts would so willingly set aside the legislation of the Westminster Parliament, particularly given the express and unambiguous assertion in the Scotland Act 1998 itself that the power of Westminster to make laws for Scotland has not been affected.[110]

Perhaps in an effort to ensure that the courts are not faced with such temptation, the government developed a constitutional convention that Westminster would not legislate on any devolved matter without the consent of the devolved legislature. This has become known as the Sewel convention after Lord Sewel's statement in the House of Lords that 'we would expect a convention to be established that Westminster would not normally legislate with regard to devolved matters in Scotland without the consent of the Scottish Parliament.'[111] The convention, unusually deliberately made rather than evolved, was subsequently included in the Memorandum of Understanding.[112] If the Sewel convention was intended to limit the instances of Westminster legislating for Scotland on devolved matters, however, it has failed miserably. Instead, there has been an abundance of Sewel motions before the Scottish Parliament, under which the Parliament has approved the exercise of Westminster legislative power to legislate for Scotland. Page and Batey discovered the astonishing statistic that the Scottish Parliament is agreeing to as many Sewel motions as it is enacting Bills.[113] In the period between June 1999 and June 2001, there were 23 Sewel motions relating to 24 different Bills, compared to 19 enacted Scottish Bills.[114] Thus, a majority of legislation *on devolved matters* was continuing to come from Westminster rather than the Scottish Parliament. Page and Batey suggest that this excessive use of the Sewel motion may be due partly to Labour being in power in both jurisdictions,[115] but they also recognise that mere expedience will be an important factor.[116] Whatever the reason, it is an unacceptable abdication of legislative

---

[109] *Ibid*, p 65.
[110] Scotland Act 1998, s 28(7).
[111] HL Deb, Vol 592, col 791, 21 July 1998.
[112] Cmnd 4806 (2000), para 13: '[T]he UK government will proceed in accordance with the convention that the UK Parliament would not normally legislate with regard to devolved matters except with the agreement of the devolved legislature.'
[113] A Page and A Batey, 'Scotland's Other Parliament: Westminster Legislation about Devolved Matters in Scotland since Devolution' [2002] *PL* 501, at 502.
[114] *Ibid*, at 303.
[115] *Ibid*, at 513–15.
[116] *Ibid*, at 516–18.

responsibility for the Scottish Parliament to permit so much Scottish legislation on devolved matters to originate in London rather than Edinburgh. It undermines the exercise of self-determination and the claims to popular sovereignty of the Scottish people when voting for a Scottish Parliament to legislate for them on matters not reserved by Westminster. In addition, there is a danger that the Scottish element of UK legislation passed by Westminster (and approved under a Sewel motion) will attract even less scrutiny than pre-1998. As Page and Batey have noted, this would be 'an unfortunate outcome for a process that was meant to reduce the democratic deficit in relation to Scottish legislation.'[117]

The endurance of Westminster's parliamentary sovereignty within the context of Scottish devolution casts light upon the legal/political distinction which has always underlain Dicey's theory. As Loveland has noted, the Scotland Act provides 'a graphic example of the way in which the constitution can be seen as harbouring a profound dichotomy between the legal and political conceptions of sovereignty.'[118] This has been explained in more detail by Bogdanor, who argues that politically devolution places a very powerful weapon in the hands of the Scottish people:[119]

> Constitutionally, the Scottish Parliament will clearly be subordinate. Politically, however, it will be anything but subordinate. For the Scotland Act creates a new locus of political power. Its most important power will be one not mentioned in the Act at all, that of representing the people of Scotland.[120]

This theory of a political sovereign in Edinburgh and a legal sovereign in Westminster, by utilising the political/legal divide, enables Dicey's conception of a legislature with no legal limits to its competence to linger on in constitutional theory. However, an important aspect of Dicey's theory is that any law passed by Westminster can be 'unmade' or repealed. Could Westminster repeal the Scotland Act 1998 and with it Scottish devolution?

Bogdanor argues that this will only be possible in extreme circumstances, such as those which occurred in Northern Ireland justifying the suspension of devolution there (although, as was discussed above, this suspension was only justifiable in strict constitutional terms, not within the international law context of the Belfast Agreement):

> It is in constitutional theory alone that the supremacy of Parliament is preserved. For power devolved, far from being power retained, will be power transferred and it will not be possible to recover that power except under pathological circumstances, such as those of Northern Ireland after 1968. Thus the relationship between Westminster and Edinburgh will be quasi-federal in normal times and unitary only in crisis times. For

---

[117] *Ibid*, at 522–23.
[118] Loveland, n 48 above, p. 673.
[119] Bogdanor, n 1 above, p 287.
[120] *Ibid*, p 288.

the formal assertion of Parliamentary supremacy will become empty when it is no longer accompanied by a real political supremacy.[121]

This 'nebulous right of suspension' is, according to Bogdanor, all that remains of Westminster's previously continuous exercise of supremacy.[122] If the Scottish Parliament is for all intents and purposes entrenched, and the suspension of Scottish devolution certainly appears unrealistic in current political circumstances, then Westminster's right to unmake all laws is more illusory than real. The dominant position of parliamentary sovereignty within the Scotland Act 1998 does present a dilemma for the constitution, because it is intrinsically at odds with the decentralisation of power inherent in the devolution scheme. Indeed, Little has argued that the central place given to parliamentary sovereignty within the Scottish devolution settlement was 'at a fundamental level, raw power politics, and an unambiguous statement of political dominance.'[123] Westminster has asserted its dominance in order to counter the threat posed to it by Scottish popular sovereignty and nationalists goals, but there is a sense of unreality about Westminster legislative sovereignty in respect of Scotland. While political limitations on parliamentary sovereignty have always existed as an aspect of the doctrine, there is a line which cannot be crossed while retaining genuine adherence to the traditional sovereignty concept. Previous chapters have illustrated that the UK constitution has evolved significantly over the last 300 years with the introduction of parliamentary supremacy, democracy, human rights, prime ministerial power, and so on. Chapter 7, on the EC, revealed that parliamentary sovereignty, which must be subject to the constitution from which it derives, is now seriously restricted by the requirement of supremacy of EC law, which the United Kingdom accepted in 1973. The Scottish people's right to self-determination will also be constitutionally protected, and thus Westminster cannot acquire constitutional support for an action which violates their freely expressed desire for a Scottish Parliament. This does not necessitate a re-evaluation of the superiority of Westminster legislation over Acts of the Scottish Parliament. Indeed, this is the central feature of the scheme agreed to by the Scottish people in the 1997 referendum. But it does mean that a Scottish Parliament is here to stay.

The implications for Westminster are substantial. Little has suggested that:

[I]t is possible that the traditional ideal of parliamentary sovereignty may become so qualified by convention in order to accommodate political reality that – in Scotland in particular – it becomes increasingly compromised as a meaningful constitutional doctrine.[124]

---

[121] *Ibid*, p 291.
[122] *Ibid.*
[123] G Little, 'Scotland and Parliamentary Sovereignty' (2004) 24 *Legal Studies* 540, at 552.
[124] *Ibid*, p 562.

The evolution of parliamentary sovereignty as a core aspect of the constitution has undoubtedly begun. While still dominant in so many areas, other constitutional principles – EC supremacy, the protection of human rights, the right to self-determination of the Scottish people – are increasingly influencing its application in practice. Indeed, Bogdanor goes so far as to claim that the Scotland Act 1998, by dividing the power to legislate for Scotland and thus creating a quasi-federal relationship between Edinburgh and London, amounts to a constitutional revolution.[125] This is reminiscent of the debate in the EC context (discussed in chapter 7) as to whether the constitution has evolved or been subject to a revolution. The former is the better view. The fundamentals of the constitutional structure remain, but are modified to incorporate new principles and constitutional ideas.

One final issue in respect of the impact of Scottish devolution on the Westminster Parliament, which may ultimately prove to be the most groundbreaking, is the potential influence of the establishment of a subordinate Parliament under the constitution. In *Whaley v Lord Watson*, Lord Rodger explained the nature of the Scottish Parliament as one which 'has been created by statute and derives its powers from statute ... In principle, therefore, the Parliament like any other body set up by law is subject to the law and to the courts which exist to uphold that law.'[126] This is an unusual status for a national legislature under the UK constitution, although it reflects a globally accepted concept. It is possible that the existence of such a subordinate legislature within the United Kingdom may broaden the concept of the legislature in general. Increasingly, the Westminster Parliament, and its claims to omnipotence, may appear unusual and even curious. As Loveland has argued, 'the notion that a 'Parliament' can and should be a body possessing limited law-making competence will begin to become normalised within British political culture.'[127] A recognition that the Westminster Parliament must be subject to the (albeit unwritten) constitution that established and bequeathed its sovereignty is long overdue and can only be encouraged by the creation of subordinate, devolved legislatures. Such recognition may also lead to an appreciation that the constitutional protection of certain fundamental principles should receive protection even from a sovereign, democratically elected, Parliament.

---

[125] Bogdanor, n 1 above, p 294.

[126] 2000 SC 340 at 348.

[127] Loveland, n 48 above, p 676. Loveland continues by writing that, 'At present, predictions as to the future development of the Scots and United Kingdom Parliaments seem to be dominated by the supposition that the former will become more like the latter. We may find in the longer term that the reverse argument acquires increasing force.'

IV. Conclusion

Numerous commentators have referred to the 1998 devolution schemes as creating a quasi-federal structure within the United Kingdom. This is a largely unhelpful description of the constitutional impact of devolution, because the United Kingdom remains determinedly unfederal in nature. A federal arrangement would require devolved legislatures to be sovereign within their jurisdictions; documentary guidance (invariably in the form of a codified constitution) as to the jurisdictional boundaries; and a settlement for England that gave it a sufficient voice within the United Kingdom without overwhelming the other component parts. The 1998 devolution schemes fall far short of this and are best analysed in their own right rather than as quasi-anything. The United Kingdom is a union state and, as such, has evolved in an asymmetrical fashion. The 1998 devolution schemes recognise this and build upon it by providing territorial governance in a form tailored to the demands and needs of Scotland, Wales and Northern Ireland respectively. The result is an extremely complex system of multi-level governance, and one made all the more complex by its contingent nature, with both England and (currently) Northern Ireland denied any form of devolved government. Such complexity – untidiness or flexibility depending upon one's viewpoint – can be accommodated within the evolving constitution but necessitates some rethinking of traditional doctrines. The constitutional consequences of devolution include the adoption of a novel approach to territorial sovereignty (in the Northern Ireland context); the prioritisation of a right to self-determination, seen particularly within the Scottish and Northern Ireland context (where it is expressly entrenched in an international treaty); a recognition of the need to decentralise the unitary state in order to ensure democratic legitimacy for the governance of the component parts of the union; and the retention of parliamentary sovereignty at Westminster, but within a more complex constitutional structure than previously existed which, within the Scottish context at least, has required a subtle evolution of its place and priority within a constitution with competing and potentially conflicting principles. Dicey's orthodox theory of parliamentary sovereignty is increasingly being overtaken by the rapid evolution of the UK constitution into one suitable for a modern, democratic, asymmetrical union state. The devolution Acts of 1998 brought with them considerable constitutional implications and, as such, 1998 justifies its inclusion as a key moment in constitutional history. But devolution remains a work in progress, and in the years to come it will be necessary to see how it develops and the impact its further development has upon the union state and constitution of the United Kingdom. The evolution will not stop here.

Conclusion:
The Evolving Constitution

I. The Substance of the Constitution

a) A Chapter-by-Chapter Overview of Constitutional Evolution

The evolutionary period covered in this book of landmark moments begins in **1688** when the revolutionary settlement transformed the relationship both between Crown and Parliament and between individual and government. The three core ideas implanted, or at least strengthened, in the constitution at that time were a constitutional monarchy, a supreme parliament, and individual rights and liberties. These three ideas are all aspects of a broader movement towards limited government. The dangers to individual liberty inherent in the divine rights of kings theory of government applied by James II and his predecessors led to a perceived need to impose some limits upon the monarchy. The assumption that the King-in-Parliament would now take over identical absolute power is a foolish interpretation of the events of 1688–89. While the idea of a supreme parliament subject to limits imposed by the constitution that created it cannot be implied by the 1688 Settlement, it was to emerge later as a viable and logical explanation of subsequent constitutional events, and nothing in 1688 disproves it. The fledging attempts to provide some legal protection for a number of specified individual rights and liberties also formed an idea which would develop in the years to come, but in 1688 can also be seen as an aspect of the broader move towards ensuring that governmental bodies would exercise more limited powers in the future.

The events of **1707** created a new union state. Although the boundaries of that union state would fluctuate (in 1800 and 1922) and the form of governing the union's component parts would be transformed in 1998, the nature of the United Kingdom as a union state endures. The asymmetry inherent in this arrangement continues to define, and create problems for, the UK's constitution today. The establishment in 1707 of a new, and purportedly limited, parliament to legislate for the new state is a further aspect of the Treaty of Union with enduring consequences. The evolving nature of the constitution enables some of the core principles of the union to find a secure place within the modern constitution. These principles include the union state, the independence of the Scottish legal system, the established churches, freedom of trade within the United Kingdom, and the evident utility protection of private rights in Scotland.

In **1721**, the new relationship between Crown and Parliament established in 1688 was subject to a logical development. The emergence of the office of Prime Minister provided a link between Crown and Parliament which made the working of the 1688 Settlement much easier. The need for Crown and Parliament to work in harmony with one another required an executive focus in the House of Commons and a strong parliamentary leader within the King's closet. The office of Prime Minister provided both of these in one person. That person would develop to pose a new threat to individual liberty, however, by combining the democratic legitimacy of the twentieth-century Parliament with the untrammelled power of the seventeenth-century monarch.

The modern form of executive power evident in the office of Prime Minister was coupled with a modernised legislature when, in **1832**, the first steps to democratic representation in the House of Commons were tentatively taken. Both the contents of the Reform Act of that year and its passage revealed that a door had been opened onto a new relationship between individual and government.

The increased legitimacy of the House of Commons after the 1832 and subsequent Reform Acts led to a formalised recognition of this House's supremacy in **1911** following a power struggle between the two Houses of Parliament. The Upper House was left in a weakened state due more to its perceived illegitimacy than the constraints upon its veto power in the Parliament Act 1911. The events of 1911, in conjunction with those of 1832 and 1721, laid the framework for a modern parliament and executive: a democratic and supreme House of Commons; a weakened House of Lords; and a leading member of the executive dominant within the supreme Lower House. These events are all aspects of the democratisation of the constitution and its institutions, but they also led to a centralisation of power in the Prime Minister and Cabinet, which would pose a new threat to the balance of the constitution. Both 1832 and 1911 also indicate the remaining role of the monarch: no longer with any practical power, the monarch is left to act as a referee of the constitution and its players.

The **1953** coming into force of the European Convention for the Protection of Human Rights and Fundamental Freedoms (ECHR) had three main constitutional implications. It introduced an external legal influence into the constitution, it entrenched the principle of a democratic society, and it transformed the nature of individual rights and liberties. The first of these implications was entirely new (and developed further in subsequent years, especially in 1972), but the other two implications built upon pre-existing values in the constitution. Both democracy and individual rights already held a prominent place within the constitution, but the significance of 1953 was that from henceforth they would be subject to external protection.

The increased influence of bodies of law external to the United Kingdom continued and heightened with the **1972** accession to the European Communities. The principle of European legal supremacy, established if unappreciated at the time of entry, necessitated a rethinking of existing core constitutional principles such as parliamentary sovereignty and state sovereignty. The idea of a parliament sovereign under the constitution gains particular weight from the events of 1972 and logically explains how parliamentary sovereignty can co-exist in a constitution with seemingly conflicting values such as European legal supremacy although, as noted in chapter 7, this theory is not universally accepted. The potential lack of democratic legitimacy for the new value of European legal supremacy is a significant problem given that it must reside within a constitution which, by 1972, has democracy as a core, if not the central, element.

The final key moment in the evolution of the constitution as identified in this book is **1998**, and the devolution schemes of that year which emphasise the union, rather than mere unitary, nature of the United Kingdom. The asymmetrical form of the union state has led to a complex system of multi-level governance which has had profound implications for the constitutional principles of state sovereignty, self-determination, decentralisation, and parliamentary sovereignty. Again, a parliament sovereign under the constitution and subject to its other core principles (such as the right of the Scottish people to self-determination) seems a logical explanation of some problematic aspects of the Scottish devolution scheme. It is particularly fitting that this most recent key moment of constitutional evolution should remain in a transitory state: failure and recrimination in Northern Ireland; further development in Wales; controversy in Scotland; and the continued search for (and failure to find) a solution fitting to England all indicate that the evolution of the UK constitution is a continuing phenomenon. The constitution itself is in a transitory state but, by piecing together recent transforming moments, we can perceive the direction of the evolution and perhaps even predict future developments.

b) Democratisation of the Constitution

Most of the constitutional evolution discussed in this book can be regarded as part of a broader democratisation process. Such categorisation depends upon an extensive interpretation of the requirements of democracy. Six main democratising influences can be identified in the evolutionary period covered. First, there has been a move towards limited government in the sense of increased limits being imposed upon the powers of government bodies, including the monarchy, Parliament generally, and the House of Lords specifically. The idea of a parliament sovereign under the constitution, encountered a number of times in this book, is one aspect of this move away from absolute dominion for our ruling bodies. A limited government, as well as a representative one, is a core component of the modern idea of democracy. Second, there has been a transformation in the nature of individual rights, and therefore also in the relationship between individuals and the government which can both protect and violate their rights and freedoms. The protection of rights is essential within a truly democratic state. The transformation in the nature of rights under the UK constitution has led to international protection of individual rights and also of the concept of a democratic state itself, most notably in the ECHR. Third, and perhaps the most obvious democratising influence, democratic representation has been gradually and incrementally introduced into the House of Commons, and that body has become supreme within the Queen-in-Parliament. Linked to this, and fourth, there has been a power shift from the hereditary parts of the constitution to those with greater democratic legitimacy. Thus power has moved away from the House of Lords and towards the House of Commons; away from the monarch and towards a democratically elected Prime Minister. Fifth, there has been a recent tendency towards decentralisation as a means of achieving greater democratic legitimacy within the component parts of the union state. Bringing power closer to the people is an obvious response to perceived illegitimacy and can be seen within the European Union (EU) as well as through the 1998 devolution schemes. Sixth, and finally, the development, and entrenchment, of a right to self-determination within the UK constitution can also be seen as a modern reconciliation of the need to pay regard to the wishes of the people (as a group, as well as individually). Within the context of devolution, especially in Scotland, the right to self-determination has constitutional influence and potentially may serve as a restraint upon external integration, for example within the EU. Through these six means, the evolutionary period of this book has seen a dramatic reshaping of the UK constitution from one based upon ancient privileges to one based upon democratic legitimacy, limited government and individual rights. The fact that the modern-day constitution seems incapable of preventing abuses of position, hereditary influence and centralisation of power cannot be denied, but equally the fact that the constitution has evolved into a form more represen-tative of the needs and rights of its citizens is a significant step. The evolution of the constitution is, of course, inextricably linked with the evolution of society over the same period. Each feeds upon the other. The modern constitution is one suitable for a democratic society although, as has been noted, it is far from perfect.

In addition to the general movement towards democratisation of the constitu-tion, we can identify two specific transforming effects of the evolutionary key moments discussed in this book. First, the relationship between the executive and legislative branches of government has been transformed to the extent that even the locale of those powers has changed. For much of the seventeenth century, the power struggle between the Crown and Parliament dominated constitutional affairs. The 1688 Settlement saw a resolution of that conflict but the relationship established – limited King; supreme King-in-Parliament – has evolved further since that time, most notably with the development of the office of a Prime Minister within Parliament and through the increasing dominance of the House of Commons within Parliament. The development throughout the twentieth century of party politics has had the unfortunate consequence of centralising political power in the small executive body of the Prime Minister and his Cabinet and advisors. The traditional conflict between the holders of executive and legislative powers has largely been deflected by their alliance in one body: the parliamentary executive. While Parliament retains the supreme legislative role it acquired in 1688, modern-day circumstances, including the party and whip system, the Parliament Acts and the personalisation and mediafication of politics, ensure that the executive is dominant in a way not so different from the seventeenth-century Stuart monarchs. The removal of the monarchy from practical power is merely a distraction, because a potent source of executive power remains in the form of the Prime Minister.

This raises the second transforming effect of the constitutional evolution discussed in this book: the citizens' relations with their government have changed. The individual, regardless of sex, wealth and race, has the right to vote for elected representatives (and, indirectly, for the Prime Minister). In addition, the individual's rights and liberties will be protected both in domestic law and in international law, as well as constitutional theory. These rights include the right to vote in free and open elections and, at international law, the right to self-determination as a people. It can thus be seen that the two transformed relationships provide a startling contrast: the relationship between executive and legislature has evolved into a dangerous centralisation of power, but the relationship between individuals and government has evolved to offer much greater protection for the individual against a misuse of that centralised power. It is a delicate balance and future evolution of the constitution may tip the balance one way or the other. It can only be hoped that the core principle of democracy within the constitution will ensure that future evolution does not endanger the individual and his vital role, and freedoms, within the society of a democratic state.

II. The Form of the Constitution

So far this conclusion has focused upon the substance of the evolved constitution but this book has at its core an argument about the form of that constitution, namely that it is an evolving one. The evolution identified in this book is in the form of a continuing phenomenon punctuated by landmark moments such as a revolution, a statute, a treaty or an individual. It has been noted at various points that the UK constitution bends but does not break when encountering a radical event. For example, the incorporation of the idea of European legal supremacy into the UK constitution in 1972 necessitated a re-evaluation of the constitutional principle of parliamentary sovereignty. While some commentators view 1972 as a constitutional revolution, having the effect of overturning the pre-existing constitutional order, the better view is of a flexible constitution which can accommodate such a radical new principle while retaining its core fundamentals. MacCormick was quoted with approval in chapter 7 as recognising that there may be moments that 'produce great constitutional change' but that do not 'thereby amount to radical or revolutionary discontinuity.'[1] The only way in which this can be achieved is by the constitution having easily identifiable key principles and values which guide the evolution of the constitution. The principle of democratisation was identified above as one such value; others may include individual rights and liberties, limited government and the union state. These core principles may be regarded as the skeleton upon which the constitution is built. They are sufficiently rigid, or entrenched, to provide adequate protection for individuals and the state. But the constitution is far more than a mere skeleton. Thus it is flexible enough to evolve in line with the changing priorities of society without endangering the core principles. The more detailed provisions of the constitution provide the flesh on the bones of the skeleton and are moulded to suit contemporary circumstances. To take an example: the 1911 Parliament Act was a constitutional addition entirely suitable for, and indeed required by, the political and societal conditions of the time. As a generally democratising measure, as discussed above, it was harmonious with the core principles of the existing constitution and thus could be incorporated into the evolving constitution. It is also possible that additions to the constitution may, over a period of time, evolve to create new core principles thus potentially changing the direction of the constitution. This is what happened with the value of democracy which has, as we have seen, tentative roots in 1832 and even earlier, but gradually evolved into a, if not the, core principle of the modern constitution.

This view of the constitution means that, although it is an evolving constitution, sufficiently flexible to incorporate, and elevate to core status, new principles, laws and practices, it is not without strength and standards. A purported change to the constitution which violates its current core principles will fail. In practice, this may mean that a constitutional revolution occurs because in the UK's unwritten and uncodified constitution the purported constitutional change, if it is a legal one enacted by a statute, will take effect within the legal system despite its unconstitutional nature. Thus, the constitutional order will have been broken. This will only happen in extreme circumstances, however, and over the period covered in this book, we have seen only constitutional evolution not constitutional revolution. This is largely due to the constitutional restraints imposed upon political actors. Even if not enforced by law, the constitution imposes very real constitutional obligations upon those who act under it, and such prevention is always better than cure.

We should not become complacent, however, that the constitution can continue to offer adequate protection against increasingly centralised executive power, especially in times when the state is perceived as increasingly under threat from disaffected groups and individuals posing genuine threats to national security. There is unmistakable irony in the coincidence that, in this human rights

---

[1] N MacCormick, *Questioning Sovereignty: Law, State, and Nation in the European Commonwealth* (Oxford, Oxford University Press, 1999), p 93.

age, when individual rights are codified, protected and relied upon to an unprecedented extent, the threat to our liberty is greater than it has been for centuries: detention without trial; erosion of trial by jury; identity cards; restrictions on free speech. The eternal need to balance individual freedom with security of the democratic state presents ever more difficult challenges for the UK's constitution and for those who act under it. But it is a challenge that the evolving constitution is well suited to meet, given centuries of development in response to the needs of contemporary society. To understand its past evolution is to begin to understand its current value, as well as its deficiencies, and to perceive the inevitability of future constitutional changes, the substance of which remain unforeseen today.

Bibliography

Introduction

Coward, B, *The Stuart Age: A History of England 1603–1714*, 2nd edn (London, Longman, 1994).

Craig, P, 'Formal and Substantive Conceptions of the Rule of Law: An Analytical Framework' [1997] *PL* 467.

Goldsworthy, J, *The Sovereignty of Parliament: History and Philosophy* (Oxford, Clarendon Press, 1999).

Griffiths, JAG, 'The Political Constitution' (1979) 42 *MLR* 1.

Hart JS, Jr, *The Rule of Law 1603–1660: Crown, Courts and Judges* (Harlow, Pearson, 2003).

Holt, JC, *Magna Carta*, 2nd edn (Cambridge, Cambridge University Press, 1992).

Kishlansky, M, *A Monarchy Transformed – Britain 1603–1714* (London, Penguin Books, 1996).

—— 'The Emergence of Adversary Politics in the Long Parliament' in R Cust and A Hughes (eds), *The English Civil War* (London, Arnold, 1997).

Russell, C, 'Parliamentary History in Perspective 1604–1629' in R Cust and A Hughes (eds), *The English Civil War* (London, Arnold, 1997).

Scott, J, *England's Troubles – Seventeenth Century English Political Instability in European Context* (Cambridge, Cambridge University Press, 2000).

Turner, RV, *Magna Carta: Through the Ages* (London, Pearson, 2003).

Warren, WL, *King John*, 2nd edn (London, Eyre Methuen, 1978).

—— *The Governance of Norman and Angevin England 1086–1272* (London, Edward Arnold, 1987).

1688

Ashcraft, R, *Revolutionary Politics and Locke's Two Treatises of Government* (Princeton, Princeton University Press, 1986).

Carter, J, 'The Revolution and the Constitution' in G Holmes (ed), *Britain after the Glorious Revolution 1689–1714* (London, Macmillan, 1969).

Dicey, AV, *Introduction to the Study of the Law of the Constitution*, 10th edn (London, Macmillan, 1959).

Haseler, S, 'Britain's *Ancien Regime*' [1990] *Parliamentary Affairs* 415.

Holdsworth, WS, *A History of English Law, Volume VI* (London, Methuen & Co, 1924).

Israel, JI (ed), *The Anglo-Dutch Moment – Essays on the Glorious Revolution and its World Impact* (Cambridge, Cambridge University Press, 1991).

Jones, JR, *The Revolution of 1688 in England* (London, Weidenfeld & Nicolson, 1972).

—— (ed), *Liberty Secured? Britain Before and After 1688* (Stanford, Stanford University Press, 1992).

Keir, Sir DL, *The Constitutional History of Modern Britain since 1485* (London, Adam & Charles Black, 1969).

Kishlansky, M, *A Monarchy Transformed – Britain 1603–1714* (London, Penguin Books, 1996).

Locke, J, *Two Treatises of Government* (ed P Laslett) (Cambridge, Cambridge University Press, 1988).

Lovell, CR, *English Constitutional and Legal History* (New York, Oxford University Press, 1962).

Miller, J, *The Glorious Revolution* (London, Longman, 1983).

—— 'Crown, Parliament, and the People', in JR Jones (ed), *Liberty Secured? Britain Before and After 1688* (Stanford, Stanford University Press, 1992).

Morrill, J, 'The Sensible Revolution' in JI Israel (ed), *The Anglo-Dutch Moment – Essays on the Glorious Revolution and its World Impact* (Cambridge, Cambridge University Press, 1991).

Nenner, H, 'Liberty, Law, and Property: The Constitution in Retrospect from 1689' in JR Jones (ed), *Liberty Secured? Britain Before and After 1688* (Stanford, Stanford University Press, 1992).

Norton, P, 'The Glorious Revolution of 1688 – Its Continuing Relevance' [1989] *Parliamentary Affairs* 135.

Schama, S, *A History of Britain, Volume 2, The British Wars 1603–1776* (London, BBC Consumer Publishing, 2001)

Scott, J, *England's Troubles – Seventeenth Century English Political Instability in European Context* (Cambridge, Cambridge University Press, 2000).

Smith, DL *A History of the Modern British Isles 1603–1707 – The Double Crown* (Oxford, Blackwell Publishers, 1998).

Trevelyan, GM, *The English Revolution 1688–89* (London, Thornton Butterworth Ltd, 1938).

Williams, EN, *The Eighteenth Century Constitution, 1688–1815 – Documents and Commentary* (Cambridge, Cambridge University Press, 1960).

1707

Addo, MK and Smith, VM, 'The Relevance of Historical Fact to Certain Arrangements Relating to the Legal Significance of the Acts of Union' [1998] *Juridicial Review* 37.

Dicey, AV and Rait, RS, *Thoughts on the Union Between England and Scotland* (London, Macmillan & Co, 1920).

Edwards, DJ, 'The Treaty of Union: More Hints at Constitutionalism' (1992) 12 *Legal Studies* 34.

Ferguson, W, *Scotland's Relations with England: A Summary to 1707* (Edinburgh, John Donald Publishers, 1977).

Kidd, C, *Subverting Scotland's Past – Scottish Whig History and the Creation of an Anglo-British Identity 1689–c1830* (Cambridge, Cambridge University Press, 1993).

Kishlansky, M, *A Monarchy Transformed – Britain 1603–1714* (London, Penguin Books, 1996).

Lynch, M, *Scotland – A New History* (London, Pimlico, 1991).

MacCormick, N, 'Does the United Kingdom have a Constitution? Reflections on *MacCormick v Lord Advocate*' (1978) 29 NILQ 1.

Munro, CR, *Studies in Constitutional Law*, 1st edn (London, Butterworths, 1987).

O'Gorman, F, *The Long Eighteenth Century – British Political and Social History 1688–1832* (London, Arnold, 1997).

Riley, PWJ, *The Union of England and Scotland – A Study in Anglo-Scottish Politics of the Eighteenth Century* (Manchester, Manchester University Press, 1978).

Scott, PH (ed), *1707 – The Union of Scotland and England in Contemporary Documents with Commentary* (Edinburgh, W & R Chambers, 1979).

—— *Andrew Fletcher and the Treaty of Union* (Edinburgh, John Donald Publishers, 1992).

Smith, TB, 'The Union of 1707 as Fundamental Law' [1957] *PL* 99.

Smout, TC, 'The Road to Union' in G Holmes (ed), *Britain after the Glorious Revolution 1689–1714* (London, Macmillan, 1969).

Speck, WA, *The Birth of Britain – A New Nation 1700–1710* (Oxford, Blackwell, 1994).

Upton, M, 'Marriage Vows of the Elephant: the Constitution of 1707' (1989) 105 *LQR* 79.

Walker, N and Himsworth, CMG, 'The Poll Tax and Fundamental Law' (1991) 1 *Juridical Review* 45.

Whatley, CA, *Bought and Sold for English Gold? Explaining the Union of 1707*, 2nd edn (East Lothian, Tuckwell Press, 2001).

Wicks, E, 'A New Constitution for a New State? The 1707 Union of England and Scotland' (2001) 117 *LQR* 109.

—— 'State Sovereignty – Towards a Refined Legal Conceptualisation' (2000) 29 *Anglo-Am LR* 282.

Williams, G and Ramsden, J, *Ruling Britannia – A Political History of Britain 1688–1988* (London, Longman, 1990).

1721

Bagehot, W, *The English Constitution* (London, Fontana Library, 1963 edn).

Black, J, *Walpole in Power* (Stroud, Sutton Publishing, 2001).

Blake, R, *The Office of Prime Minister* (London, Oxford University Press, 1975).

Carter, BE, *The Office of Prime Minister* (London, Faber, 1956).

Crossman, RHS, 'Prime Ministerial Government' in A King (ed), *The British Prime Minister*, 2nd edn (London, Macmillan, 1985).

Dicey, AV, *Introduction to the Study of the Law of the Constitution*, 10th edn (London, Macmillan, 1959).

Hennessy, P, *The Cabinet* (Oxford, Basil Blackwell, 1986).

—— *The Prime Minister: The Office and its Holders Since 1945* (London, Allen Lane, 2000).

Holmes, G, 'Sir Robert Walpole' in H Van Thal (ed), *The Prime Ministers, Vol 1: Sir Robert Walpole to Sir Robert Peel* (London, Allen & Unwin, 1974).

Jennings, I, *The Law of the Constitution*, 5th edn (London, Hodder & Stoughton., 1959).

Jones, GW, 'The Office of Prime Minister' in H Van Thal (ed), *The Prime Ministers, Vol 1: Sir Robert Walpole to Sir Robert Peel* (London, Allen & Unwin, 1974).

—— 'The Prime Minister's Power' in A King (ed), *The British Prime Minister*, 2nd edn (London, Macmillan, 1985).

King, A (ed), *The British Prime Minister*, 2nd edn (London, Macmillan, 1985).

O'Gorman, F, *The Long Eighteenth Century – British Political and Social History 1688–1832* (London, Arnold, 1997).

Williams, EN, *The Eighteenth Century Constitution, 1688–1815 – Documents and Commentary* (Cambridge, Cambridge University Press, 1960).

1832

Aspinall, A, *Three Early Nineteenth Century Diaries* (London, Williams & Norgate, 1952).

Bentley, M, *Politics Without Democracy 1815–1914: Perception and Preoccupation in British Government*, 2nd edn (Oxford, Blackwell, 1996).

Brock, M, *The Great Reform Act* (London, Hutchinson & Co, 1973).

Clark, JCD, *English Society 1660–1832: Religion, Ideology and Politics During the Ancien Regime*, 2nd edn (Cambridge, Cambridge University Press, 2000).

Cunningham, H, *The Challenge of Democracy: Britain 1832–1918* (Harlow, Pearson, 2001).

Dinwiddy, JR, *From Luddism to the First Reform Bill: Reform in England 1810–1832* (Oxford, Basil Blackwell, 1986).

Gash, N, *Politics in the Age of Peel* (London, Longmans, 1953).

—— *Reaction and Reconstruction in English Politics 1832–1852* (Oxford, Clarendon Press, 1965).

Harden, I and Lewis, N, *The Noble Lie: The British Constitution and the Rule of Law* (London, Hutchinson, 1986).

Held, D, *Models of Democracy*, 2nd edn (Cambridge, Polity Press, 1996).

Holden, B, *Understanding Liberal Democracy* (Oxford, Philip Allan, 1988).

Hunt, A, 'Evaluating Constitutions: The Irish Constitution and the Limits of Constitutionalism' in T Murphy and P Twomey (eds), *Ireland's Evolving Constitution 1937–1997* (Oxford, Hart Publishing, 1998).

Lardy, H, 'Democracy by Default: The Representation of the People Act 2000' (2001) 64 *MLR* 63.

LoPatin, ND, *Political Unions, Popular Politics and the Great Reform Act* (London, Macmillan, 1999).

Maehl, WH, *The Reform Bill of 1832 – Why Not Revolution?* (New York, Holt, Rinehart & Winston, 1967).

Morison, J, 'Models of Democracy: From Representation to Participation?' in J Jowell and D Oliver (eds), *The Changing Constitution*, 5th edn (Oxford, Oxford University Press, 2004).

Newbould, I, *Whiggery and Reform 1830–41: The Politics of Government* (London, Macmillan, 1990).

Pearce, E, *Reform! The Fight for the 1832 Reform Act* (London, Jonathan Cape, 2003).

1911

Lord Bingham of Cornhill, 'The Evolving Constitution' [2002] *EHRLR* 1.

Blewett, N, *The Peers, The Parties and the People: The General Elections of 1910* (London, Macmillan, 1972).

Bogdanor, V, *The Monarchy and the Constitution* (Oxford, Clarendon Press, 1995).

Bradley, AW and Ewing, KD, *Constitutional and Administrative Law*, 13th edn (Harlow, Longman, 2003).

Brazier, R, 'The Monarchy' in V Bogdanor (ed), *The British Constitution in the Twentieth Century* (Oxford, Oxford University Press, 2003).

Clarke, P, *Hope and Glory: Britain 1900–1990* (London, Penguin Books, 1996).

Cross, C, *The Liberals in Power 1905–1914* (Westport, Greenwood Press, 1963).

Dicey, AV, *A Leap in the Dark on Our New Constitution* (London, John Murray, 1893).

Dicey, AV, *Introduction to the Study of the Law of the Constitution*, 10th edn (London, Macmillan, 1959).

Douglas-Home, C (and Kelly, S), *Dignified and Efficient: The British Monarchy in the Twentieth Century* (Wiltshire, Claridge Press, 2000).

Egremont, M, *Balfour: A Life of Arthur James Balfour* (London, Collins, 1980).

Ewing, KD, 'The Politics of the British Constitution' [2000] *PL* 405.

Grigg, J, *Lloyd George: The People's Champion 1902–1911* (London, HarperCollins, 1978).

Heffer, S, *Power and Place: The Political Consequences of King Edward VII* (London, Weidenfeld & Nicolson, 1998).

Hood Phillips, O and Jackson, P, *Constitutional and Administrative Law*, 8th edn (by P Jackson and P Leopold) (London, Sweet & Maxwell, 2001).

Jenkins, R, *Mr Balfour's Poodle* (London, Collins, 1954).

—— *Asquith* (London, Collins, 1964).

Jennings, I, *The Law and the Constitution*, 5th edn (London, University of London Press, 1959).

Loveland, I, *Constitutional Law, Administrative Law and Human Rights: A Critical Introduction*, 3rd edn (London, LexisNexis Butterworths, 2003).

Murray, BK, *The People's Budget 1909–1910: Lloyd George and Liberal Politics* (Oxford, Clarendon Press, 1980).

Nicolson, H, *King George V: His Life and Reign* (London, Constable & Co, 1952).

Owen, F, *Tempestuous Journey: Lloyd George – His Life and Times* (London, Hutchinson, 1954).

Philipson, G, 'The Greatest Quango of them all, a Rival Chamber or a Hybrid Nonsense? Solving the Second Chamber Paradox' [2004] *PL* 352.

Russell M and Cornes, R, 'The Royal Commission on Reform of the House of Lords' (2001) 64 *MLR* 82.

Spender, JA and Asquith, C, *Life of Herbert Henry Asquith, Lord Oxford and Asquith, Volume 1* (London, Hutchinson, 1932).

Wade, HWR, 'The Basis of Legal Sovereignty' [1955] *CLJ* 177.

Walters, R, 'The House of Lords' in V Bogdanor (ed), *The British Constitution in the Twentieth Century* (Oxford, Oxford University Press, 2003).

Weill, R, 'We the British People' [2004] *PL* 380.

1953

Attlee, CR, *As It Happened* (London, William Heinemann Ltd, 1954).

Beloff, MJ and Mountfield, H, 'Unconventional Behaviour? Judicial Uses of the European Convention in England and Wales' [1996] *EHRLR* 467.

Bingham of Cornhill, Lord, 'The Evolving Constitution' [2002] *EHRLR* 1.

Burgers, JH, 'The Road to San Francisco: The Revival of the Human Rights Idea in the Twentieth Century' (1992) 14 *HRQ* 447.

Childs, D, *Britain since 1945 – A Political History*, 5th edn (London, Routledge, 2001).

Ewing, KD, 'The Human Rights Act and Parliamentary Democracy' (1999) 62 *MLR* 79.

Feldman, DJ, *Civil Liberties and Human Rights in England and Wales*, 2nd edn (Oxford, Oxford University Press, 2002).

Howarth, TEB, *Prospect and Reality: Great Britain 1945–1955* (London, Collins, 1985).

Irvine of Lairg, Lord, 'The Development of Human Rights in Britain under an Incorporated Convention on Human Rights' [1998] *PL* 221.

Johnson, MG, 'The Contributions of Eleanor and Franklin Roosevelt to the Development of International Protection for Human Rights' (1987) 9 *HRQ* 19.

Lauren, PG, *The Evolution of Human Rights: Visions Seen* (Philadelphia, University of Pennsylvania Press, 1998).

Lester, A, 'Fundamental Rights: The United Kingdom Isolated?' [1984] *PL* 46.

Lester of Herne Hill, Lord, 'UK Acceptance of the Strasbourg Jurisdiction: What really went on in Whitehall in 1965' [1998] *PL* 237.

Lester of Herne Hill, Lord, and Clapinska, L, 'Human Rights and the British Constitution' in J Jowell and D Oliver (eds), *The Changing Constitution*, 5th edn (Oxford, Oxford University Press, 2004).

Mandelson, P, and Liddle, R, *The Blair Revolution – Can New Labour Deliver?* (London, Faber & Faber, 1996).

Marston, G, 'The United Kingdom's Part in the Preparation of the European Convention on Human Rights, 1950' (1993) 42 *ICLQ* 796.

Merrills, JG, *The Development of International Law by the European Court of Human Rights* (Manchester, Manchester University Press, 1988).

Moravcsik, A, 'The Origins of Human Rights Regimes: Democratic Delegation in Postwar Europe' (2000) 54 *Int Org* 217.

Nicol, D, 'Original Intent and the European Convention on Human Rights' [2005] *PL* 152.

Roberts, FR, 'Ernest Bevin as Foreign Secretary' in R Ovendale (ed), *The Foreign Policy of British Labour Governments, 1945–1951* (Leicester, Leicester University Press, 1984).

Robertson, G, *Collected Edition of the Travaux Préparatoires* (The Hague, Martinus Nijhoff, 1977).

Simpson, AWB, *Human Rights and the End of Empire: Britain and the Genesis of the European Convention* (Oxford, Oxford University Press, 2001).

Szabo, I, 'Historical Foundations of Human Rights and Subsequent Developments' in K. Vasak (ed), *The International Dimensions of Human Rights (Vol 1)* (English edition by P Alston) (Westport, Greenwood Press, 1982)

Teitgen, P-H, 'Introduction to the European Convention on Human Rights' in RStJ Macdonald, F Matscher and H Petzold (eds), *The European System for the Protection of Human Rights* (Dordrecht, Martinus Nijhoff, 1993).

Verzijl, JHW, *International Law in Historical Perspective (Vol V)* (Leiden, A.W. Sijthoff, 1972).

Wicks, E, 'The UK Government's Perceptions of the European Convention on Human Rights at the Time of Entry' [2000] *PL* 438.

—— 'Taking Account of Strasbourg? The British Judiciary's Approach to Interpreting Convention Rights' (2005) 11 *European Public Law* 405.

1972

Allan, TRS, 'Parliamentary Sovereignty: Law, Politics, and Revolution' (1997) 113 *LQR* 443.

Alter, KJ, *Establishing the Supremacy of European Law: The Making of an International Rule of Law in Europe* (Oxford, Oxford University Press, 2001).

Beloff, Lord, *Britain and the European Union: Dialogue of the Deaf* (London, Macmillan, 1996).

Benn, T, *Office Without Power: Diaries 1968–1972* (London, Hutchinson, 1988).

Bradley, A, 'The Sovereignty of Parliament: Form or Substance?' in J Jowell and D Oliver (eds), *The Changing Constitution*, 5th edn (Oxford, Oxford University Press, 2004).

Craig, P, 'Sovereignty of the United Kingdom Parliament after *Factortame*' (1991) 11 *Yearbook of European Law* 221.

Craig, P, 'Britain in the European Union' in J Jowell and D Oliver (eds), *The Changing Constitution*, 5th edn (Oxford, Oxford University Press, 2004).

Craig, P, and de Burca, G, *EU Law: Text, Cases and Materials*, 3rd edn (Oxford, Oxford University Press, 2003).

De Witte, B, 'Direct Effect, Supremacy, and the Nature of the Legal Order', in P Craig and G de Burca, *The Evolution of EU Law* (Oxford, Oxford University Press, 1999).

Donoghue, B, 'Harold Wilson and the Renegotiation of the EEC Terms of Membership, 1974–1975: A Witness Account' in B Brivati and H Jones (eds), *From Reconstruction to Integration: Britain and Europe since 1945* (Leicester, Leicester University Press, 1993).

Ellis, E and Tridimas, T, *Public Law of the European Community: Text, Materials and Commentary* (London, Sweet & Maxwell, 1995).

Goodhart, P, *Full-hearted Consent: The Story of the Referendum Campaign and the Campaign for the Referendum* (London, Davis-Poynter, 1976).

Gowland, D, and Turner, A, *Reluctant Europeans: Britain and European Integration 1945–1998* (Harlow, Pearson Education, 2000).

Heath, E, *The Course of my Life: My Autobiography* (London, Hodder & Stoughton, 1998).

Hibbert, R, 'Britain in Search of a Role, 1957–1973; A Role in Europe, European Integration and Britain: A Witness Account', in B Brivati and H Jones (eds), *From Reconstruction to Integration: Britain and Europe since 1945* (Leicester, Leicester University Press, 1993).

Jenkins, R, *A Life at the Centre* (London, Macmillan, 1991).

Lord, C, *British Entry to the European Community under the Heath Government of 1970–1974* (Aldershot, Dartmouth, 1993).

MacCormick, N, *Questioning Sovereignty: Law, State, and Nation in the European Commonwealth* (Oxford, Oxford University Press, 1999).

Robins, LJ, *The Reluctant Party: Labour and the EEC 1961–1975* (Ormskurk, GW & A Hesketh, 1979).

Wade, HWR, 'Sovereignty: Revolution or Evolution?' (1996) 112 *LQR* 568.

Wicks, E, 'State Sovereignty: Towards a Refined Legal Conceptualisation' (2000) 29 *Anglo-Am LR* 282.

Wilson, H, *The Labour Government 1964–1970: A Personal Record* (London, Penguin, 1971).

Young, H, *This Blessed Plot: Britain and Europe from Churchill to Blair* (London, Macmillan, 1998).

Young, JW, 'Britain and the European Economic Community, 1956–1973' in B Brivati and H Jones (eds), *From Reconstruction to Integration: Britain and Europe since 1945* (Leicester, Leicester University Press, 1993).

—— *Britain and European Unity 1945–1999*, 2nd edn (London, Macmillan, 2000).

1998

Blair, T, *New Britain – My Vision of a Young Country* (London, Fourth Estate, 1996).

Bogdanor, V, *Devolution in the United Kingdom* (Oxford, Oxford University Press, 1999).

Bort, E, 'The New Institutions: An Interim Assessment' in M O'Neill (ed), *Devolution and British Politics* (Harlow, Pearson Education, 2004).

Brazier, R, 'The Constitution of the United Kingdom' (1999) 58 *CLJ* 96.

Burrows, D, *Devolution* (London, Sweet & Maxwell, 2000).

Campbell, C, Ni Aolain, F, and Harvey, C, 'The Frontiers of Legal Analysis: Reframing the Transition in Northern Ireland' (2003) 66 *MLR* 317.

Curtice, J, 'Is Scotland a Nation and Wales Not?' in B Taylor and K Thomson (eds), *Scotland and Wales: Nations Again?* (Cardiff, University of Wales Press, 1999).

Hadfield, B, 'The Belfast Agreement, Sovereignty and the State of the Union' [1998] *PL* 599.

—— 'The Nature of Devolution in Scotland and Northern Ireland: Key Issues of Responsibility and Control' (1999) 3 *Edin LR* 3.

—— 'Seeing it Through? The Multifaceted Implementation of the Belfast Agreement' in R Wilford (ed), *Aspects of the Belfast Agreement* (Oxford, Oxford University Press, 2001).

Hazell, R, 'The English Question: Can Westminster be a Proxy for an English Parliament?' [2001] *PL* 268.

—— 'The Unfinished Business of Devolution' in A Trench (ed), *Has Devolution Made a Difference? The State of the Nations 2004* (Exeter, Imprint Academic, 2004).

Jones, TH and Williams, JM 'Wales as a Jurisdiction' [2004] *PL* 78.

Keating, M, 'What's Wrong with Asymmetrical Government?' in H Elcock and M Keating (eds), *Remaking the Union: Devolution and British Politics in the 1990s* (London, Frank Cass, 1998).

—— 'The United Kingdom as a Post-Sovereign Polity' in M O'Neill (ed), *Devolution and British Politics* (Harlow, Pearson Education, 2004).

Little, G, 'Scotland and Parliamentary Sovereignty' (2004) 24 *LS* 540.

Loveland, I, *Constitutional Law, Administrative Law and Human Rights: A Critical Introduction*, 3rd edn (London, LexisNexis Butterworths, 2003).

Mitchell, GJ, *Making Peace* (London, William Heinemann, 1999).

Mitchell, J, 'Scotland: Expectations, Policy Types and Devolution' in A Trench (ed), *Has Devolution Made a Difference? The State of the Nations 2004* (Exeter, Imprint Academic, 2004).

Morgan, A, *The Belfast Agreement: A Practical Legal Analysis* (London, Belfast Press, 2000).

Morgan, KO, 'Welsh Devolution: The Past and the Future' in B Taylor and K Thomson (eds), *Scotland and Wales: Nations Again?* (Cardiff, University of Wales Press, 1999).

Naughtie, J, *The Rivals: The Intimate Story of a Political Marriage* (London, Fourth Estate, 2001).

O'Leary, B, 'The Character of the 1998 Agreement: Results and Prospects' in R Wilford (ed), *Aspects of the Belfast Agreement* (Oxford, Oxford University Press, 2001).

Oliver, D, *Constitutional Reform in the UK* (Oxford, Oxford University Press, 2003).

O'Neill, A, 'Judicial Politics and the Judicial Committee: The Devolution Jurisprudence of the Privy Council' (2001) 64 *MLR* 603.

O'Neill, M, 'Great Britain: From Dicey to Devolution' (2000) 53 *Parliamentary Affairs* 69.

—— 'Reforming the British State: The 1998 Watershed' in M O'Neill (ed), *Devolution and British Politics* (Harlow, Pearson Education, 2004).

—— 'Britishness and Politics: Towards a Federal Future?' in M O'Neill (ed), *Devolution and British Politics* (Harlow, Pearson Education, 2004).

Osmond, J, 'Nation Building and the Assembly: The Emergence of a Welsh Civic Consciousness' in A Trench (ed), *Has Devolution Made a Difference? The State of the Nations 2004* (Exeter, Imprint Academic, 2004).

Page, A. and Batey, A, 'Scotland's Other Parliament: Westminster Legislation about Devolved Matters in Scotland since Devolution' [2002] *PL* 501.

Taylor, B, Curtice, J and Thomson, K, 'Introduction and Conclusions' in B Taylor and K Thomson (eds), *Scotland and Wales: Nations Again?* (Cardiff, University of Wales Press, 1999).

Tierney, S, 'Reframing Sovereignty? Sub-State National Societies and Contemporary Challenges to the Nation-State' (2005) 54 *ICLQ* 161.

Walker, N, 'Beyond the Unitary Conception of the United Kingdom Constitution?' [2000] *PL* 384.

Wicks, E, 'State Sovereignty: Towards a Refined Legal Conceptualisation' (2000) 29 *Anglo-Am LR* 282.

Wilford, R, 'Northern Ireland: Resolving an Ancient Quarrel?' in M O'Neill (ed), *Devolution and British Politics* (Harlow, Pearson Education, 2004).

Wilson, R and Wilford, R, 'Northern Ireland: Renascent?' in A Trench (ed), *Has Devolution Made a Difference? The State of the Nations 2004* (Exeter, Imprint Academic, 2004).

Winetrobe, BK, 'Scottish Devolved Legislation and the Courts' [2002] *PL* 31.

Index